ROUGHING IT
IN AFRICA:

"Roots, Roads, and Revelations"

Katherine Krige

Twin Horseshoes Publishing
www.twinhorseshoes.ca
Ontario, Canada

Krige, Katherine
Roughing in in Africa: Roots, Roads, and Revelations
Includes bibliographical references.

eBook ISBN 978-1-7775345-3-0
Paperback (Colour) ISBN 978-1-7775345-2-3
Paperback (Black and White) ISBN 978-1-7775345-7-8
Paperback (Novel) ISBN 978-1-990831-06-5

Nonfiction | Travel | Africa | General
Nonfiction | Biography & Autobiography | Personal Memoirs
Nonfiction | Travel | Special Interest | Family

TABLE OF CONTENTS

PROLOGUE

Africa is my quiet obsession. It has been since my South African born father died when I was five years old. His covert absence sparked my curiosity and fueled a preoccupation that only grew over the years. This is ultimately where the story begins, but plenty of other factors put my tale in motion. Young, beleaguered love was the final straw that pushed me headlong towards a continent over 13,000 kilometers away…time to go.

A handful of clothes, a couple of books, my trusty journal; that was everything needed. The timeworn stuffed bear propped on my headboard and unwieldy university textbooks weren't going anywhere. If I was lucky, perhaps someone would tend to them, if they tidied while I was gone. If not, no loss.

I slung the backpack over my shoulder, careful not to brush the tender spot on my arm. Typhoid, yellow fever, meningitis, hepatitis A and B; all the shots I received the day before to protect me while I was in Africa. It was the reason I had returned to Richmond Hill. At present though, I returned to Jack.

That was a journey unto itself—an hour-ish to get downtown to the bus station followed by another hour and a half more to Peterborough. From there, who knew where we would toss up. His lifestyle made for an uncertainty that I had to accept to be with him. It was exciting at times, but the glamour had waned over the summer months. Now I wearily boarded the many buses that would take me back to him.

Jack's guitar case was propped open in front of him when I found him. Loose bills and scattered coins littered the bottom of the tattered case.

Playful songs greeted passersby with spirited lyrics and silly jigs. A promising sign. It meant he was in good spirits. And that no demons darkened his soul that day. Then the music changed. The first few familiar bars of 'Home for a Rest' by Spirit of the West reached me.

He had seen me. A conspiratorial smile played across his lips.

His voice rang loud and beckoned with its infectious lyrics, but it only took a glance to see that the song rang true. Dark circles ringed his eyes. The beginnings of scruff and a fresh wave of acne shadowed his face. He hadn't taken any better care of himself while I was away, than when I mothered him at his side. Late night music sessions, too much drink, and nightmares kept him company always.

I couldn't resist that smile though. I joined him for the chorus and danced to the spirit of the song.

"Hi," I laughed breathlessly as the song ended. I nuzzled in for a kiss, careful to not bump the guitar strung around his neck.

"Rrrr," he whispered in my ear as he pulled me in close. "Give me half an hour to busk up a little more for dinner." With a quick kiss, he turned back to the new wave of people who approached and right back into his next song for his audience—the passing pedestrians.

With that, I was dismissed. Any words I had died on my lips. This was how it went. Music first, everything else second.

"I don't suppose we have a place to sleep tonight," I grumbled to myself as I turned towards 'The Only'. It was one of many never-ending questions—what are we going to eat? Where are we sleeping tonight? How long can we stay there? It was exhausting. The answers depended upon how much he made, who he ran into, and how generous those friends felt. There was always a new friend with an empty couch to be had.

No matter. I could find my own table to prop my journal on, not to mention a drink to whet my own thirst until Jack found me again. I had never-ending lists to check for my pending trip out of country. And until he joined me, there was only one tab to pay.

"Hey!" rang out a friendly voice, as I pushed open the door at the bar. "Pull up a stool and join us for a pint."

"Hey, Rick!" I replied with a smile.

Jack's lacklustre greeting slipped from me. Here were welcoming faces happy to see me. It would be a while before my less-than attentive boyfriend was ready to join me with puppy dog eyes and poems about our undying love to make up for his lack of presence now.

"Sounds good," I said as I pulled out a stool beside him at the bar.

Later that night I drifted off to sounds of Jack and Sebastien jamming upstairs. I nestled deeper into a blanket cocoon on the floor below. It would be hours yet before he would crawl into bed beside me. He would pull me to him for the rest of the night and hold me close as long as he could the next morning. Until I couldn't take it anymore and disengaged in search of coffee—always long before he was ready to face the day. So it went once more.

As much as I thought I had love at Jack's side and ached for the sweet moments, it was the flaws that helped nudge me on my journey. I wanted more than to be a mute bystander to the angry musical rants that consumed him. I knew better than most what dark secrets fuelled them, but ultimately couldn't reach him there.

And back home in Richmond Hill, the Reader's Digest *Southern Africa: Land of Beauty and Splendour* by T.V. Bulpin (1976), which had sat on the coffee table for as long as I could remember, beckoned me. Exotic flowers, animals, and landscapes illustrated its pages. I needed only to flip through it to step into the world my father had left behind when he made Canada home. The book tempted me to believe I could exist in a bigger world than the one at Jack's side.

There were more reminders and silent motivators at home. Across the room, '*Die Familie Krige*' sat on a shelf. Written in Afrikaans, it held my family history from the first Krige to land in South Africa in 1721, down to my father, born in 1938. His marriage to my mother was noted in 1968. I failed to make the list in our genealogical tome due to the publication deadline. Both the book and I came into being in 1973. I would have been H1—the term of reference for the eighth generation of Krige—in Die Caledon-Tak (the Caledon branch of my family). Like the language itself, the connections were lost to me, but I planned to change that. These tokens of my family roots were a constant reminder that there was more to me than just being my mother's daughter or a boyfriend's mate. I had other far-flung family and an identity I didn't even know. The ties were lost when my father died in 1978, but threads still clung to me and I couldn't let them go. A piece of my father and my long-lost roots begged to be explored, more than just by skimming the pages of a coffee table book. I longed to see his homeland in person. The ache to reconnect with family only grew stronger the older I got. I needed that personal reunion.

So, when the end of my university days loomed, and a small inheritance materialized from my paternal grandmother, I jumped at the chance to make my dreams a reality. It seemed fate had presented a window. I had the time and money, plus encouraging letters from the virtual strangers who were my aunt and uncle in Cape Town. Not to mention the fact that I had yet to step into a career and the responsibilities that came with 'real' life. It was now or never.

The only thing that stood in my way was of course Jack. Once I was gone, I suspected he wouldn't remain single long. As much as I played second-fiddle to his music, without the steadying influence of a partner, he invariably slid back into old depressions. He needed a partner to give him the stability to explore his creativity and ground him after bingeing on jam sessions. Without one, his world became too dark for any of it.

Comparatively, my suffering was from the existential crises that came with studying Descartes and Freud. It didn't stand up to the leitmotif of playing guitar on street corners. And while I loved his music, I didn't fit in with his tortured artist mystique. When I tried to find the middle ground between his fight against the system and my newly opening eyes to the world beyond my mother's apron strings, the compromises seemed mostly to be mine. His feelings were louder, thoughts more expansive; mine, just quiet concepts I didn't have the strength or voice to share.

Hence when the idea of exploring my roots finally crystallized and I realized the journey was mine alone to make, I knew the sacrifice would be his love. There was no other way. And it was the chance I had to take.

If given the choice, I would do it again in a heartbeat. Africa awaited.

*****

GOODBYE

Once upon a time, a young woman sat waiting for the call. The bustle of the airport surrounded her, but she was immune to its din. She huddled, lost in thought.

Yes, it was I, but so long ago as to be almost unrecognizable as such. Eyes downcast, I poured my heart into the journal on my lap. Teardrops dried on the page as I wrote. Hugs received but moments before still wrapped themselves around me, my arms still warm in remembrance. I had bid farewell to my mother and sister, but it was my boyfriend who tugged at my heartstrings. I would miss them all of course but was uncertain whether the same three would greet me again at the end of my journey. The bittersweet moment would carry into my days to come—tarnished love traded for an adventure of a lifetime.

"First boarding call for flight number 475 to Frankfurt, Germany..."

My flight. It was almost time to go.

I tucked the bag looped securely around my ankle further under my chair. People milled everywhere. A voice of wisdom droned in my head: *When travelling, always be cautious.* You never know what or whom you are going to run into. Strangers might steal your purse, luggage, or heart.

My father learned that the hard way. He left South Africa when he finished school, worked in the mines of Rhodesia for three years, lived in England for three more, then travelled throughout Europe. Canada was supposed to be the last stop on his tour of the world before heading home.

It was indeed the last stop, but not in the way he envisioned. My father stumbled home one night after a few drinks with friends and found he had lost his keys. After pounding on the door of his apartment building in hopes someone would let him into his flat, a young woman came to the door with a disapproving frown. He managed to convince her to let him in, but the door opened to a whole new world. They were married within the year. Canada changed from a destination to a new home.

While I was a consequence of that story, I did not learn the tale from my father. He died shortly after I turned five and his stories went with him to the grave. His spirit didn't though, and it was inspiration for my own journey. Like him, I too burned to travel as he had. I sought adventure, excitement, but even more so, the piece of my father that had been lost with his death. My brand-new BA in English encouraged me to analyze and expound on the world around me. I thrilled to put it to use further afield and hoped it would help me tell stories of my own as I delved into a foreign land and a history I hoped to uncover.

But first I had to leave behind the romance that was doomed to never bear fruit, a directionless life on the verge of becoming or unravelling (what *did* I want to be when I grew up?), and the days of my youth, which were rapidly winding down. I couldn't live under my mother's roof forever, after all. It would have been easy enough to stay on my current path and start a passage into adulthood, but my past nagged at me to explore it. And if I was honest with myself, I knew my relationship wouldn't last. I wanted more of life and, more importantly, more of my father's story. The only place to find that was where he had come from - South Africa.

So, on a cool November day, I set off to find my roots. I pondered what I would see and do. Would I reconnect with the lost pieces of my childhood—family I hadn't seen since I was five? Would my father breathe to life, as he'd been unable to do in reality? Would it fill me, shock me, or change me? Only time would tell.

The excitement should have been palpable. Almost was. But the hugs that faded held sorrow in their wake. I was heartbroken and couldn't shake it. As much as I knew we had problems, Jack was my first true love, and it was difficult to walk away from that. Too many demons poisoned him though.

Oh baby. You wanted to change the world but didn't have more than a change of clothes to your name. You spurned the working world, a tool of the government to keep the people down but accepted alms of space on people's couches and food your friends worked hard to earn. It was a dichotomy. If only they listened to you, their lives would be spiritually richer, if not monetarily so.

I wanted to listen to Jack too but got lost in his rhetoric that didn't jibe with what I knew of life so far. I loved him, but ultimately couldn't live with his skewed view of the world. This trip seemed the only way to let him go. It didn't curtail the tears that fell and would continue to do so for many days to come.

When my section was called, I joined the queue. Hurry up and wait. People shuffled forward pushing boarding passes in front of them. All I wanted to do was get on the plane, get on with my journey and go, even while another piece of me panicked as I left behind my home, my security—my life. I wanted to, had to, but sorrow overflowed my aching heart. There was no turning back now though.

I found my seat on the plane and settled in for the flight. Through the view from my prized window seat, people bustled about on the tarmac.

All I saw was a lover's eyes staring through me. Abandonment. I could do nothing to forestall the forlorn feelings.

All night those eyes watched me, as I flew through inky skies away from him. Sleep teased and gave comfort for a few measly hours. Mostly I watched the midnight sky. The full moon guided me to a new life. Adventure had begun, and I could not close my eyes to it.

"Welcome to Frankfurt, Germany. The local time is now 7:10 am."

My next flight wouldn't leave until 9:50 p.m. I had plenty of time to distract myself from thoughts of Jack. A lack of sleep, and the shift in time zones left me decidedly apathetic though. There wasn't enough time to properly explore the city, and the effort seemed pointless. Too many hours stretched in front of me to just sit idle in the airport though. Sleep seemed my best bet, but just as I drifted off, a security guard shook me awake again.

"Du kannst hier nicht schlafen," he announced.

Whatever that meant. But I could tell from his frown that it wasn't good.

"Guten tag[1]," I stammered. "Do you speak English? I am waiting for my next flight. Is there anywhere I can rest until then?"

It was obvious even without a translation that the answer was no. He pointed an incontestable finger away from the bank of seats I had appropriated. Under dark brows, the security guard glared at me as I shuffled off.

---

[1] good day.

The flight from Germany to South Africa brought even less sleep. The second leg of my journey followed the moon and try as I might to close my burning eyes, I was too enthralled by its light, as we travelled down the continent together. I imagined deserts, nomads, and tiny villages held close in slumber's grasp and began to comprehend that I approached a far different world than the one I had left behind. It grew closer by the moment. In a matter of scant hours, I would touch down in the land of my father's birth. I would meet his brother—my Uncle Jock—and numerous other family members who had been nothing more than abstract concepts a short while ago. Excitement finally began to seep in.

As we alit in Johannesburg, I got my first taste of the changes that my preconceptions were to undergo. My visions of Africa came from *The Land of Beauty and Splendour*, National Geographic photo spreads, and infomercials portraying drought and famine. The sight of lush, purple jacaranda trees in full bloom erased the dry deserts from my staid imagination. It seemed improbable, but they painted a violet carpet that filled my window as the plane descended towards them. Swimming pools dotted the cityscape, and it was obvious that no camels wandered freely here. What else would I discover when I finally got off the plane in Cape Town and land in the arms of my kin?

Once the plane refueled, we were off to find out.

*****

FAMILY

"Touchdown"

As I blinked in the glare of near-forgotten sunshine, I stared out at a new world. The moisture that escaped my strained eyes now had more to do with a need for shade, rather than sorrow. On the other side of the world, my home was headed into the cold embrace of winter. Here in Africa, the spring rays drove sharp daggers into my tender eyes. Already there was a need for adjustment, for change.

In the blink of an eye, I would find myself walking off the plane and down a ramp to the tarmac below. This was a novel experience, as back in Canada I would have drifted leisurely through a long tunnel attached to the parked plane, before reaching the airport building proper, followed by a pell-mell rush to be first at the luggage carousels.

Not here though.

On this day, a flight attendant called my name before I had a chance to exit the plane.

"Katerina Krreeha, please report to the flight stewardess."

The accent was lost on me. Several summonses went out in both English and Afrikaans before I realized it was myself being paged on the intercom. It was my first awkward language lesson, as I had never heard my last name pronounced in anything other than a garbled Canadian version before.

I finally awkwardly raised my hand.

"Ja[2], good!" she declared with a smile. "Follow me please."

In a daze, I gathered my things and trailed behind the pretty woman who expertly steered me off the plane. Once outside, she stopped in front of a burly, goateed man.

"Velcome[3]!" the man shouted as he scooped the carry-on bag from my arm.

Pure joy and vibrant life sparkled in his eyes. Apparently, he was happy to see me. As his pull from his job at the airport got me off the plane first, I was pretty pleased to see him too.

"I'm Weppie," he said as he gathered me into a bear hug. "Your cousin Marianne—Jock's oldest daughter—she is my wife."

And so, it began. We quickly whisked through security with much laughter and pleasantries to all and sundry. It seemed he knew everyone we passed.

"How is your wife, Willem? Has she forgiven you for your bit of fun at the braai last weekend?" he laughed.

"Good to see you, Jakob! Don't you give my friend a hard time today. She has come all the way from Canada," he admonished. "Ja!"

The stories flowed fast and furious. I was the centre of it all and couldn't help but feel bedazzled.

---

[2] yes.
[3] Welcome.

I desperately tried to keep up with the jovial banter and quick pace. Weppie's open nature was infectious though and he quickly propelled us along. We cleared customs, then gathered my luggage, all as the conversation danced ahead. Despite my sleep-addled brain, it was impossible not to like him already. I nodded and squinted through bleary eyes, happy to be there regardless.

Before my exhausted brain could catch up, we stopped again. This time it was in front of another group of strangers. Their faces seemed somehow familiar though.

"May I have the pleasure to introduce you to your Uncle Jock," Weppie declared as he introduced his father-in-law with a small bow.

Here was my father's brother. Beside him stood his wife, Elsa, and my Aunt Linn, my father's sister. They were the closest relatives I had on my father's side, and they were alive and in the flesh in front of me.

A crooked smile crept across my face. I was home.

"Arrival"

"My dear," Uncle Jock declared as he pulled me into an embrace.

It had been 17 years since I had seen any of these relatives, but might as well have been never, as I was barely five years old when last we met. My uncle's squeeze let me know he had not forgotten though.

"How was your flight?" Aunt Elsa asked politely when she got her turn at a hug. Aunt Linn just beamed.

For most of my life, these relatives had been nothing more than fabricated stories gleaned from rare letters. Now four of many stood in front of me. It seemed impossible that they were real. That this was finally happening. But it was and here was not the place to get reacquainted. It was time to move on again. We made our way to the airport's exit.

"We will see you later then, after I get home from work," Weppie promised, as we bid him adieu and stepped outside.

And I faltered all over again.

The world was blinding. I cannot do justice to the agony, as sunlight hit my eyes once more. I reared back, my hands instinctively flying to my face. To no avail. My eyes instantly cringed and flooded in the strong southern sunshine. It burned! Visions of dark tinted sunglasses sprang to mind.

"My first purchase," I promised myself.

Meanwhile, Uncle Jock prattled away as he stowed my bags in the boot of the car.

"We'll get together with your Aunt Linn in a few days," Uncle Jock said, as we bade goodbye to her as well. "Give you a chance to rest and get settled in."

I didn't care, as long as they got me out of the searing sun. I blindly followed them, utterly useless by that point.

"There you go," he said as he held the back door open for me.

A vague thought struck me that the car seemed peculiar, but I couldn't place why, until he slid into the front seat and slipped the keys into the ignition. The steering wheel was on the wrong side! Another difference from me to get used to. It wasn't until the car pulled onto the highway though, that it truly struck home though.

"Oh!" I exclaimed with a violent start.

I grabbed for the door with eyes squeezed shut, my heart beating madly in my chest. A vehicle barrelled directly towards us! When the explosion of metal upon metal didn't happen, I peeped an eye open. I glanced out the rear window, then back to the road in front of us again.

"... and the poor girl completely missed her flight, so we took her back to your house in Richmond Hill..." Uncle Jock continued to chatter without missing a beat.

Breath slowly seeped back into my strained lungs as understanding washed over me. I really was in a different country. I was in a different world, and it wasn't just the steering wheel. Driving on the left-hand side of the road was a first for me. It was the first of many experiences to come.

While my tired brain tried to adjust to the onslaught of new stimuli, I desperately tried to follow my uncle's anecdotes without having further panic attacks over the traffic. I opted to watch him instead. I examined his profile as we zipped along. Did I have his nose? Were my cheekbones akin to the ones that rounded his face? It was hard to tell. But the same blood flowed through both our veins.

"We got to see your Niagara Falls; quite impressive that, ja," he nodded. "And they took us to Ontario Place."

He was bursting with stories. They had visited Canada when I had been much younger, only a child. I did not truly remember the visit, nor him for that matter, but that didn't prevent my glow at the connection that was already there. He was a link to a past that I did not know. My father had died within the month of my uncle's last visit to Canada, and with his death, he took the vital connection to a family that resided thousands of kilometers away. It had taken 17 years and a full two days of travel, but I finally had the chance to reconnect.

"What was the name of that restaurant we always went to?" he asked Elsa. "It was your Dad's favourite," he commented as he glanced back towards me. "You got to choose your hamburger toppings..."

"Harvey's," I exclaimed with a thrill.

He recollected places and people that were vividly familiar. I soaked in pictures of the father that had been but a ghostly image to me for most of my life. He ate hamburgers, drank Labatt's Blue, and enjoyed the role of tour guide apparently. A portrait of a man formed in my consciousness. My father filled out in my mind and gained the flesh and blood I had craved. It was magical. It was surreal. It was just too much.

I brushed aside a tear. I was in Africa. It was a dream I had held for more years than I could remember. At that moment, I zipped through the Cape Province with family at my side. I closed my eyes and listened, the better to create my own pictures of the stories. It was all very real, and I gloried in the moment. I had finally arrived.

"Shanty Town"

When I opened my eyes again, the landscape had changed. Table Mountain was still visible in the rear window, but the city had been left behind. The first of the terrain that would become so familiar started to creep in. What surprised me most was the buildings that began to dot the landscape. The red soil gave way to decrepit lean-tos with tin roofs. A few of the shacks merged into many, and then many more. We drove and drove, and the shanties took over the world.

"What is this place?" I quietly asked with a wave of my hand.

"Khayelitsha," was the curt reply.

A sudden silence filled the car. Here was the dark secret of a nation that desperately wanted to hold onto its former glory. My uncle could not sugar-coat what lay in front of me, as desperately as he might have wanted to. I was viewing a shantytown.

Kilometers of scabbed together houses, made from whatever materials that could be salvaged, schemed for, or stolen, were the sad evidence of South Africa's less-than-ideal present. Barbed wire was liberally scattered everywhere. It was shocking. Poverty was not unknown back home, but not visible on such a level. Here were thousands of structures that all looked like a gust of wind or drop of rain would level them to the ground. These were people's homes.

As he couldn't deny the reality, my uncle chose to explain it the best he could.

"Nelson Mandela was elected last April. The elections were tough; they were the first multi-racial elections we've had. There were threats and scares, but ultimately they went off well enough," he claimed.[4]

---

[4] Nelson Mandela Foundation. (2014, October 29). Biography of Nelson Mandela. https://www.nelsonmandela.org/content/page/biography.

"But the extent of the atrocities that came before were awful! I had no idea!" he exclaimed. "I don't think any of us did really. The torture and ill-treatment? Shocking. Now they are in the process of setting up the Truth and Reconciliation Committee to deal with the worst of it."

He grimly shook his head.

The election had succeeded in ending 46 years' worth of a separation of the races, but the bad blood behind those measures was far from forgotten, nor should it ever be. You cannot erase, nor make amends for the effects of that level of government-sanctioned apartheid overnight. How does one explain why people were beaten, tortured, or simply disappeared over such a long time period, not to mention the blatant disparity in basic human rights? How could they possibly ever make it better?

The answer was to start the conversation.

The slum we zipped past on the highway suggested it wouldn't be easy though. Khayelitsha, like much of South Africa, was home to a predominantly black population and widespread poverty. My uncle went on to tell me of recent issues that had befallen the area.

"The government-built homes, but they quickly filled up and overflowed. When the homes ran out, people made their own out of whatever they could get." He added, "Construction companies got upset when building materials disappeared in the middle of the night."

I imagined that was when broken glass started getting embedded into the tops of walls and barbed wire became so popular everywhere— except in shantytowns, of course.

"When the demand outweighed resources, running water became harder to find. Public taps were set up but couldn't keep up. Electricity was the same. They couldn't get enough in. There were too many people," he noted. "Violence wasn't far behind. People got frustrated. They stopped paying bills and utilities got cut off. Oh, you should have heard the howls then!" he exclaimed. "It didn't get any better though. Last month there was a garbage strike. The workers couldn't get into the squatter camps, as people attacked them or threw things at them. Eventually they stopped trying. People got angry, but in the interim, the waste piled up."

"It's the same everywhere. There have been four teacher strikes this year. They want more money, but there isn't more money to be had. Unemployment is high, so the government puts money into job creation, but takes it from education and health care. When those workers get upset, they strike," he continued. "And when the hospitals strike, *everything* stops. Not even the Emergency Department is open."

"What do people do?" I asked.

"They go to private hospitals or get taken care of by family," he stated. "Or they die. It is not the strikers' concern."

I was chilled and couldn't help but think of our public health care and education back home. Jack was just one of the many who moaned about it, but comparatively our world was the furthest thing from this cluttered community that made up people's homes. How many trips to the doctor alone had I made before I left to ensure I remained healthy here? It cost me time, but not dignity nor money. I was sobered by the thought.

When we accidently drove into it a week later on our way to Cape Point, Uncle Jock quickly made a three-point turn, but not fast enough to shield me from a glimpse of some of Khayelitsha's inhabitants. Three bedraggled young boys walked barefoot along the dirt road we travelled. When they spied our white faces driving towards their home, and then hastily beating a retreat, they did the only thing they could to show their frustration—the littlest one mooned us as we passed. His friends laughed at our discomfort, but I was shaken by the experience. Even the children seemed to understand their dismal lot in life and were angry. How long would it take to change that?

While I would never get used to it, sadly I would find that poverty and frustration in far more places than I could ever have imagined. These shantytowns were one face of South Africa. But they weren't the only one.

As we continued towards Uncle Jock's home, Khayelitsha eventually disappeared behind us and was replaced by suburbia. Dry scrub gave way to shopping plazas and gated communities. Manicured lawns and familiar fast-food restaurants confused my sense of whereabouts once again. Surely lions and elephants did not graze through KFC's parking lot? Would ostriches bury their heads beside a mall's receiving area? And one would assuredly not imagine vultures perched atop walls with broken glass embedded into them to discourage scavenging trespassers.

I watched the world glide by my window. South Africa was a dichotomy of realities that I only just touched on. Home might as well have been on another planet.

"Blame the Kumquat"

The first few days in South Africa were a barrage of experiences. I fell in love with my Uncle Jock's big belly laugh and felt at home in his warm presence. He was eager to talk and show me his world. We wandered around the back garden where he showed me his strawberries (which I devoured),

Cape gooseberries (that I had never seen before, let alone eaten), and other plant life. I was introduced to paw paws (like papaya) and oranges like I had never tasted before. They were so sweet and juicy. I couldn't resist! Neither could he. He ate several pieces of fruit every day after dinner. "Doctor's orders," he explained with a laugh.

The food did not stop there. Aunt Elsa had a knack for cooking new and intriguing dishes. She insisted I try them all. I tried skilpadjie (liver wrapped in fat and braaied – kind of gross, sorry Aunt Elsa!), rooi hakskoentjies (translation: small red heels – a pickled onion dish), homemade rusks (dried crusts of bread), bobotie (curried meatloaf with egg topping), and brawn (gelatinous curried sandwich meat made of calf's heels and pig's trotters). I also had more recognizable dishes, like spaghetti, but the new foods made more of an impression on me. It was a smorgasbord of flavour sensations! As you might have guessed, not all of them good.

While those dishes were all from the women's domain, the men cooked too. Their implement of choice though was the mighty braai. And it didn't take long before I was privy to exactly what that was.

One evening Marianne and Weppie came over with their children, my second cousins Francoise and Ilse. A few other friends from the church rounded out the guests for dinner. While the women busied themselves in the kitchen, the men tackled their dinner responsibilities outside.

It was quite the sight to behold. The beefy, meat-loving men stood around the braai pit, laughing and joking, with a beer or whisky in hand. It seemed drinks were the mainstay of any braai experience. Uncle Jock held a long set of tongs. As man of the house, he oversaw the fire and vleis (meat). It was an important job and apparently one that only *he* could do. The tongs held sway over the action and whosever's house the braai was held, was the one in charge.

As the women came in and out with the many salads and sides that went with the vleis, the real show was in front of the wood-fired grill on the outdoor hearth. No gas barbecues here. The wood was lit and burned down until it reached the perfect temperature. And while the braaier (head barbecuer) was the only one who could ascertain that, any man present had to weigh in on this important decision. Only then was the hallowed meat brought forth.

"I think it's time Jock."

"Hmm, net oor," he replied as he peered at the embers.

What was that, I wondered? How many times did I get lost in a conversation, whether due to pronunciation or the fact that so many mixed English and Afrikaans together?

"Elsa, now now," he finally bellowed. "Bring die vleis!"

Now, it was time.

Ilse followed Marianne, both laden with heaping platters of meat. And what a variety there was! While a coiled sausage (boerewors) is the headliner of any braai, it's only one of several meats featured. There was marinated chicken, lamb, steak, pork, fish and sosaties (like kebabs). Afrikaners love their meat. More importantly, they are masters of how to cook it.

Once Uncle Jock made the call that the braaivleis (barbecued meat) was done, then the women could finally relax and join the men in the social affair. Their laughter was added to the men's as they brought out the last of the salads and everyone grabbed a plate to tuck into the feast.

"Lekker[5] braai Jock!" Weppie exclaimed with a clap on his back.

It was indeed a good barbecue and worth the many cheers it received.

I had more than food to discover though. There was a whole new language to learn—Afrikaans. From the moment I first heard my name pronounced, I knew that I needed to pick up even a small piece of my father's native tongue. I took baby steps to acquire words for the objects around me.

"Chicken - *hoender*. *Katjie* - kitten. *Hond* - dog." I stated. "*Een, twee, drie…* One, two, three," I intoned to the mirth of relatives who watched on. "Dankie," I beamed to their claps. "Baie dankie[6]!"

Yes, thank you. Thank you very much. My pronunciation was horrible. I had to learn that a "tjie" combination made a sound like "key" in English. The letter "V" was now pronounced like an "F" and "G" more like an "H". And then there was the matter of rolling "R"s. I quickly learned that even my last name, that I had happily pronounced my whole life, was something which I said horribly wrong.

"*Kri-g\ä*," I pronounced. And was corrected to something closer to "*Kr-/i:/-xə*" – with rolling 'r', guttural 'g' and an 'e' pronounced more like an 'a' in a̱bout. Yeah, I wasn't ever going to master that.

How embarrassing. My family took it in stride with ready laughter.

---

[5] good; pleasant.
[6] many thanks.

They were happy to teach me about their culture and world. Initial lessons were filtered through a foggy brain, but I was keen to learn as much as I could. I took notes on pronunciation. I read books written by local authors, including one by Uys Krige, a distant relative. I plotted our family tree to help me figure out whom I had met and how they were related to me. I listened to tales of relative's adventures in Canada; I was surprised to learn that Marianne and Weppie had honeymooned there. We plotted where I might like to go in South Africa; perhaps winetasting, to the top of Table Mountain, or to Etosha National Park in Namibia with Marianne. I shared plenty of tales of my own; of my country, culture and more familiar family who were so far away. And of course, I asked questions, questions, and more questions.

It all exhilarated me! It also exhausted me. I made it to 7:30 the first night, before I finally gave in to sleep. After my extensive trip to get there, I slept straight through to 10:30 the next morning. It is a wonder I had the strength to function at all the first day, but sleep was only a minor setback to survive.

After about a week in the country, I slowly got over my jet lag. My renewed strength gave me courage, so one Sunday while Uncle Jock and Aunt Elsa were at choir practice, I decided to venture out of the house on my own. I opted for a walk to the store, for both the exercise and adventure. What it was though, was an exercise in stress.

I reached the end of the subdivision and came to a busy road. I had to cross it to get to the store. A light stood a way off, but the store was directly across from me.

"I'll just cross here," I innocently decided.

I looked left, right, left again, then started to cross. A car laid on its horn and I jumped back to the safety of the curb. It had veered at me from the "wrong" direction. That is, it drove on the left side of the road when I was expecting to see it come from the right. Lesson learned. It took much perseverance and practice getting used to the new road rules, but the experience empowered me and set me on a path for the independent travel that was to come.

Sadly, there was another lesson I didn't learn in time: moderation. My experiments with new food slowly began to catch up with me. I might have managed to cross a road, but finally one too many kumquats pushed me over the edge. My first tentative soft bowels were soon replaced by a full-on case of Traveller's Trots. It had nothing to do with poor sanitation or contaminated water. It had everything to do with my love of new foods and lack of forethought before ingesting mass quantities of fruit to a body that still thought it would go into winter hibernation. Regret did nothing to assuage my pains.

As spasms wracked my body, everything refused to stay in me, including water. I dropped over 10 pounds in less than a week.

"Would you care for some dry toast dear," my aunt fretted. She worried that my mother would be horrified by their lack of care in poor little me during such a short time. It wasn't her fault though and I feebly tried to ease her conscience between trips to the "water closet". As I pushed away her offerings and desperately tried to keep down sips of water, I thought again about the adventure I was on.

"Thank god for indoor plumbing," I moaned as I braced myself once again on the toilet. The bubbles that shifted around in my tummy and fierce assault on my digestive system did not celebrate the journey I heralded. The only thing that kept me going was the knowledge that this too would pass. And of course, it did.

Flush...

"Another Branch on the Family Tree"

As the burbles slowed, I embraced the world again. I vowed to take it a little slower this time but was ready to move beyond my uncle's house. It was time to connect with another branch of the family tree. So, once I could stomach water and dry crackers again, Aunt Linn picked me up to take me to brunch at the Mowbray Golf Club.

Home to several South African Opens and Bells Cups since its opening in 1910, apparently Mowbray was the place to be. The newly renovated clubhouse was pristine, and I felt a little daunted by its presence as we approached. I suspected that this step up into the upper echelon of South African society was just one example of the differences between my aunt and uncle.

Despite only four years separating them, there was a marked difference between Uncle Jock's Afrikaner traits and my Aunt Linn's staunch English ways. While laughter and cheer were the hallmarks of my uncle's family, I wondered what I would find at my aunt's table. She had written letters to my mother religiously over the years, but they had always seemed polite, proper, and distant. Would her family be the same? It was time to find out.

We were quite the gathering for lunch. I double-checked my confusing pencil-sketched ancestral tree before heading out but was still lost immediately. This side of the family represented Aunt Linn's kin, none of whom I had met yet. It was time to change that.

"Pleased to meet you," my cousin Robin said as he shook my hand firmly.

Robin was my father's name. Aunt Linn had named him after her brother.

"I do hope you are enjoying our country so far," his wife Jill remarked from his side.

"How very exciting of you to undertake this adventure!" Anna Maria exclaimed.

She was Pieter's wife, Aunt Linn's youngest child of three. So far, they were polite through and through, with stiff smiles and handshakes all around. I desperately tried to remember names, as I ticked off cousins, spouses, and their subsequent children. Nametags and a cheat sheet would have been handy, but not surprisingly I couldn't remember which children belonged to which adults, let alone what their names were by the end of the afternoon.

No matter. It didn't prevent me from enjoying the posh buffet brunch, which I delicately sampled. As my stomach had shrunk to the size of a dried-up kumquat, I rationed myself to a humble plate with the bare minimum of offerings; nothing too racy and nothing with a hint of acidity. I was rewarded by not having to madly scramble to the WC once food passed my lips. Small victories!

As I nibbled at my small pile of fluffy scrambled eggs, Anne chatted at me from down the table. She was Aunt Linn's oldest and the only one who seemed fallible, therefore more real and approachable. Where everyone else was prim and proper, without ill winds ever having apparently touched them, Anne frequently squeezed Graham's hand seated beside her—her second husband! She wasn't embarrassed at all to share that her first marriage had ended in divorce. They had even had a fourth child—young Paul.

"You must come stay with us for a spell," she insisted. "You need to be around people your own age! You and Greg are only a few months apart and Richard is a few years younger again."

Greg and Richard were her two oldest boys. In fact, I had met Anne and Greg when I visited South Africa as a baby. There is a picture of Mom and Anne holding Greg and I, as we sat around a pool celebrating our first Christmas. I had seen the photo often. Somehow, it gave me a stronger connection to her. Anne was the same age as my mother in fact. Plus, she seemed more open and inviting than her two younger brothers. She had a warmth that naturally eased the shyness from me. Regardless though, they were all family and meeting them was the point of my trip in the first place.

"We live at the base of the mountain," Anna Maria chimed in from the other side of the table. "You can walk into downtown Cape Town from our stoep[7]. There is so much to see and do. You really must stay with us as well."

"Thank you," I replied.

I was touched by all the attention from my brand-new family. The offers were appealing too. If I stayed with them, I would get to know them

---

[7] stoop; porch.

all better and that had been the plan from the start. More than that though, it gave me something else to look forward to.

Truth be told though, it was also a great distraction from my homesickness. I constantly dreamed of home. And Jack. And wondered what he was doing, who he was with, and if he thought of me as much as I did him. Exploring the waterfront with Anne or Anna-Maria would push those thoughts out of my head, if only for a while. Plus, I wanted to see more, do more, live more. The longer I was there, the farther away home seemed, and I still wasn't sure if that was a good thing or a bad thing. I needed something to reignite the spark that had brought me to Africa. Family was a big part of that.

"Greg," Anne said. "Why don't you take Katherine out to show her the course? Go find Richard and get him to take her around."

"Come then," Greg said with a smile, as he pushed back from the table. "Let's see if Richard can give us a tour."

I was ready. As much as I loved getting to know family, I relished the idea of hanging out with people my own age. I was happy enough to play at being prim and proper myself but loved the idea of hitting the town. As we drove around the grounds, the boys painted visions of Cape Town's nightlife, complete with dancing, music, and clubs.

"It sounds awesome," I agreed, as I envisioned a bit of fun and frolic with them. "Definitely when I get back."

Another adventure was slated first. I was headed to Botswana in less than a week. The wilds of Africa awaited.

"Jo'Burg"

"Let me book you a flight," Weppie insisted. "It is too long to go across country on the bus."

"I appreciate it Weppie, but it's alright" I replied. "Honestly, I'm fine on the bus. I want to see the countryside."

While it might only be from the window of an Intercape Mainliner, I figured the bus would give me more of a perspective of my father's homeland. There were over 1300 kilometers between Brackenfell and Johannesburg, and I wanted to see them for myself, not just fly over them in a hurry. This trip was not about taking the easy or fast route. It was about being in the moment and experiencing all I could. Plus, the bus gave me a taste of independence. In theory anyway.

So, I waved goodbye to Uncle Jock and Aunt Elsa and climbed aboard the massive double-decker luxury bus that would take me across the country. Not exactly how the lower class travelled. Posh seats and friendly attendants greeted me.

"Would you care for a beverage?" the smiling woman asked as she paused at my seat.

"I would love a coffee," I replied. Anything to wake me up after our early start to the day.

I almost choked when she handed it to me though. The coffee was served the African way; extremely sweet and white. There was no question of how you took it. The rich black coffee I had conjured in my mind disappeared in swirls of the caramel-coloured chicory blend in my hand. It had nothing on Tim Hortons. If I wanted a caffeine fix though, I had to suck it up and get over it. It was a 15-hour bus ride and Timmies was nowhere in sight. The South African landscape was all that was on offer, and I had no choice but to sit back and enjoy the ride, sickly sweet coffee and all.

Blech...

After a few tentative sips on my brew, I laid the java aside. It just wasn't worth it. Never mind that I would have killed for the luxury months later. For now, I perked up for the journey ahead. I was single, mobile, and free!

As a rule, bus trips didn't faze me. I had taken my fair share of Greyhounds to Peterborough and back. This was comparable, if just a little longer. And more excitingly, it was through brand new terrain. I would cross through the Western and Eastern Cape, the Free State, and into Gauteng. It sounded exotic.

My excitement wore thin quickly though. In the grand scheme of things, the Mainliner was little better than the Greyhounds I was used to, and the hours ahead of me were long. Way too long. I recalled Weppie's offer but reminded myself that I had pointedly made this choice.

"Adventure," I muttered out the big plate glass windows.

Instead, I absorbed myself in the view. Red soil raced beside us, interspersed with dry scrub. How could someone grow crops in this vastly different loam? Back home, rich brown humus invited a wide variety of produce. Would carrots or potatoes grow to be a different colour or taste in this earth? My musings were the only answers I would get.

One can be fascinated by soil for only so long though. Soon enough my mind's eye was focused on the future. I shifted my weight from cheek to cheek and imagined what Botswana would hold. A brochure for Victoria Falls, Zimbabwe lay across my lap, and I dreamt of the possibilities depicted in its glossy pages—animals, white water, flora, and fauna galore! But my butt gave up caring about all of that long before we would arrive.

Out! my body screamed, as it itched to be free of its confines. *I need OUT of this chair. Out. Please God, let us stop soon, so I can at least stretch and breathe a moments peace...*

My ass was flat and refused to be ignored. No amount of subtle massage or squirming relieved could relieve the 10+ hours of confinement. Trips to the WC only offered temporary reprieve and it just wasn't enough. I needed to walk. I needed to run. I needed to get off the damn bus and out of the captivity of my seat!

"Not long now", I muttered to myself unconvincingly. What I wouldn't have given for the comparative puddle-jump that was my usual bus trips. Why had I not taken Weppie up on his offer? How could people subject themselves to trips like this on a regular basis? These questions would become clearer in time, but not today.

When Johannesburg finally came into sight, I breathed a sigh of relief for my cramped muscles. The bus wheezed and then issued a timely goodbye, with a squeal of airbrakes.

"Thank God," I murmured as I collected my belongings from the seat beside me.

I blissfully stepped into my cousin Naudé's waiting arms not a moment too soon. We exchanged hugs and pleasantries, then headed towards his car. As torturous as another trip in a vehicle was so soon after my release, at least this one would be quick and end in a bed. The pillow was a blissful companion.

I had two nights ahead of me to spend with Naudé before my trip into Botswana. It wasn't much of a window, but he was keen to give me a taste of Johannesburg while I was there. Before that could happen though, we had to go to the airport.

"Erica is coming home from a business trip to Italy," Naudé explained. "Once we pick her up, we'll show you Jo'burg."

"No problem," I replied.

I was at his mercy after all. A trip to the airport wasn't exactly exciting, but it was only a brief interlude before the show. And it meant I would get to meet his wife—more family. While we waited, he regaled me with stories about her and his stepchildren, Johannesburg, and his version of the politics of the country. Everyone had a different story to tell, and it was these stories that began to shape my views on what life in South Africa really looked like. Not just what I had heard from newsreels over the years. I was greedy for that bigger picture. I wanted all the stories I could find. I listened, rapt, then stared off into the crowd.

Naudé paused, staring in the direction my gaze lingered.

"What do you see?" he asked. "Who are you looking at?"

I shook myself free and smiled back at him.

"Oh nothing," I replied. "It's just someone who looks remarkably like someone I went to high school with."

"Go and talk to them," he exclaimed, as he peered into the crowd.

What are the odds of bumping into someone in the middle of a busy Johannesburg airport? Someone you know from home, thousands of miles away. Slim, at best.

I shook my head and said, "It can't be her. What would she be doing in South Africa?" But I couldn't help peering in her direction. I could not get over how familiar the woman looked. It couldn't be her though, I rationalized.

I turned back to Naudé and continued our conversation, but kept glancing in her direction, until I heard...

"Katherine?"

Oh my God! The familiarity wasn't just a figment of my imagination. It was real. I stared at the waving figure across the room.

"Miki?!"

We rushed to each other and couldn't resist hugging in disbelief.

"What are you doing here?" I asked when I pulled away.

"My brother is flying in to meet me," she explained. "He was in England but decided to fly here so we could explore South Africa together."

I was floored. She was waiting for her brother. He was flying in from England, while I waited for my cousin's wife who was flying in from Italy. They were on two separate flights, but coincidence had both flights arriving at approximately the same time. I bumped into a high school acquaintance on the other side of the world, by the sheer luck of timing.

The coincidences did not stop there though. Miki turned to her travelling companion.

"Katherine, meet Martin. I met him last year when I was in Europe. He's from Cape Town and convinced me to come see South Africa. Once Taro arrives, we plan to travel down the coast and hit Cape Town for Christmas."

"Nice to meet you Martin," I replied.

"Ya, and you," he said. "So where are you headed?"

"I'm staying here with my cousin Naudé for the moment but leaving for an overland trip to Botswana in a few days," I said. "I'll be back in Cape Town too though by Christmas."

"Oh?" he said with interest. "Whereabouts?"

"My Aunt and Uncle live in Brackenfell," I replied.

"Oh ja, whereabouts?" he inquired again. I was impressed. He knew the suburbs of Cape Town.

"They live in Protea Heights," I said.

"Oh ja, whereabouts?" he asked.

Ok, now I was officially freaked out. He knew the town, subdivision, and then asked for the street. And you know what? He knew exactly where that was as well. It had gone past coincidence, in my mind. Now the meeting with Miki seemed more like fate, kismet, destiny even! I was flabbergasted. How was it that I not only bumped into her in South

Africa, but that we both planned to be back in Cape Town at the same time? It didn't feel like mere coincidence.

As Taro arrived, followed shortly thereafter by Erica, we quickly ended the conversation. Miki and I exchanged phone numbers and addresses, then snagged another quick hug amongst the now teeming throng of people, who jostled towards luggage carousels. Would our destinies intertwine again? Time would tell, but other excursions were slated first. It was enough for now to have bumped into an old friend from high school.

Naudé, Erica, and I spilled out of the airport into Johannesburg's glare. I rode the wave of excitement at having met Miki, but Naudé promised more immediate adventure. We were off to Sun City for the afternoon.

Sun City. I had heard of it. Anyone who had listened to the radio in the 80s had heard of it. But not for the reasons my cousin was excited about. I had a song stuck in my head, and its accusations played in a loop in my mind. Artists United Against Apartheid recorded 'Sun City' in 1985. In the accompanying music video, dozens of musicians sang accusing lyrics, while images of barbed wire, police brutality, and overwhelming violence against blacks were juxtaposed against inviting swimming pools, engaging musicals, and the overall opulence of the ostensibly white resort. The popular artists who helped produce the song proclaimed they weren't going to play 'Sun City' in protest to South Africa's apartheid policies. The trick was, several other musicians had, and received extremely generous pay for their time. But these artists were standing up for the subjugated masses and were urging others to join them. Now I was headed there.

Guilt filled me, but didn't prevent us from going to the jewel of the North West province. I tried to reason that apartheid was over, but then remembered Khayelitsha. Apartheid was over in formal practice, but the

42

effects would linger for a long time to come. Was I right in going to a resort that had glorified the divide between blacks and whites? It didn't matter at that point because we were almost there.

Sun City was a beautiful amusement park, with several hotels, casinos, a golf course, and water parks on the sprawling property—probably along the lines of what I imagined Vegas to be like, not that I had been there to compare. Just two hours north of Johannesburg, this playground for the rich sported waterfalls, murals, and intricate statues everywhere you looked. It was enchanting and I almost forgot that it had been built during the dark days of apartheid—designed to be a place where you could gamble and see topless shows (activities banned in South Africa but allowed within Bophuthatswana's borders). That was over with now though and South Africa was doing their best to forge a new image for themselves in the world.

It was hard to forget the past though. In contrast to the luxury of Sun City and relative safety of Cape Town, I found even more barbed wire in Johannesburg. There were heavily-gated communities, with not one, but two check points that only allowed in residents and select visitors. I was informed that the number of car-hijackings, which happened all too frequently, were part and parcel of the reasoning behind these measures. It painted a bleak picture and a tough road to shake off South Africa's ugly past. I prayed for its future.

So, while I struggled with the places and pictures that Naudé drew for me, I looked for brighter spots where I could. Isn't that what food is for? When we fetched up at a 'King Pie', I knew something was right in the world. And I've always felt pie was perfect, so a fast-food chain devoted to pies? Heavenly! Their flaky pastries came in a multitude of savoury flavours that I couldn't resist; chicken, spinach and feta, cheese, pork pasties, and more. And everyone ate there. Pie had broken the colour barrier.

43

What can I say? I am a sucker for food. There would be plenty more of their delicious pies in the months to come too, but at the end of the day, a dash of fate and a pillow of pie made Jo'burg more memorable than I ever could have guessed.

*****

OVERLAND ADVENTURES

"Enter the SAMIL"

"Rise and shine," Naudé called as he knocked on the bedroom door.

I dug deeper under the blankets in protest. The sun wasn't even up yet. That left me incapable of words on a good day. But today I was headed to Botswana, so I had to get up. I threw back the covers and quickly got dressed, then joined Naudé for the drive to the Drifters headquarters. As we drove, the sun inched into the sky. As I slipped my sunglasses on, I reluctantly admitted that it would probably be a perfect day. How little could I realize.

Naudé lifted my heavy backpack out of the boot of his car once we arrived.

"Go talk to someone," Naudé encouraged.

"Yeah," I mumbled, but didn't move. The introvert in me was screaming in protest, but I feigned aloof to stall for time. As much as I paid good money to be there, I wasn't quite ready to commit myself to the adventure I had signed up for. I knew no one and couldn't muster up the courage to change that just yet. I felt like I needed to suss out the group before I stepped in. At least that was the reasoning I hid behind. And there was plenty to look at while I stalled.

Central to the activity around me was the monstrous vehicle I would call home for the next two weeks. A black and white striped truck stood amidst the waiting cluster of people. Two men busily stowed bags in the compartments under the seating area. One was a young, lithe, white man, heavily tanned from many days spent in the sun. The other stout individual was as black as night. They matched the zebra stripe of the truck in a conspicuous way.

My eyes moved from these two strikingly different men to our mode of transport. Here was a thing to be reckoned with. The vehicle was nothing like I had ever seen, let alone ridden in. It was a nine-foot-tall truck, or overland cruiser. In other applications, it is used as an army personnel carrier or as a service truck for construction or mining. This one would carry us through game parks and other rough terrains. I didn't doubt that it could handle anything thrown at it. It certainly looked sturdy. And big!

Bench seats faced one another in the back, with nothing but air and the height of the massive tires to protect passengers. Bulging canvas at the top of the windows hid the rolled-up flaps, which would protect us from the elements, as necessary. I wondered if they would give any protection from the animals the brochures promised we would spy. Not likely.

While the vehicle appeared to seat 20 people, it didn't look like that many travellers milled about. As I scanned the group, I saw a couple in their late forties, another in their early fifties, two similar-looking young women that could have been in their late teens or early twenties, another couple in their twenties, a tall blonde man in his late twenties or early thirties, a single young man, a single young woman, and myself. I would learn we were a diverse group collected from Austria, Germany, South Africa, Switzerland, USA, and of course Canada, but for now all I knew was that they were strangers to me.

A voice startled me from my contemplations, "Are you ready to go?"

Beside me stood one of the men who had been stowing luggage earlier. He faced me with a grin.

"Karel," he stated as he thrust his hand out at me.

"I think so," I stammered as I shook his hand. "My name's Katherine," I remarked with a hesitant wave of my arm. "There's plenty of people here."

"Ja[8]," Karel remarked as he nodded at the group of expectant travellers. "We'll be picking up one more in Maun too." Then he turned and clapped his hands, as he called out "Lekker[9]! Are we ready to go?"

Heads swivelled in his direction and nodded with murmurs of assent.

"Alright then. All aboard!"

And with that, it was time to go. We bid farewell to friends and family, then awkwardly clambered up wherever we saw fit. Karel and Masters, our other guide, swung into the front of the cab, and with a rumble the truck sprang to life. There was no turning back now.

I couldn't resist the smile that played across my lips, as I waved Johannesburg goodbye. From the looks of our guide and his assistant, plus the grins on the faces around me, I suspected true adventure was now upon me. Next stop; Nata Lodge, Botswana.

---

[8] yes.
[9] good; pleasant.

"Girls to the Right, Gents to the Left"

The truck bounced along the highway but could not succeed in bouncing the grin off my face. I had left the safe confines of my relatives to venture out on safari. I was headed to Botswana to explore Maun, the Okavango Delta, Moremi, Chobe National Park, and the famous Victoria Falls in Zimbabwe. No seat belts tied me down in this open-air transport, and I felt free and alive.

My companions chatted amongst themselves, as we sped along the highway. Still feeling timid, I instead attempted to capture the experience thus far in my journal. I quickly gave up however, as the pen sprawled illegible across the jouncing page. Apparently, it was time to take in the world around me from my non-existent window instead.

Be in the moment Katherine…

A voice broke my reverie.

"Where are you from?" a woman asked.

"Canada," I answered, as I turned to her. "And you?"

"Tristan and I are from Austria," she replied. "My name's Sassa. This is extremely exciting, yes?"

It was indeed. We were strangers thrown together by circumstance of adventure, and that was all that united us at that point. Tentative conversations would change that, but for now we were mostly polite. The further we got from Johannesburg the more arid and isolated the landscape became, but the richer was our banter. Before I knew it, we reached the border, and another stamp was added to my passport. We entered Botswana and I couldn't have been more excited. A new country! It was a new world, like nowhere I had ever been, and I loved it.

With South Africa behind us, Karel seemed to relax into his role of tour guide. He turned in his seat to chat with us, but soon enough jumped through the window in the back of the cab to join our space.

"So, are you ready for adventure yet? Hmm?" he asked. "Today, it's a long travel day, but it won't be so bad after that. Tonight, we spend in style at Nata Lodge; there's a pool, restaurant, bar... All very nice, really. Ja! But tomorrow—that is the end of luxury," he warned with a shake of a finger. "The *real* adventure begins then. I hope you all like to camp! There will be plenty of it over the next 16 days."

His stern looks were tapered with raucous laughter that eased tensions in the group. I couldn't help but like him already. As we bounced along, he shared more snippets about Botswana, its people, and the animals that called the flat, arid country home. Details like that Botswana gained independence from England in 1966, but that people had lived there for over 400,000 years.[10] Britain's influence meant that the official language was English, but Setswana was widely spoken across the country, as well as several other local dialects. It meant that when we went into the Okavango Delta in a few days, we would be able to communicate with the guides who would paddle us in, not to mention have them point out the many animals we would spy along the way.

"What about the Big 5," Pete asked. "Will we see them?"

---

[10] Parsons, N. (2021, May 24). Botswana. Encyclopædia Britannica. https://www.britannica.com/place/Botswana.

"Elephants, lion, buffalo; no problem," he replied. "Leopards are harder to spot, as they are night hunters and sleep hidden in trees during the day. As for rhinos, our best bet will probably be when we go into Moremi. But they are rare! Sies."

Apparently, nothing stumped him. He cajoled everyone into joining the conversation and helped make our reticent group a little more relaxed. Once laughter filled our midst, he left us to peruse the guidebooks and climbed back into the front seat. You could feel the tension drift away behind us. We had indeed become Drifters.

The thoughts he left us to daydream over were visions of camping in game parks with the sound of animals as backdrop, seeing those same animals at daybreak, and relaxing at the end of the day with a meal cooked over an open fire. It was my idea of a perfect vacation, if not everyone's. This was the Africa I had envisioned in my youth. Now I was here and about to immerse myself in all its offerings.

My delighted musings slowly dissipated the longer we bumped and bounced along without stop. A scan of the horizon failed to materialize any towns in sight, and I began to squirm on my bench. The day shone hot and many of us doffed layers as we streamed through the countryside. The removal of my sweater did not dispel the tightening around my mid-section though. My discomfort led me to notice other's wiggles as well. I began to reach a saturation point. How was I to delicately ask for a bathroom break within a group of relative strangers, I wondered?

"Karel, when are we going to stop next?" Sue piped up.

Yes, I thought. *Thank God!* Disappointment wrenched my tortured bowels (barely recovered from their previous ordeal with traveller's trots), as Karel stated it was still a ways to our destination.

"I have to use the toilet," Barb stated.

"I do too!" I desperately added.

Several other murmurs of the same ilk filtered up to the front of the cab. Karel turned around and waved his hand out the window with a huge smirk.

"There is nowhere to stop," he said. "If you have to go, this is your water closet."

Desperation was amongst us and agreement went out. "Stop," was the resounding answer. Masters pulled the mighty SAMIL (South African MILitary) truck to the side of the dirt road we now travelled on. As soon as it stopped, people hastily dropped from the sides of the truck to relieve themselves.

"Girls on this side," Karel hollered out. "And gents to the other."

Roughing it struck home, as the ladies sought out scrub brush to squat behind. Privacy and decorum disappeared, as relief washed through our band of travelling companions. For this is what we were now. Kleenexes were shared around to those in need, with embarrassed looks offered as thanks. We stretched legs and numb bums. Laughter aided in letting go of a few more tensions. This was Africa. It was the start of our 16-day excursion, and it would surely get rougher from here. With an empty bladder, my smile returned.

"Ok. Let's go!" Karel yelled to our little bunch of tourists.

We climbed back up a little less hastily than our descent moments before and were back on the rough road again. The day passed in a blur of occasional villages, rare people, and lots of scant brush as landscape. The picnic lunch we enjoyed on the side of the road quickly became a memory, as we resumed our goal for Nata Lodge. But as the sun dipped low in the sky, we finally reached our destination after a long first day on the road.

The day was not done with us yet though. Oh no. Despite Karel proclaiming this was our luxury stop, we had lessons to learn on how to survive in the backcountry.

Lesson number one—how to pitch a tent. They would be our homes from here on out, so this was a valuable lesson.

"Okay. Everyone get into pairs and grab a tent. Once you have a tent, I will show you how to put it up."

We paired up as instructed and grabbed tent bags, then followed Karel to where Sue and Barb had lain their canvas puddle. They were our lucky demonstration tent.

Karel stood with arms akimbo and stared hard at his inexperienced tourists. We were all neat, clean, and looked woefully unprepared for the travails we were to face. He shook his head and unfurled the tent onto the ground. Before he unfolded the big canvas though, he paused dramatically. Here was our second important lesson of the day.

"Always check for scorpions!" he cried as he went into an in-depth arthropod lesson which detailed their claws, stingers, and the poisons they could inflict.

Apparently not only did we not want sticks and stones to break our bones as we slept, but woe be to the hapless camper who erected their tent in a scorpion's domain. Karel went on to state that the prudent camper should check the area they chose to put up their tent beforehand to ensure no creepy crawlies lurked there.

"Really! Believe me," he exclaimed with an almost amusing wide-eyed passion and wave of his hands. That is if you weren't suddenly terrified of every bump, bug or branch you came across.

His lecture didn't end there. While you might have been lulled into a sense of security that you had somehow miraculously picked the prime campsite, you weren't out of the veldt yet.

"In the morning, check underneath your tents again," he admonished. "Scorpions like warm places to rest their own heads after a night of hunting and your tents are perfect for them. You don't want to start your day with a fierce pinch or sting."

It certainly wasn't worth reaching a blind hand or foot into a concealed space. Hence you also didn't leave your shoes outside your tent overnight. No need to find a scorpion via unprotected toes.

"Look, then shake, shake, shake!" was Karel's motto.

He had a way with words that made everything seem hazardous. I realize it was prudent to have us aware of the potential dangers that could befall us on this very real tour into the wilds, but I also think he enjoyed the looks of trepidation that crossed his nervous patrons' faces when he proclaimed, "Ja. Really!"

Spiders, snakes, scorpions, and spaghetti; these were all things to be feared, if not respected in the proper light. We would be cooking our own meals and too bad to those who feared their turn at the potjie pot. I would quickly come to learn that a potjie pot (pronounced poy-key) was a heavy, three-legged cast-iron pot with a handle; a staple for cooking over campfires.

That would be another night though. Nata Lodge had most of the comforts of home, so a cold beer, hot meal, and washrooms were enjoyed on our first evening together. No scorpions interrupted our dinner or sleep. And enjoy it we did.

"Blinded by the Baobab"

I stood at the edge of the Makgadikgadi Salt Pan in the middle of Botswana. A sign board claimed it was one of the world's largest salt pans, among other fun facts. It was also the site of a huge former inland lake the size of Switzerland. Of course, it had dried up several thousand years ago and now was just a series of flat salt pans interspersed by desert. During the wet season, a thin layer of water covered the pans creating an oasis of sorts. Now though, a dredging of blue-green algae was all that could be seen. This didn't deter visitors to Makgadikgadi Pans National Park though and it certainly didn't deter us.

The Makgadikgadi was our first taste of nature and game viewing. It was flat and seemed to stretch forever. Aside from a nearby observation tower, which gave visitors some much-needed height to see birds and game, no other significant structures could be seen. No trees blocked this view. In fact, very few scrubby plants could be seen at all. Dry, dusty-looking sand provided a tenuous hold to sparse vegetation that often looked not far from fossilization. In fact, the lack of moisture made the area inhospitable to most living creatures during the dry season. When the rains finally trickled down from the north it was a different story though. The salt pans came alive with flamingos, zebras, and wildebeest in the thousands. It was a feast for the visitor's eyes.

It was far from that the day we were there though.

"You have an hour to explore," Karel stated as we climbed down from the SAMIL.

People nodded and waved to him as they went in their own separate directions. Some headed for the observation tower. Others made straight for the sludge, cameras, binoculars, and determination at the ready. It was our first taste of the wilds of Africa and our enthusiasm buoyed us up, even as watery mirages wavered and teased on the super-heated horizon.

"There," cried Eric with an outstretched finger.

I squinted at the dot he pointed to and trusted his judgement that he actually saw something more than dubious visions.

"What am I looking at?" I queried.

"Some kind of deer?" he answered uncertainly.

"It's a springbok," cried Pete. He held a pair of binoculars pressed to his face scanning the horizon.

Of course, it was a springbok. They are the most common and abundant antelope in Southern Africa. We would see thousands of them across the many parks scheduled for our trip. Despite the apparent barrenness though, we did manage to check a few other animals off our safari checklists; Kori bustard, secretary bird, reedbuck. They were hard to spy against the glare of the salt pans, but they were there. And more importantly, it served as a taste of what was to come. Other than just dust and salt.

"Ach, mein steifel[11]," cried Jens from further out in the pan.

We laughed, as he hopped on one foot, attempting to extract his boot from the mud. Despite a lack of rain to fill the dusty pans, the area remained stubbornly mucky. Once you wandered away from the edges, your shoes gave proof to that. Everyone was covered in dust and sticky, salty mud.

It was nothing as compared to what it would have been with a little rain though, but we wouldn't get the chance to experience that. Or see the legions of flamingos and other birds which came to the area to breed in the short-lived wet season. Not that the lake would ever return, but the salt pans would be more hospitable for hopeful mammals looking for love. Sometimes location is everything for amorous intentions.

My gaze drifted to the tall, blonde specimen beside me. Timing is everything and I wasn't sure what to make of mine. Eric definitely drew my eye, and try as I might, I couldn't see Ron anywhere on the horizon. It was hard not to return the attentions of this handsome man, despite the quiet nagging reminder of my love life back in Canada. That was problematic. And quite possibly wouldn't withstand me being gone for six months. But still…

"Time to go," called Karel.

I dragged my gaze from Eric's blue eyes and trudged back to the SAMIL. Saved for the moment.

"Keep your eyes open," Karel said, as we slowly left the salt pans behind.

---

[11] my boots.

56

While Masters had a keen eye and pointed out the occasional impala or springbok, for me the most awe-inspiring sight on our way out was a tree. While most trees in this area were rather meager, in part due to infrequent rains, one species stood out from the rest. Rising majestically above the world was a most unique tree—the baobab. And it was monstrous.

The distinctly African baobab is a tree which appears to have been flipped upside down by Gods pulling pranks in an arid land. The upper sparse branches appear more like a root system, with what should be the main part of the tree, living underground. Leaves were in short supply as a result of the dry season, but never abundant on a good day. I imagined catching sight of Alice chasing the white rabbit from a hole at the base of one.

We came across one giant which had succumbed and was lying on its side.

"Can we get out and look at it?" I called up to Karel.

While he had probably seen plenty of the giants before, we were in awe. It looked almost two stories high lying prone!

As soon as Masters stopped, we raced to the tree. Several of us attempted to scramble up the smooth sides of it, to no avail. These behemoths had time spans that surpassed whole lineages of locals in the area, perhaps growing a thousand years or more. I was mesmerized by the magnificent piece of nature that seemed so stark, yet somehow survived in this desolate land.

Again, the rumble of the SAMIL's engine called us back to the truck though. The road lay ahead of us, and another traveller was to join our midst in Maun. With a laughing black-backed jackal trailing behind us, we settled back onto our benches and dreamed of drifting through the Delta in the days to come.

"Drifting in the Okavango"

Marjory and I leaned back in our mokoro, as the still waters of the Okavango Delta drifted by us. From the back of the boat, Oscar casually pushed us along with a long pole that dug into the depths of the river. We weren't breaking any speed records, but the pace was perfect. Sunshine filled our eyes and hearts.

Occasionally, Oscar would point to a distant dot that moved on the horizon and whisper "Look impala!" or "Wildebeest". I was constantly amazed by all our guides' keen vision. They could spot an animal large as an elephant or small as a jackal from what seemed like miles away. I had a hard enough time keeping track of the other boats, let alone anything else.

"This is a piece of heaven," I remarked, as I trailed my fingers in the warm water.

From under the brim of Marjory's straw hat, she murmured "Absolutely" with a sigh.

Marjory was our newest addition. She had joined our travelling group the day before in Maun. Her arrival was met with toasts aplenty, which made for a rough start to the following day, but no matter. Nothing that a little water sipped from the clear Okavango River couldn't dispel. Karel considered it team building. I considered it a breakdown in my hard-crafted decorum but couldn't help but love every minute of it. I felt like I was supposed to be the nice, polite Canadian girl, but the castle of Castle beer cans which I had a hand in helping erect, suggested that perhaps I was not as demure as I felt I was meant to be. But we all enjoyed letting our hair down, and that was the point of the trip in the first place. To see, experience, be ourselves, and own every minute of it.

For the moment, the warm breeze blew any lingering bits of hangover away, as we watched the world glide by from the relative safety of our mokoros. No cries of "Hippo!" interrupted our reveries.

Of course, Karel had made sure to warn us of their dangers as well.

"No cute Disney hippos here," he said. "They cause more human deaths than any other animal in Africa. Really! An adult male can reach up to 2,000 kilo! And don't think that slows them down. Nee! Those stubby little legs can reach speeds of 30 kilometers per hour and leave you trampled in their wake. Ja! Never get between a hippo on land and their route back to water. Or near their young. They are dangerous and unpredictable. You don't want to mess with them!"

He had a way of making everything seem treacherous. Which I suppose was warranted. It was better to be safe than sorry when we were hours from proper help and only had the security of our wooden canoes to keep us away from their grinding teeth. Thankfully the grey and pink submarine-like mammals were spied from a safe enough distance away to satiate our curiosity, but not tempt fate. We could soak up the sun and serenity of the Okavango Delta and relax into the sense of security we chose to surround ourselves with. It worked for me.

As Marjory and I rounded a bend in the stream, we spied the lead boats beached in a shallow area ahead of us. Jens and Elvira stood on shore, while Tristan and Sassa stepped out of their mokoro and waded onto the sandbar. Their polers scurried to empty supplies onto the beach beside them. It was one of few spots we had seen that looked solid enough to stand on, let alone set up table and chairs. Everywhere else had been either waterway or lined with tall reeds along the edges of the swamp.

Oscar pushed us hard into the shallows and jammed us into the soft bottom of the Botswana superhighway. Freedom was ours! Marjory and I gratefully stepped out of our boat into the warm waters of the Okavango and waded toward the little group that formed on shore. Food hampers, stools and folding tables emerged from the boats that had sped ahead to set up our lunch siesta.

"Make yourselves useful," cried Karel as he and Masters set up our temporary kitchen.

Right. I grabbed a knife and sliced tomatoes for sandwiches, while Mino and Eric set chairs out for everyone. Sue and Barb reached for cheese and bread for assembly detail.

Once the last of our straggling crew joined us, we all tucked into sandwiches ravenously. It's funny how a little fresh air can create an appetite unrelated to our sedentary activities. Or was it because no one had had the stomach for breakfast after our castle of Castles? Regardless, once the crumbs were licked off sticky fingers, it was time to play.

"Can we go for a swim?" Sue asked.

"Oh, yes!" Sassa added.

"Sure, ja[12]," Karel said. "You can swim in the beach area, but don't go far. Stay in the shallows where we can see you."

---

[12] yes.

"And watch out for hippos, right," added Sue.

"Yes, man!" exclaimed Karel. "Those hippos are bad don't. You don't even know!"

We all laughed as we streaked into the water. Bath time! We splashed like preschoolers at a water park, as the warm water washed away the last of the previous night's cobwebs. Sighs of ecstasy were the loudest roars to be heard in our vicinity.

When we finally emerged wrinkled and happy, it was time to pack up the lunch debris and head out again. A bit of land in the middle of the swamp was our destination and it was time we got there. As it would be our home for the next few nights, we needed to get there to set up our first bush camp. Once there, we would be busy, so a little more lazy poling along sounded good to me in the interim.

Before long, our polers maneuvered us to the spot of land we would call home for the next few days. Gone was leisure hour. I spilled out of my mokoro and re-joined Eric to erect our tent and roll out the beds. Lucky Marjory got a tent to herself, as she had been the last to join our band of merry travellers.

Did I mention that Eric and I had shared a tent the previous nights? Everyone had to pair up, and him and I were both single. Well, without travelling companions anyway. Jack was on a different planet in my mind now. I had slipped out of civilization and wasn't looking back. Not that anything had happened. Yet. He was 1.93 meters, blonde haired, blue-eyed, and just the right amount of muscle. And when he stretched out on his roll mat, then immersed himself in a book, I couldn't help but notice. I could feel the heat of his body from my own sleeping bag a mere few inches away. Occasionally our arms brushed one another with an electric jolt when either of us turned the pages in our books. I couldn't have written him any better if I was creating a character for myself. He was a classic dreamboat.

But thoughts of home, and my erstwhile boyfriend, kept me to my own side of the tent for the time being. Eric's smile threatened to change that, even as I grappled with my undulating willpower. I wasn't sure if I would win the battle or if I even wanted to mount a defense.

I was in Africa. Jack was not. I didn't know when I would return home or if I even wanted to. Here, I was surrounded by friendly faces and exciting adventure. Thoughts of home only reminded me of the emotional struggles that Jack and I might never move beyond. Would he still be there with open arms when my plane even landed? I knew that was highly questionable.

There was nothing to be gained by going there though, so I consciously put him to the back of my mind. No judgement. What I did or did not do was my choice to make. I would live in the moment and deal with the consequences later. If I had to. Maybe...

Back to that moment. It was time for us to set up the rest of our camp. It was an excellent distraction.

"We need a firepit," Karel said. "We'll need wood for the fire too. Get on it. Collect rocks, brush, and someone put up the laundry line too."

Masters showed us how to hack away with a machete at the brush collected, in order to make sizeable pieces for the fire. The polers set up their own camp, plus took on the heavier jobs at our site. It wasn't a free ride though. We were expected to help, regardless of the fact we had paid to be here. We all took turns with dinner prep. We all washed and put away dishes. We were all part of the team. And so far, I loved every minute of it.

Except maybe one little part. We were on this adventure to be exposed to the beauty of Africa and were expected to leave nothing behind to mar its beauty. Everything brought in, must be taken back out again. To a point.

"Karel, ummm," Barb stammered. "Uh, where do we go to... um, relieve ourselves?"

Ah yes, a latrine. We knew there were no water closets at hand. No fully stocked porta-potties hid behind the next tree or bush. And Karel was adamant that we had to minimize the footprint of our journey. This was as much for our safety, as for the enjoyment of the pristine beauty for others. And so, to not attract wild animals with our scent, we needed to lessen it.

Karel pointed into the bush.

"Help yourself!" he declared.

"But uhhh," her eyes darted in the direction he pointed, then dropped to the ground. "but what about if, err..."

She was the first to ask, but not the only one who would need to know. Karel threw his head back in a mighty laugh and walked over to one of the totes full of equipment. He rummaged about then emerged with a shovel. Apparently, we wouldn't have to pack everything back out again.

"You need this!" he chuckled. "Now don't go far, as we don't want to have to rescue you from lions on the prowl. And I want you all to use the same general area for shovel detail, ja. So. Dig yourself a hole. And don't forget to bury it after. We don't want to attract animals with our scat."

The poop shovel could not be avoided or denied. Modesty still existed but handing off the shovel to a squirmy face was done with knowing eyes, and the reality that we were roughing it to the extreme. I was not averse to squatting in the bush, but this proved to break down any last vestiges of reserve that existed between us. All you could do was hope that not too many eyes followed your path as you trudged off to take care of business.

And we paid good money for this.

"Don't forget the TP[13], Bubs," yelled Sue after her sister, as she slinked into the bush to the sound of our laughter.

In the interim, the busyness of setting up camp slowed as the sun made its way across the horizon. A simple meal was created, and we tucked in with relish. The fresh air had whetted our appetites well. I took my first turn as dish washer with Elvira, while some of the others gathered more brush for the fire. It was our security against the animals that awoke once the sun went down. But a campfire and stars naked of city lights were a treat, nonetheless.

The occasional cry of lions in the distance served to remind us that we were not alone at our circle of light though. Vulnerability lay beyond the fire's glow and Karel had plenty more cautionary tales up his sleeve to warn us with. We hadn't seen his scorpions yet, but he reminded us that they were definitely still around. Bigger threats now though were the animals that surrounded us in the wilds.

"We are in their home now," Karel stated. "No more city life for you. Remember that and be respectful."

---

[13] toilet paper.

Crocodiles and lions would dominate the ghost stories around our campfire in the days to come, but for the time being, a plan was set in place for the next day. People wearily drifted off to their waiting tents, as more wood was added to the fire for protection. I eventually joined them too.

The polers played double duty as babysitters to guard us as the night grew long. Their camp was a short distance from ours, but close enough for security's sake. Insurance aside, it would not look good in the adventure brochures to have a running death tally en route. So, they took turns stoking the fire and guarding the perimeter of our camp throughout the night. It was an assurance that the safety of all of us would be maintained. And I slept a little sounder knowing that.

"Survival of the Fittest"

"Rise and shine, my friends," Karel quietly called with a shake of our tents the next morning. "Time for a game walk."

It was pitch black. Dawn nowhere in sight.

"Didn't we just go to sleep?" I mumbled to Eric.

"Come on," he nudged me playfully from across the tent.

Suddenly, I felt a little more alert and smiled in the darkness. How was it that he had that effect on me? Instead of being grumpy at being woken up, I put on my game face and aimed to exude fun-loving traveller, ready for anything. Knowing that our other travellers also waited served to get me moving though, and soon enough we were all standing outside our tents staring blearily at Karel and Masters. I shouldn't have worried about impressing though, as it was early for all of us. I wasn't the only rumpled camper to crawl out of a tent with blank face and less than chipper attitude.

"No talking as we walk," Karel instructed as he led us away from camp.

No problem, I thought, as my drowsy brain shuffled along on autopilot. None of us were capable of stringing a conversation together yet anyway.

Karel turned and motioned for us to follow, with Masters bringing up the rear. Despite being in the middle of a swamp, Karel led us to an incongruously dry plain. We made our way on foot; no boats or polers for exit strategy. Our best defense was a quiet passage, so conversation was kept to a minimum. Pointed fingers served for direction with few whispered words.

We didn't need anyone to help identify the giant, grey, tusked mammals we spied though. As the first light of day began to illuminate the world, elephants appeared. They seemed much larger than from the safety of the SAMIL. Their majesty left us speechless.

As the hike progressed, we saw even more. There were Gemsbok and buffalo; never quite far enough away to be called distant. Wildebeest and impala moved along with herds of zebras in plain sight. Solitary Rothschild Giraffe trimmed leaves off trees 20 feet in the air. We diligently remained quiet, as we watched on a mere few hundred yards away.

I refused to consider that we might stumble across anything as dangerous as a leopard or hyena, as we walked along on foot. The fierce lullaby of roaring lions from the night before? We would never see those predators either, I prayed. I knew it was possible, but also knew nothing could be done if we did see them. Our protection was to shout, clap our hands, or attempt to look bigger than we felt. I didn't feel excessively big or mighty though, so opted for stealth and quiet voices. I also stuck pretty close to Masters.

After our silent journey looped us closer to camp once more, tensions eased, and conversation broke out.

"Alright," Karel called, back to his usual jubilant tone. "Who's ready for lunch and a siesta?"

"Me," we echoed along the line.

"This is so cool," Sue exclaimed, as she fell beside me in line.

"Oh my god! Right!" I replied. "I've always dreamt of this, but never thought it would actually happen. Being in Africa? Wandering around the Okavango Delta?! This is surreal! No pamphlet or zoo can prepare you for this…"

I waved my arms around me. African air filled my lungs, as the Okavango River slowly burbled nearby. The sound of animals grunting in the bush surrounded us. Fresh footprints around camp gave proof that they came even closer than that. This was something I had always imagined, but never thought would actually come to be.

"You think this is a zoo?" Karel interrupted, as we entered camp. "Not likely! Ach, far from it. On our last expedition, one of the guides told a story about a man who ventured too close to the river alone. Esel! A crocodile snatched him from his feet in the blink of an eye. Not a sound…"

I was sufficiently chastised. More importantly though, the story effectively kept us together in groups whenever we ventured close to shore, even when allowed into bathe. The stories didn't stop there though.

"Pasop[14]! Your splashing won't protect you," Karel called out. "Ag man, it'll attract crocs. They'll think your splashing is a wounded animal and hap—give you a bite. Really!" He added, "We don't have thick skins or sharp tusks either. You'll be sommer buggered. Sies, we're vulnerable, ja. Definitely not the top of the food chain, nè."

Thanks for making bath time a precarious adventure Karel. It's a wonder we didn't drink more in fear of every rustle and bump we came across. The Okavango camp was a dry one though. Philosophy was our poison now.

We had slipped into a primordial time. Survival of the fittest was a fact of life and the reality was not lost on us. No one cared to push their luck and see if's Karel's tales were true or not. Better to be safe, than sorry. There weren't second chances for sorry here.

So, in my free time I updated a log of the animals we spied on our walks, read, or snuck in a doss (naptime). It didn't hurt that Eric was nearby either. As the days passed, we gravitated closer and closer together. Dangerously so for my moral predicament, but everything came down to primal levels in the bush. And so, the days passed.

By evening, the fire stoked conversation about our primitive history. Seeing a plethora of animals in their natural element made Darwin's Theory of Evolution seem entirely plausible.

---

[14] beware.

"It's easy to believe in survival of the fittest here," Pete said. "The old, slow, and weak keep the rest of the herds alive. There is no denying the existence of predator versus prey, and the checks and balances that go with them."

Resonant grunts, roars, and howls punctuated our conversation.

"Where did it all begin though?" Bubs asked.

"That's easy," Eric commented. "Evolution."

"Nope," Karel countered. "I've read a little story from a book called the Bible. Ever heard of the Miracle of Creation?"

"But look at the animals," Barb said.

"What about creatures that crawled from the ocean," I added.

Had we once been simple protozoa? Were we more closely related to the animals that roamed beyond our flames than we realized? The flickers of fire might have been unchanged from the ones which warmed our prehistoric ancestors years before, but what exactly did they look like; Hominoid, Neanderthal, or Ape? Could Man once have dragged his knuckles through this awesome land, or perhaps crawled out of these very swamps?

"Eish, man! I was never sand or a fish!" Karel shouted. "And I'm *not* a blooming ape! You won't find any monkeys in my family tree! Sies…"

And with that it was time for bed.

"Ooh, oooh, Ahhh," screeched Sue as we all dragged our knuckles back to our primitive lairs for the night.

"Stroppy moegoe," Karel grumbled as he made his own way to bed. "Jislaaik, I'm gatvol with the lot of 'em…"

Yea, he wasn't impressed.

*****

While Karel might have wanted to wash his hands of our heathen thoughts and ideas, after three nights he still deigned to deliver us out of the Okavango Delta. Our mokoros were beached for the last time and we climbed back up onto the SAMIL to return to Maun. The next leg of the journey awaited.

"We're going to take the flight over the Delta," Babs said to me. "You have to come with!"

"Janee, it'll be lekker[15]," added Sue.

"Eish, but it costs 175 Rand (ZAR)!" I pointed out. I had begun to pick up the catchy Afrikaans lingo already and couldn't resist throwing in some slang when I could.

"Ag man, you only live once," Sue chided. "Com!"

"Fine!"

Who needed more convincing than that? Not I apparently. Before I knew it, Barb, Sue, Elvira, and I were climbing into a tiny six-seater plane to view Botswana from the sky.

---

[15] good; pleasant.

With everyone strapped in, the little plane rumbled along the rough airstrip, then bravely leapt into the sky. The world instantly transformed into a grainy Natural Geographic television special, as we swung between touching the heavens and flying low enough to almost brush the ground. Equal parts awe, exhilaration, and dizziness filled me.

We saw massive herds of zebras intermixed with wildebeest. Our pilot banked steeply for the best view possible of vultures dining on a fallen giraffe. The small plane dropped lower, as we herded a tower of gangly giraffes across the plains, before rising into the cerulean skies once more. The money spent seemed a paltry exchange now.

Of course, I don't think my flight mates entirely agreed on that point. Elvira was yellow by the time we landed an hour later. And Bubs ran to the toilet as soon as the plane's little doors opened. But to see the swamp that we had just spent the last four days in was incredible! It took my breath away. Even if it took away the other ladies' appetites.

Meanwhile back in town, as we grazed the African skies, the rest of our group toured around Maun while our guides stocked up on supplies. There were no shops where we headed to next; Moremi, Savuti, and Chobe. We had to have everything we needed before we left, as there would be no last-minute trips to the store to pick up milk or bread. If we didn't have it, we wouldn't be getting it where we were going. So, by the time we met back up, the SAMIL was restocked and ready to go.

Before we set off for the bush once more though, we took advantage of one more night in town. Who can resist a meal prepared by others with cold drinks to wash it down with?

"Anyone ready for a pint?" Sue asked as we headed to the bar after dinner.

"I'm in," I chimed in.

My hand was just one of many that shot up. The beer flowed fast and free, and I was belly up to the bar. The first month of sobriety at my aunt and uncle's house was forgotten, as my poor liver got a proper workout. Being a little worse for wear in the morning was a small price to pay for an experience of a lifetime in the heart of Africa. It certainly didn't stop me from enjoying another night in Maun. And by morning we would be off again, so there would be plenty of time for recovery to come. We had to take advantage of Botswana's hospitality while we could get it after all. We were headed into the heart of Botswana's renowned game parks, and there were no pubs there. What was one more for the road?

But you know it still hurt the next morning. No matter. By the time we stopped to set up camp, I would be fine. Really, by the time we hit the game park, I would forget my woes altogether. Because, well, animals...

Botswana's game parks were incredible, to say the least. Using the label "renowned" didn't do justice to the experience. We were inundated with animal sightings almost upon arrival. These animals weren't just distant brown dots either, that I would have no hope of recognizing once pictures were developed. The SAMIL got us within mere metres of animals. Plus, the height of the truck gave us a bird's eye view. We looked down on warthogs, lions, cheetahs, sable, hippos, vervet monkeys, baboons, and bushbuck.

"Look there," Masters whispered more than once. I was in awe of his keen ability to spot wild animals I never would have glimpsed without his help.

"What? What does he see?" I whispered back.

"A leopard," Tristan said, as his arm mimicked Masters' own.

There in a tree, a leopard lay working his way through an impala. It balanced itself between thick branches high up in the canopy, but not high enough to hide it from our sight in the tall SAMIL. I marvelled at the sight, as we sat watching the leopard devour its prize. Unlike other predators, leopards were solitary hunters. They didn't feel the need to share.

Time and again, Masters spied animals. A short while later, his arm shot out again, this time pointing into the veldt. There were no trees for animals to perch in. No hills to hide behind. Again, I struggled to see what his practised eye spied, twisting this way and that.

Marjory gasped, "Oh my god! Look!"

And then I saw them; a pack of wild dogs trotted out from behind nearby bushes. We fell silent, as their yips and barks filled the air. They were moving fast. We trailed along behind the energetic pack, as closely as we dared. They seemed unphased by the bulk of the SAMIL, but I suppose they had seen plenty of game trucks before. It helped that they were laser-focused on the task at hand.

This was not a family trot for fun. African wild dogs are highly skilled hunters and travel in packs of up to 20 dogs to chase down their prey. They had their sights set on a small family of impala that bounced into view and now scrambled to escape. With quick precision and intricate teamwork, the dogs went to work. As with most of life in Africa, it was survival of the fittest. The slowest and most feeble were always at greatest risk. The youngest too.

As we watched, the pack divided the family up. Their barks and yips served as instructions to their pack, but for the confused antelopes, they were terrifying cacophony. A baby veered away, and its decision sealed its fate. The wild dogs swiftly attacked and ripped it to shreds.

While some of us gasped and turned away in horror, I couldn't help but be awestruck by the sight. Cameras flashed in succession as we captured the scene. Pete paused to peek out from behind his lens and captured the moment for all of us.

"Wow," he said softly. It was nothing short of phenomenal and we knew it.

Survival of the fittest gained new significance. These were experiences that one just did not come across every day in suburban Ontario, Canada. Life and death were directly linked. The survival of one being was dependent upon the sacrifice of another. The thin line that separated predator from prey was played out every day here and we were but brief visitors to the never-ending drama of it.

In Africa, those that used their skills most effectively—speed, size, sharp horns/antlers/teeth, thick hides, camouflage—they might live to see another day. The young, old, sick, and weak did not. It wasn't personal. It wasn't pretty. But it was life. And I would never quite look at it the same way again.

There was something about a brush with death that made you cherish life that much more.

"When the Rains Come…"

The game parks of Botswana were incredible. We were no more than a breath away from throngs of animals who could make a meal of us at any given moment. Our SAMIL and cautionary stories were all that prevented worst case scenarios from coming to pass. I continued to be gobsmacked every step of the way.

But even as we travelled, there were moments of unexpected joy. It was hot in December—the start of their summer. Rain was hard, brief, and the effects of it disappeared almost instantaneously, as the baked earth failed to be a match for the punishing sun. So, when the clouds did break, you needed to take advantage of it. An afternoon shower was just the thing.

We were taking advantage of the shade to escape the heat of the day after a morning game drive. I perched atop the SAMIL, chatting with Eric who balanced on a chair below me. A shadow crept across the veldt and Karel called out a warning.

"Oi! Rain is coming," he cried. "Time for shelter!"

"What?" said Sue. "Why's that?"

And then the skies burst. Buckets of rain soaked us to the skin in moments. I squealed, as I scrambled down off the top of the truck, for fearing of slipping off inadvertently. But as I ran towards shelter, Barb called to me.

"Grab the soap!"

And that changed everything. We were drenched anyway, so why not wash off the road grime while we had the opportunity?

"I'll grab shampoo too," I cried with a laugh.

Soon enough I had a head full of bubbles and was laughing away memories of Africa's harder lessons. The land greedily sopped up the precious moisture, as my travelling companions grappled to scrub down before the rain stopped. Buckets captured water just in case we needed help, but we needn't have worried.

"Right then," Sue called as the last of the suds washed away and shivers threatened to take hold. "Jumping jacks... Hup!"

I laughed and followed along, as Karel and the older members of our group hid in tents or under awnings.

"Gek," he laughed with a shake of his head. "Crazy women."

How could you not make the best of that gift though? Rain was a blessing that revitalized the land and my spirits. It seemed wrong to fail to recognize that. Plus, we were headed from Moremi into Zimbabwe shortly.

"Mosi-oa-Tunya"

Mosi-oa-Tunya—or "the smoke that thunders"—is magnificent to behold. When David Livingstone arrived in 1855, he was awestruck. So much so that he renamed the falls in honour of the reigning monarch at the time. Victoria Falls kind of stuck.

To be fair, Livingstone was right to be captivated by Victoria Falls. UNESCO agrees with him. They declared it a World Heritage Site in 1989. It is also considered one of the Seven Natural Wonders of the World. Why? It isn't the highest waterfall in the world, but the long curtain of water that cascades over its steep edge gives it the distinction of being considered the largest, at 1,708 metres long. With a height of 108 metres tall, it dwarfs Niagara Falls at approximately twice the height. And the "smoke" that rises from the sheer volume of water which tumbles over the lip can reach up to 400 metres high. You can see it from upwards of 60 kilometers away.

And we would get much closer than that.

When our SAMIL pulled into the dusty campground in the middle of Victoria Falls, its contrast to the magnificent parks we had recently been through was glaringly obvious. The ground was hard and barren of even a blade of grass from constant use by tourists. Oversized trucks and a never-ending stream of tents flattened everything. The draw here though was the Falls. The campground was quietly excused its failings.

What I couldn't excuse any more though was my tent mate. I had gotten over his originally appealing looks and found him increasingly lacking. There was no pretense at romance. Eric was nice, but dull. Worse, his flirtations made me increasingly uncomfortable to be alone around him. The more he pressed for my attention, whether it was in the group or after dark in our tent, the less I wanted to be around him. He was an alright guy, but I couldn't help but compare him to Jack. Which then brought on new waves of guilt. Despite not receiving a letter from him since I left home a month and a half earlier, I still cared about Jack and the relationship we had. I was done with my part in any flirtations that had danced between Eric and I and couldn't face spending another night fighting with myself, and Eric's hopeful hands. It was time to do something about it.

I sidled up to Karel, as he pulled his own gear out of the SAMIL.

"Karel," I said, as tents popped up around us. "Is there anywhere else I can sleep? Aside from… with Eric?"

With a laugh, he shook his head. I'm sure he had seen his fair share of short-lived overland romances in his days as tour guide, but he wasn't in the business to cater to them. We carried only the barest amount of equipment, so no extra tents were available. Options weren't plentiful.

He pointed behind him at the SAMIL.

"You're welcome to join me open-air, topside," he said with a chuckle as he pointed behind him. "That is the only free space."

The roof of the SAMIL. It was a long way to the ground from up there, but I didn't hesitate.

"Deal," I said.

One of us would sleep above the truck cab. The other at the rear. Not exactly cozy, but at least I would be alone. Hopefully, Eric would take the hint.

With that settled, it was time to explore.

The contrast between the arid campground and the nearby national park was striking. Less than six kilometers away, the landscape surrounding the falls became a lush rain forest. A constant mist shrouds the area due to the more than 1,000 cubic metres of water which falls over Mosi-oa-Tunya per second. Graceful ferns and other flora thrive where a few miles yonder the earth was scrubby and dry. It was a world transformed from the savannahs we had just left.

We soaked it up. Literally. Our shirts clung to our backs as a group of us wandered through Victoria Falls National Park.

Truth be told though, even the vegetation was not what brought us to Victoria Falls. Sure, it was beautiful, but the plans for the next day were the big draw for everyone. Although I wasn't sure how keen I was to be a part of it.

"Howzit?" Karel called, as we ambled up to camp after our wander through the park. "Let's go!"

"This'll be awesome," Sue gushed, as we walked across the street to the Frontiers Rafting office.

I didn't say much. I still wasn't sure if I wanted to part with the money. Or with one of my nine lives. But everyone had a smile on their faces, and it seemed unlikely that I would be able to wiggle out of things. So, I stayed silent, as we were ushered into the theatre to watch a promotional video demonstrating the majesty of white water rafting on the Mighty Zambezi.

As the lights dimmed, 'Joyride', from Swedish pop band Roxette, quietly filled the small auditorium. On a screen, unsuspecting rafters waved to the camera as they made their way to boats. As the song built in crescendo, so too did the action onscreen. I watched in horror, as the rafting company's version of the hook was shown. But catchy lyrics weren't enough to convince me that all the flipping rafts doing grotesque twists and spins were safe. Over and over again, people spit out of rubber dinghies, flying through fast-moving rapids at terrifying speeds. What madness was this?

"No way!" I cried when the lights came back up. "Uh, uh. Nope. No way!"

"You have to go," Barb pleaded.

"Ja! Everyone is going," Sue said with laugh.

Karel just pushed me into the queue with a grunt. "Sies man, don't be a baby. It's lekker[16]. You'll love it! Won't she Max?"

---

[16] good; pleasant.

79

Karel was no stranger to Victoria Falls, white water rafting, and the many guides who ran the rapids there. Max was one of them. And his smile made my reserve melt. I knew I was in trouble, even as upbeat tunes continued to blare out their call to action. They might have drowned out the sound of rushing water, but they couldn't mask the sound of my beating heart. But why had it suddenly sped up a notch?

"Don't worry," Max said with a wink. "I'll take good care of you. I haven't lost anyone yet."

His eyes. Oh man. Hadn't I just gotten myself out of this situation?

"Fine," I mumbled.

As we waited to pay, I reluctantly looked around the office. Graphic pictures of rafts bent double or standing on their end did little to convince me that I had made the right decision. A map on the wall showed the route we would take; rapids with names like "Overland Truck Eater", "Oblivion" and "Devil's Toilet Bowl" didn't make me feel any better. Hearing that over half of the rapids were class five (class six is considered unrunnable), made my hands that much sweatier when it came time to sign the waivers to participate in this madness.

Everyone cheered when Max took the signed contract back with a smile.

"See you tomorrow," he said with a twinkle in his eyes.

I felt like I was going to throw up. The natural cure—a drink. Sadly, no number of drinks furnished the courage I sought. It also didn't help me sleep better, as I lived in fear of rolling off the side of the truck as I dreamt.

Not enough hours later, Karel roused me from sleep on my side of the SAMIL's roof.

"Rise and shine, sleeping beauty," he said with a nudge. "It's time to meet Nyami Nyami[17]. See if the 'River God' likes you or no. You will meet your rafting guides at the bottom of the ravine. The path starts there."

"Nee – what?" I asked despite myself. "See if who likes me?"

"You'll see," he replied with a wink. "Com!"

The sun wasn't even up yet. And coffee didn't ease my dry mouth nor still my shaky hands; both only partially to blame on the rounds of courage from the night before. After far too short a drive, we arrived at the gorge.

What was I getting myself into, I wondered? *That was our instruction? The path was seriously steep and plummeted 400 feet down to the river's edge!*

"Ag man, let's go," Karel remarked, as he pushed me in front of him.

I wanted to hate him. I really did. But I didn't have the energy to do that and force my quaking legs down the steep path. In for a penny, I guess, I sighed.

Max greeted us at the bottom of the gorge with the same smile he had charmed me with over Zambezi beer the night before. After dinner, Karel

---

[17] VictoriaFalls24. (2014, March 21). The Legend of Nyami Nyami. https://victoriafalls24.com/blog/2014/03/21/the-legend-of-nyami-nyami/.

had suggested a pint for liquid encouragement. He knew this group was always up for one and Vic Falls had no lack of places to enjoy them. The local guides did their part to schmooze the tour operators in hopes that they would use their companies, so often showed up at the favourite haunts of the overland companies. And it was obvious that Max was well-versed in schmooze of everyone he met. We had chatted a lot the night before.

"Good morning," he exclaimed, as he tossed a life jacket towards Tristan. "Are you ready to raft?"

He looked no worse for wear, unlike my pasty self. A pile of life jackets lay beside a jumble of helmets. He pointed to another pile of paddles and said, "You'll need one of those if you plan to help paddle. Or for those who prefer, you can ride in the raft with a central guide." I gazed towards the raft he pointed out longingly. Before I could say a word though, Max dashed my hopes of only having to hang on for dear life.

"Oh no my friend," said Max with a wicked grin of his pearly whites. "I've got a seat for you in my raft."

He held out a life jacket to me in one hand and a paddle in the other. I slumped my shoulders in defeat, even as I met his smile with a sigh. How did I get myself into this?

"May I?" he cordially asked, as he slipped the jacket on, then wrenched the breath out of me.

"Oh," I gasped, as he cinched the life jacket tight. "Thanks," I peeped. "I think…"

"Need to keep you safe," he said, as he patted my arm.

It was buck up or get bucked out on the first rapid. I tightened the helmet around my chin and waded towards the rafts with a paddle in tow. It was time to go.

"Wet and Wild"

We awkwardly scrambled into the solid PVC boats and plunked ourselves around the raft. I ended up at the front; first in, first out? So be it, I thought. It wasn't a leisure cruise anyway, even though we drifted lazily along in the river while Max explained the boat and what to expect from the day. He pointed out the orange cordial, holy-shit rope, throw bag, first-aid kit, and then himself.

"Listen hard for my instructions," he said. "I'll tell you when to steer left, right, when to drop into the boat, and when to pop back up and start paddling once more." It sounded easy enough, but I wasn't sure how comforting any of it was. Realistically, his words meant nothing. We needed practice.

"Alright, are you ready to give it a go?" Max asked. Then he shouted, "Dig in!"

And we paddled like mad, splashing like fiends with little effect.

"Back paddle!" he screamed.

Flailing like drunken windmills, we desperately tried to keep up the pace, as we reversed direction. Coordination was not our strong suit. Shouts of "Hard left" and "Hard right" had my reeling head pounding, but adrenalin kicked in and we began to have a semblance of synchronicity.

I looked over my shoulder at Max. He was smiling and laughing, giving the illusion that we would be fine. His muscular build looked impressive tied into his own life jacket. How could anything go wrong with the obvious strength he wielded? He would surely look after us and not let anyone come to harm. But the twinkle disappeared when he described what to do when someone fell out of the raft. Not if, but when.

"So, if someone falls out of the boat right beside you, you need to grab them quick and pull them back in. Push down hard, so that they'll pop up and launch back into the boat. Make it count. If you fall out and are too far to grab back into the boat, we'll throw you a line. Catch it the first time. There won't be a second chance."

He didn't miss a beat as he continued, "If you miss it, one of the kayakers will attempt to guide you through the rapid, if they can get to you in time. Don't try to climb onto their kayak, as that will just put you both at risk and we don't need more people to rescue. Just hold on for the ride."

There was still more though.

"If no one is close enough, keep your head up. You are going this one alone. It might not seem like it, but you *will* pop back up in the water. That's what the life jackets are for. Hold your breath and kick your feet hard. Try not to panic and just ride the rapid out. We'll pick you up at the end." He finished with, "You've got this! Just don't forget to breathe."

His laugh didn't make anyone feel better. He was dead serious and this all of sudden didn't seem like the picnic that people had signed up for. I laughed nervously glancing at Marjory beside me.

"Right," he called. "Let's get this party started! First rapid of the day up next."

We got a quick lesson on what to expect and how we would tackle the rapid. He detailed its holes, eddies, and the chutes we would try to skirt. Before actually seeing the rapid, it meant nothing to me.

Our little raft of eight people seemed to speed up and suddenly we were wet and going wild. Max's screamed directions fell on deaf ears, as a wall of water crashed into us. We hit the water like it was a bucking bronco and Marjory disappeared over the side from where she had sat moments before. I desperately tried to push my paddle into the onslaught of water that threatened to flip our craft and caught site of Max throwing a line to our escaped paddler, to no avail. We smashed right, left, then straight through a sheet curved like glass, before getting swallowed by waves again. As we spluttered and braced into the boat, we shot out the far end of the rapid and finally slowed. We made it!

Well, all minus one.

"Holy shit," I exclaimed. "That was awesome!"

My heart pounded in my chest, and I felt more alive than I'd ever been. It had been a crazy onslaught, but we did it. I was soaked, but instantly addicted and needed *more*. It was so wicked cool that I couldn't contain the energy that flew out of me.

"How far is the next rapid?" I asked. "How many are there altogether? Are they all that intense, or was this one just a tester? Do they get bigger from here?"

"Let's pickup Marjory first, shall we?" Max replied. "Right, let's go!"

We backpaddled towards a nearby boat and kayak and got some of the story on poor Marjory. She had travelled most of the rapid solo. Our line was shot out in vain, and the kayaker only reached her in time to travel the last chute with her. She was picked up by another raft before we even spit out of "Morning Glory".

When we finally made it to the boat she was in, Marjory sat lifeless and glassy eyed. She was physically fine but gone for all intents and purposes; vacant and mute remembering the horror of her ride. When she finally spoke, she stammered out the details.

"As soon as we hit the rapid, I flew out of the boat. I didn't even see the throw bag. Rushing water sucked me under and I didn't know which way was up." Her pale face was drawn in the telling, but she continued, "I popped up, but immediately got sucked under again. I couldn't breathe. I thought I was going to die. I had no idea which way to turn."

Tears glistened on her wet face, as she choked back a sob. Her story was sobering for the rest of us. We could see her terror, but it was not quite enough to quell the adrenaline that coursed through me. I still wanted more.

"What do you think Marjory?" Max asked. "Do you want your paddle back? Or would you rather stay in the other raft?"

The oar boat she was in only required you to hold on. A guide in the middle of the raft steered you through the rapids with one large set of oars. There was no option to get out and return to the safety of land.

Marjory stared glassily at us and our raft. A visible shudder ran through her. She could not speak. Slowly, she shook her head.

Poor Marjory, as we knew her, was not back until lunchtime.

While Marjory may not have enjoyed our white-water rafting trip, I was an instant convert. For each rapid we approached, Max laid out a game plan that we bunglingly tried to follow. By the time we shot three or four rapids, we slowly started to get the hang of it, despite losing the occasional passenger to the mammoth waves that crashed over us. Somehow our little craft didn't flip like some of the other boats, and thankfully we didn't get caught in any eddies.

"We have to portage around the next rapid," Max announced after catching our breath coming out of *The Midnight Diner*. "Commercial Suicide is unrunnable."

"Unrunnable?" I said. "What does that mean?"

"No one runs it. It is a class six rapid that is far too dangerous. You'll see when we walk around it."

To call it a rapid was a stretch. To my eye it looked more like a waterfall, and it was sobering to think that anyone had ever tried to attempt it. I might have felt like an adrenaline junkie in the moment, but I didn't have a death wish.

"Whoa, no thank you…" I mumbled as one of our safety kayakers launched themselves into the abyss.

Solid ground had never felt so good.

Soon enough our boats were back in the water for a few more rapids before lunch. The rest of the day brought more white water and plenty more adrenaline rushes. To survive made you feel like you had accomplished something, even if it was only conquering your worst fears. The bonding of working hard with your team to find success (even marginally), at the mercy of thousands of litres of water flowing through the gorge, was enough to make you feel alive. And by the end of the day, I would say that we all were successful in that.

"Baboons, Beer Drinkers, Bee-Eaters & Bungee Jumpers"

I wearily reclined in my seat, as the road wound out behind the Intercape Mainliner. My overland trip to Botswana was over; new friends all dispersed back to whence they had come. My journal lay open on my lap, where I caught snippets of my adventures, as we headed back to civilization. As much as I felt like the memories would live forever, I knew that a few words written now would help retain the moments far longer.

I worked backwards from our white-water rafting trip.

We conquered 17 of the most challenging rapids in the world, only portaging around one, due to its class six rating. Despite my initial doubts, I was instantly addicted to the exhilarating experience and longed to try it again. It was hard and fast and incredible all around. Even a brief dip into the warm Zambezi River couldn't wash the smile off my face. We laughed, paddled hard, ate like champs at lunch, and paddled some more.

The worst of the day was the 250-metre slope we had to scale to walk out of the gorge. While brochures claim it takes an able-bodied person 20 minutes to walk out, my exhausted body begged to differ. Let me tell you, it was a struggle. The vicious hill was a gradient 1-3; I'm not sure if that makes you feel better or worse for me, but after a few cutbacks back and forth, I was certain I would never make it. I wanted to puke, to lay down and die, or perhaps hire a porter to throw me over their shoulders and run me to the top. They didn't seem to break a sweat as they ran up the hill laden with our gear. What was one more thing?

Not that I had the breath to ask anyway. I paused, gasping for breath or death. Whichever came first.

"Howzit?" Karel asked as he stopped beside my bent form. "Ag man, why have you stopped? You've got a ways to go yet before you reach the top, my friend."

There was not enough air in my lungs to breathe, let alone respond to his mockery. I panted with hands on knees, waiting for my heart to burst from my chest. There was no way I could make it to the top.

"C'mon meisie. There's icy cold lager in the bakkie topside," he commented as he continued up the hill.

"Bugger," I mumbled.

Nothing else could have motivated me more in that moment. I might have hated every step I took, but Karel's prod gave me the superhuman strength to carry on. Beer and shame were befitting bribes.

Plenty of other memories filtered through to my journal though. So many, I took to simple summaries to jog my memory later. I recalled the fear that we would be stuck in the middle of nowhere when the mighty SAMIL bogged down in the mud on the way into the Okavango. Masters rocked the mighty truck forward and back to no avail, forcing us to scramble out and use other measures to free us. With large rubber mats and a little extra muscle and teamwork, we managed to free ourselves and continue on our way. Which led us to the Delta itself and the quaint mokoros we rode in next. I couldn't help but laughing as I recalled Jens' shocked look, as he stood in a mokoro with two broken halves of the boat's pole in his hands. Oops! He had taken a boat out during our lunch break to see how difficult it was to maneuver them and discovered it was harder than it looked, when he broke the pole. Laughter followed us everywhere though, including during never-ending games of 21 and the rules that came out every round. Although it wasn't always fun and games. Marjory was not the only one to push fear to the test. After bungee jumping 111 metres off the bridge at Victoria Falls, Tristan also had a case of the shakes and a glazed look in his eyes. The challenge was to remember it all.

I had seen baboons, beer drinkers, bee-eaters, bungee jumpers, crocodiles, Castle castles, elephants, eagle-eyed guides, lecherous men, lions, mongoose, mokoros, sables/lechwe/puku (forms of antelope), potjie pots (cauldrons), rondavels (circular hut), rapids, vultures, and of course Victoria Falls. The memories were vivid and would take a heck of a lot of elbow grease to remove from the creases of my body. And while my liver begged for mercy, I suspected that a return to family would help placate its pleas.

The bounce of the SAMIL might have been gone, but adventures still lay ahead. In truth, it felt like the adventures had just begun. Christmas was a week away. I had spoken of game parks, wineries, and Table Mountain with family before heading into Botswana, and now itched to see those too. That was just the tip of the iceberg though. There were infinite other options I hadn't even contemplated yet. So much to see and do!

If only my sister was by my side to partake in the adventures with me, life would be perfect! Funny enough though, I didn't pine for a certain someone like I had before I ventured off on my overland trip. Jack was noticeably silent from my thoughts. I tried not to worry about what that meant, but my journal knew. I had received no letters, phone calls, or contact of any kind. That was not lost on me. Nor was the attention that creeped up on me when I allowed myself to be in the moment.

Home, as I knew it, was forever changed. The tears I shed on leaving, were my way of grieving a lifestyle gone. I could never return to who I was. More importantly, I didn't want to. I had awoken a desire for adventure, and a platform that now held more time for me. It was impossible to consider going back to the life of a quiet sidekick of my passionate, but complicated former lover.

With one month of my six-month adventure tucked under my belt, I dreamt of all the potential moments-to-be. Africa filled me, and I still wanted more. What would the next chapters hold?

*****

ON THE MOVE

"Christmas"

After my 14-hour marathon journey across the country, I finally dismounted the bus and fell exhausted into my aunt and uncle's arms. I babbled about the animals I had seen and the adventures I survived; a PG-13 version, minus the questionable activities they didn't need to know about. They met a vastly different niece than the one who had left three weeks previous. They were happy to see me return with such excitement and let me prattle on, but when I paused for breath, they had a story to share as well.

"You've had a visitor," Uncle Jock announced. "A young woman popped by yesterday to say hello. She said she'd seen you in Jo'berg, ja? We told her you'd be back today."

"Miki!" I exclaimed.

She hadn't forgotten. In fact, when we got home, a note peeped out of the mailbox from her. My priorities instantly changed again. She was now on the top of the list of people to see. Once I washed the last of Botswana's dirt out from under my fingernails that was.

The next morning, I rang up the number she had left.

"We're coming to get you," Miki stated. "I need to hear all about what you've been up to."

"And you as well," I added. "I can't believe we bumped into each other in South Africa and that we are only a few minutes apart."

True to her word, they were there within the hour. They whisked me off to Martin's house where we swapped stories of each other's adventures thus far, hers along the coast and mine throughout Botswana. Miki and I had never been close, but the coincidence of being in South Africa, in the same suburb of Cape Town, at the same time was not lost on either of us. The hours flew by as we chatted, but it still wasn't enough. I had plans for the next couple of days, so we made a date to go for drinks on Christmas Eve. It would have to do for the time being.

The following days flew by. Next up was a trip to some local wineries. I piled into a vehicle with Uncle Jock, Weppie, Jannie, and Jeannette and we toured a sampling of some of Cape Town's finest. The Cape region is well known for its incredible wineries, many of which have been around for hundreds of years. There was no way we could see them all, but we managed to sample Chardonnays, Chenin Blanc, Cabernet Sauvignons, and more at several. We even sampled South Africa's famous Amarula, which my Mom had insisted I bring back for her; she remembered its distinct taste from her visit in 1973. It wasn't the only thing I planned to bring home though.

My cousin Anne picked me up a few days later to tour me around the Waterfront. Her and a girlfriend treated me to the ultimate tourist experience, as we visited several upscale shops and boutiques in the trendy downtown core, including a stop for a posh lunch. At day's end, we drove through Somerset West to see Christmas lights twinkle in the well-to-do neighbourhood. It was different from the snow-covered displays back home, but a nice reminder of the season at hand.

I must admit that it hardly felt like Christmas at all though. No decorations adorned Uncle Jock's house. Summer weather called for short sleeves and swimming whenever you could get it. Outside at that! There was not an icicle or snowflake in sight, unlike back home. The only thing that was the same was Santa. Even though he would have overheated immediately in Cape Town in December, he still wore his traditional red and white fur-lined suit in any adverts I spied.

By Christmas Eve, more festivities arrived. I went out for lunch to the Mowbray Golf Club once more with Aunt Linn and her side of the family. They brought me home, where I dialed into Christmas carols in front of the tube with Uncle Jock and Aunt Elsa. And then the phone rang.

"Join us for a glass of Christmas cheer," Miki suggested.

"Alright, but I have to be up early," I replied. "We've got church at 7am."

I wasn't home early. Not even close.

"I've never been away from my Mum or Kerry before on Christmas," I said to Miki over the first pint. "Of course, I've never spent it in the tropics either. Not that I should complain. Everyone is so nice. The whole family will be around for dinner poolside tomorrow. It'll be good. It just seems weird is all."

"I know," Miki acknowledged. "I'm glad Taro is here, but I miss my Dad."

"It's all part of the adventure," Taro remarked.

"I know," I nodded, as another pint showed up.

"There's a band playing at the Purple Turtle," Martin ventured. "Anyone up for checking it out?"

So, check it out we did. And after that, we swung by The Greenhouse Effect, for some late-night smart drinks to finish the evening off. Or rather the early morning hours. They just seemed to disappear into mist and before I knew it, it was 3:30 a.m. What would Santa say! Quite sure he passed my house by that night. But it was worthwhile, to cheers in the holidays with friends and make more plans for the days to come.

"Brett is flying in on New Year's Eve," Miki said on the car ride home. "I met him in Europe last year and we made a plan for him to come join me to tour around South Africa. You'll love him! You have to come out with us New Year's to meet him."

But I wasn't thinking about New Year's anymore. Now I was more worried about the impending toll of church bells.

Despite a throbbing headache to greet the rising sun, the day was pleasant enough. No lightning struck me down for my late-night festivities, and soon enough I was lazing poolside at Marianne and Weppie's. Who can be melancholy when cannonballs splash away any remaining vestiges of nausea?

As the day unfolded, things got more festive. A tiny artificial tree hid in the corner of the airy living room, as the token decoration for the holidays. It was sufficient to anchor the celebrations, as everyone tore into presents for all and sundry. While the children received the bulk of the gifts, I received several thoughtful gifts as well; a beautiful springbok hide from my cousin Anne's family (her husband Pieter shot and dressed the hide himself), a calendar with native flora and fauna from Marianne's family, and a homemade sweater that Aunt Elsa had knitted herself. It was touching.

Christmas dinner was a cold buffet lunch eaten atop TV tables and laps, with everyone scattered around the house and poolside. It was far too hot for the lavish and formal turkey dinners I knew and loved. This feast included chicken, lamb, leg of gammon, corned beef, and salads galore. I piled my plate high anyway. As plates were cleared, the doorbell rang. Marianne opened the door to another wonderful surprise.

"Naudé!" Aunt Elsa exclaimed with shock.

"Ag, we couldn't miss this family get-together," Naudé chuckled. "And it wasn't all my doing. Weppie arranged a flight for a special Christmas surprise."

"Oh, that's wonderful," Aunt Elsa burbled, as she stepped up to hug him and the rest of the family as they stepped in the door. The treats didn't end there though. As the cousins excitedly milled around, he handed out brightly wrapped presents to the youngsters. Then turned to me.

"I have something special for you too," he said. He pulled out a small, wrinkled, silver-wrapped package.

"Oh!" I cried.

I instantly knew what it was and couldn't stop the tears, as I sniffed the precious bundle. A small portion of leftover turkey and stuffing from an earlier Christmas dinner was nestled inside. I couldn't have asked for anything more to complete a perfect Christmas with my father's kin. I was graced with a love I would never forget. And cherished every minute of it.

"A Change in Plans"

Cape Town faded into the distance behind us. It was January 15th and Mossel Bay was our first destination. Behind me lay family, former ideas of what my trip would hold, and faded snapshots of home. I didn't need any of it where we now headed. Not that much of a plan existed as of yet; just hug the shore along South Africa's coastline in our newly purchased little baby blue kombi.

Everything had happened one step at a time though. New Year's Day was when plans started to shift.

"We should get a vehicle," Miki announced as she stared at the sky from her prone position on a park bench.

We were scattered around an out of the way park, wearing off the effects of the New Year's Eve rave we had attended the night before. Clouds lazily tumbled over Table Mountain, as the sky lightened from indigo to the most amazing pink. Everything was pretty amazing at that point though. The clouds, the sky, and last night's music had drawn us up, pulled us in one direction, then scattered us in another. People floated through the night in a throbbing haze of noise.

Now we contemplated our next steps.

"That's a bloody good idea, Miko!" Brett remarked from where he lay on a picnic table. "We could go on a walkabout of South Africa." I had only known him two days but loved Brett already. He was quick to laugh, ready with ideas, and all in with the best of them.

"I bet it wouldn't cost much with all of us kicking in," I added from my swing.

We let the thought wash over us, as the morning's light slowly crept across the park. It truly was an excellent idea. One so far from my original plan that I had hatched months earlier back in Canada: leave boyfriend, meet family, and see animals. I had gone beyond, to embracing whatever life presented in the moment. Plans were fine, but sometimes more interesting ideas stumbled onto the table and were worthy of consideration. Buying a vehicle and exploring Africa in a far more independent way than tucked under my uncle's care certainly held a lot of appeal.

I was in.

With the thought put out to the cosmos, it didn't take long for the Universe to respond. After a brief search, on January 6th we signed a handwritten note to transfer ownership of Arnie—a 1972 baby blue Volkswagen Kombi bus—into our names. Arnold was the proper Afrikaner who brought the vehicle round for us to see it, so it seemed natural to name the van after him: Arnie. Our test drive was just a formality, as we knew it would be ours as soon as we saw it out the hostel window.

"Oh, my God," I squealed. "It's perfect!"

"We can make curtains," Miki said. "Buy a stove and a tent." She planned it all out as we drove along.

"There's room for my board even," Brett giggled from the driver's seat, as we drove around the block.

There was. There was room for all four of us—Brett, Taro, Miki, and me—plus our gear. We all had backpacks, but Miki was right. We would also need camp gear, if we were to stretch our travel dollars and camp along the way. Hostels were fine for cities, but game parks were expensive enough without paying for pricey lodges. A tent would be perfect to really feel at one with the land and expand where we could go and stay. I couldn't wait.

Everything was coming together. Catriona loaned us her tent. Uncle Jock gave me an old sleeping bag. Miki and I hit the market and bought material to make curtains, a dish rack, cheap dishes, and some canned goods. The rest would come.

The only thing left was to say goodbye. I trekked back out to Brackenfell, where I dropped off items I wouldn't need and collected well wishes from family for the road. It seemed odd that I was leaving so soon after getting to know them, but I was being pushed along by fate now. My plane ticket left from Cape Town, so I knew I would be back at some point. I just had no idea when that would be. And that was the least of my concerns.

Once back downtown, it was time to bid adieu to our friends at the hostel. While I was sad to say farewell, this was life on the road. Instant connections were formed, but those connections only lasted as long as your stay in the same location. And there wasn't room for everyone in the van. As it was, Taro was iffy. He decided not to chip in for a share of the van (a steal at 7500R, even without his help), but Miki insisted he come with us. For them, travelling through Africa together was part of their original plan after all. As for the rest of our mates, they all had directions of their own, so this was the end of our journey together. It called for a celebration.

"Let's have a paella feast," Catriona suggested.

"With sangria," Miki added. "From the wine we picked up on the wine tour."

"I'm in," Luke said.

"Us too," chimed in Enar and Kurt.

A new shopping list was formed with Catriona at the helm. She had worked in kitchens, so knew her way around them. We were happy to play her obedient sous chefs. The lot of us minced garlic, chopped tomatoes, and sliced all the fruit for the sangria. We needed the lubrication to get the night started after all. And man, was it good!

Eventually the wine was gone, our bellies were full to bursting, and there was nothing left, but to pass a joint around the outdoor stairwell, as we watched the stars wink into existence. People shared their travels up to that point, stories from their past, and plenty of laughs. We bonded in a way that travellers have a knack of doing, sharing innermost thoughts with virtual strangers, partly because you won't ever see them again. It was special and intimate, and left me oddly melancholy for home.

Home. Dreams of it filled my nights once more, after a lull during my time in Botswana. My downtime while I house sat in Mowbray, before moving to the hostel downtown, helped that too. Vivid images of friends and family back home seemed a portent of fate. As I counted down the days until we left in Arnie, the visions whispered for me to reconnect.

I hadn't heard anything from Jack. No calls, letters, or moonbeam connections. I had to take matters into my own hands for peace of mind before we hit the road. I might not be able to ring him up direct, but I could track down someone who might know more about where he was as.

After the third ring, Sheila answered the phone.

"Hi."

"Oh my God!" she cried. "Katherine, how are you? Where are you? What have you done? What have you been up to?"

The questions were fast and furious, but I had limited time on my phone card. After giving a brief summary, I quickly steered the conversation to the meat of the conversation.

"How's Jack?" I asked.

She paused before answering.

"He wrote you a letter," she said hesitantly. "Haven't you gotten it yet?" I didn't want to hear any more. I could tell I wouldn't like anything more she had to say. "He couldn't be by himself. He's not strong like you. I hate that I have to be the one to tell you all of this." And the clincher, "He's dating someone new..."

My heart stopped. I couldn't hear anything else. The phone fell from my hand and swung loose at the end of its cord. There was no breath for goodbye, as I slipped aimless into the night.

He's dating someone new...

I was broadsided. Cape Town kept me company, as my head swam with the news. I slipped past dark streets unseeing, as I vacillated between hurt, anger, and a profound forlornness. A piece of me knew it was coming, but the bit of my heart entrusted to Jack was still shattered. There was no going back. It was now official; I was single.

While logically a piece of me suspected our love wouldn't survive, hearing it like that—from a mutual friend and without any way to confirm details directly from him—it crushed me. Visions of our last days together tumbled together with images of him with a new partner. When had it begun? Had she moved in on him as soon as I left? Did his eye already notice her and her smooth guitar playing even before I flew off? Was it convenient that I was out of the way then? I couldn't compete musically, but never felt I needed to. Should I have though? Would it have made a difference? In the grand scheme of things, did it even matter? Those questions would remain unanswered.

As minutes turned into hours, I sank even further into the news. I understood only too well what had happened. He was lonely. He needed grounding. He needed someone there to listen, to love, to heal with. I got it. And as much as anger flashed through me, he didn't deserve all the blame. I might not have slipped between the sheets with anyone, but temptation had been strong. On more than one occasion. We were human and wanted to be loved. And by Jack's side, I never felt worthy. It wasn't fair to either of us. And it wasn't right for me to expect him to wait for me, as I traipsed across another continent with not a care in the world.

By the time the slowly fading twinkle of the night sky winked out from atop the hostel roof, my trusty journal had absorbed the wrath that ebbed and flowed from my pen. My whys would remain unanswered. All I could do was contemplate where his head was at and the history of us. I knew I would cry eventually, but not then. Not for several days.

In the interim, I had to finish packing and prepare for our departure. Our first stop was Mossel Bay, a short trip of less than 400 kilometers. It was the first of many surf towns that Brett lusted after, but for me, they would be days lost in contemplation of a love lost. Or a life freed? Eventually. I had to get my heart back into the adventure at hand first though and all I could see in the moment was my glazed eyes reflected back at me in the kombi's windows.

As fate pushed me to make the phone call in Cape Town, days later it ushered me to the ocean's edge in Mossel Bay. In the dim mists of morning, I perched on a gray boulder staring glassy eyed at the pounding surf. Tears finally slipped from me, but maddeningly failed to purge the raw emotions that left me inert.

I was in Africa, goddammit. Be present!

A swift movement drew my gaze. As I watched, a family of small furry dassies emerged to start their day. As if in greeting, they paused on hind legs to stare at me. And suddenly, I was alone no more.

And with that, I turned the page onto the next chapter of my journey.

"The Eastern Cape"

The road spilled out in front of us again. We hugged the coast of the Western Cape, as South Africa rolled by. After five nights in Mossel Bay, we veered north to Oudtshoorn for a look at the Cango Caves. Eerie stalactites dripped from the ceilings, as craggy stalagmites sprang from the floors of the cave. The ancient caverns were strategically lit to highlight its unique beauty, as the tour guide talked about their formation over millions of years and subsequent rediscovery in 1780. Jacobus Van Zyl wasn't the first one into the caves though, as cave paintings gave evidence of previous visitors. We were just a handful more.

Our pit stop only lasted an hour though before it was time to hop back into the kombi again. We had a five-hour drive ahead of us before we would reach our next stop—Tsitsikamma National Park. The park straddled the Western and Eastern Cape provinces, but also served as a special treat, as it was our first game park. While we didn't see many animals, we did get a chance to experience the beauty of the area on an 11-kilometer hike along the rugged coastline. It was magnificent, but as we trudged back into camp something else caught my eye. A truck I couldn't help but recognize sat parked alongside a group of milling tourists.

"Karel," I cried, as I spied him alongside the familiar SAMIL, which had been my home in Botswana.

"Oh ho!" he replied with a hug when he saw me. "Howzit? How is my favourite pax?"

His honest happiness at seeing me was a balm on my soul. It felt like running into a long-lost friend, even though we had only spent two weeks together the previous month. His genuine smile filled the hole that lingered in my heart.

"Ag man, this group is a bunch of dwankies. Not like you dronkies and all the fun we got up to," he remarked with a chuckle. "So, what are you doing here?"

"Oh, you know. Travelling the coast in a baby blue kombi. Learning to surf. Seeing the sights. A little of this and that…"

He laughed.

"I'll be doing a little of that shortly myself," he added. "My girlfriend is flying in from Australia at the end of this tour. We've got a month together. Headed into Botswana to tour about."

"That sounds awesome," I replied.

"Hey, Karel," came a cry from one of his passengers.

It was time for him to get back to work. I wished the moment could have lasted longer, but my own travelling companions were probably waiting dinner on me as well. Sadly, time to move on. The quick hug goodbye was a great reminder though that friends were always right around the corner, sometime when you least expected them. It helped put a little lighter bounce in my step and a smile in my heart.

After two nights in Tsitsikamma, we briefly stopped in Cape St. Francis on our way to Jeffreys Bay. Brett was in heaven along this stretch of the Garden Coast, considered by many to be a surfer's paradise. He was like a kid in a candy store, constantly remarking on the amazing surf and lack of competition from other surfers.

"Back home, they ride you off the waves. Some blokes carry knives to cut your leash to get rid of you. But here, you don't have to wait your turn on a good wave. They're all aces and open!"

Fine for him, but none of the rest of us surfed. Brett attempted lessons for Miki, but Taro was always off exploring and hanging with locals. I worked on finishing up drapes for Arnie and collected seashells along the beach. There were lots of pretty shells, but the weather wasn't conducive for much else. Three nights wasn't enough for Brett, but there was more of the Eastern Cape to explore.

Next up was Port Elizabeth. To my excitement, the first night there I found a small pocket of my tribe...a group of students were having a braai across the street from the hostel where we camped, and the sound of Nine Inch Nails drifted across the road to tempt me. I couldn't resist. I loved Trent Reznor's industrial scream. Taro accompanied me over to play chaperone, wary of a young man who paid me special attention. While he seemed harmless enough, Taro had a bad feeling about the guy. It probably had more to do with the fact that he knew how heavy and vulnerable my heart still was. I begrudgingly appreciated his concern, even as I longed for the attention. No matter. We were on the road again soon enough.

The stops flew by. After a few nights in Port Elizabeth, we detoured to Addo Elephant National Park for more game viewing. We spied elephants, black-backed jackals, kudus, bush bucks, vervet monkeys, and even a rare white rhino. We caught a couple of bull elephants playing and revelled in the fact that we all can use a little fun sometimes. It was an experience like no other.

The trip wasn't all over-the-top adventure though. There were the highs of strenuous hikes, game viewing, and surfing, mixed in with the mundane; writing post cards, catching up my journal, cooking meals, and cleaning house. Port Alfred and East London were much the same. We would spend two or three days in one town before tearing down camp and setting up in the next a few hundred kilometers down the road. It began to wear on us.

Squabbles erupted between Miki and Taro. Brett was pissed by the constant bickering. I brooded over my failed relationship and wondered if I could blame my moodiness on my late period. There was a general state of grumpiness all around. Our grand adventure started to feel like a cage, with no escape route from each other's moods and tempers. We all needed a break from each other.

And that is when we entered the Wild Coast.

"Port St. Johns"

With the Sunshine Coast behind us, we entered South Africa's Wild Coast. Located on the eastern edge of the Eastern Cape, the area was formally known as the Transkei. It was a semi-independent black homeland, which had only been reabsorbed back into South Africa in 1994; the same year that Nelson Mandela was elected President and less than two years before our arrival. Before that it had been a Xhosa homeland, prone to violence and plagued by a poorly run self-government. It was said to suffer from corruption, economic dependence on South Africa, and a decided lack of options to rectify its woes.

And we were headed for the middle of it.

"Don't go into the Transkei," people warned us. White people. Relatives.

"If you must drive through it, don't stop for anything. No hitchhikers. Avoid dirt roads and backcountry. And if you hit something, *anything* – DO NOT STOP!"

The message was chillingly clear. They weren't referring to deer or other wildlife. From their perspective, the Transkei was dangerous and full of peril. Entering it was akin to taking your life in your hands. But Port St. Johns was the next stop on the map and the Indian Ocean still lured us.

In February, we entered the Wild Coast. And for that I will be forever grateful. Port St. Johns is on the coast of the Indian Ocean in the middle of Pondoland. Its location in the heart of a traditional black homeland made for a minimal white population. The primary language in the area is Xhosa; a dialect filled with clicks and tonal nuances lost on me. Between our limited ability to communicate, our ethnicity (two white and two Japanese people), and our mode of transport (a baby blue kombi), the odds seemed stacked against a good experience in this land.

As we slowly motored into the small town, it felt like all eyes were upon us. The road had turned to dirt, as we wheeled towards the hub of the area—the market, of course. We figured that was the best spot to get the lay of the land and decide where to go from there.

You could immediately feel the difference.

Women walked by in sarongs balancing goods on their heads on their way to the bustling downtown market for bolts of colourful cloth or a fresh supply of fruits and veg. A long queue stood patiently waiting to get into the nearby bank. Tinny ghetto blasters belted out Bob Marley and other local musicians; a cacophony of sound that was infectious in its dissonance. The music was a way to lure you in to buy tapes, t-shirts, and miscellaneous other bits and bobs. Over it all, laughter permeated the air.

"Let's get out and pick up supplies," Miki suggested. "Before we get to the hostel."

"A'right," Brett replied, as he slowed down to avoid dogs that wandered across the square. "Keep your eyes on the lookout for a carpark."

"Oh, there!" I cried. He followed my finger and maneuvered us off to the edge of the epicenter of it all.

"This is wicked," Taro remarked, as we spilled out of the hot kombi. "I am so going to get lost checking out this town."

Miki shot him a quick look, before letting go with the feel of the place. Its laid-back vibe was filling us already. And, ultimately, Taro was right. We would get plenty of time to explore. We hadn't spent more than a few nights in any location since leaving Cape Town and needed a break from the pace. Here was just the place. Despite earlier warnings, we would spend the next two weeks there.

After hitting up the grocery store and taking a cursory look at the market, we found a quaint hostel on the edge of town. Even better, it was only five kilometers from a gorgeous beach full of sand, surf, and seashells. Everything was vibrant, lush, and had an incredibly peaceful vibe too. The limited connection to the outside world only drew us in that much more. It was perfect.

As I soaked it all in, I tried to let go of the many prejudices that had dominated conversations since arriving in South Africa.

"The (black) maids steal from you."

"They're lazy."

"They won't hesitate to strike. Better to steer clear or beat them to it."

"You haven't lived here. You don't know how it is."

The last point, I couldn't deny. Without living in a place and knowing someone's experiences, how could you rightly cast judgement against them? But the fear and anger seemed disconcertingly disproportionate to the cultural divide that marked the whites from blacks, the haves from have nots. I listened to travellers around me share their own stories and turns of events.

"The violence is exaggerated!"

"You can see the fear in white people. They don't even get it. They don't see what they have done or how unfair everything is."

"I feel safer walking around here, than I do in some American cities."

One of the more telling conversations I had was with a white man who had lived in the Transkei for the past 11 years.

"The reputation of violence isn't deserved," Pete said. "Violence exists, sure, but not to the extent the media portrays it. They demonized the area and created an aura of fear."

I could believe it after hearing the horror stories about the area before arriving—robbery, rape, and worse.

"A system of self-governance was established, but corruption crept in. It never really had a chance, as the local government was just a puppet to the federal government. It's no surprise then that there was unrest and the white population in the area caught the backlash. The blacks were angry about the injustices meted out by the white government. They reacted and struck out at their perceived enemies—whites. As the Transkei was their homeland, they made to take it back however they saw fit." But he had happily lived and worked there for many years and wasn't planning on going anywhere any time soon.

He wasn't the only one charmed by the area.

"Where's Taro," I asked Miki one evening.

"He's at the movies with some local kids," she replied. "He met them while he was skateboarding, and they hung out; invited him to see a movie at the Town Hall."

In fact, when Taro left his shorts behind one day after swimming, his new friends promptly returned them to him—in the Transkei! The simple kindness wasn't lost on me. I wanted to call my African relatives and shout, "Can you believe it?!" I could. The people weren't blood-thirsty monsters intent on violence. They were curious, friendly, and helpful whenever possible. They greeted us as we passed in the street. They were people, just like us, if not more solicitous.

I struggled to justify the fear my relatives held of this beautiful region. Simply entering the area terrified them. Why, I wondered, as I looked around? I had to continually remind myself that theirs was a different experience.

My father was born and raised in South Africa. Racial segregation wasn't anything new, even when he was born. In 1913, a Land Act passed which started the ball rolling. Blacks were forced to live on reserves and not allowed to be sharecroppers. In 1948, the Afrikaner National Party won the election and took the concept of "apartness" even further with the beginnings of apartheid. Not only were blacks kept away from whites, but blacks were further quantified and divided along tribal lines. By 1950, mixed marriages were deemed illegal, and everyone had to have documents proving their race—bantu (black), coloured (mixed), or white—with non-whites required to carry passbooks allowing them to enter certain areas (for example, to work/be in white neighbourhoods). In 1959, Bantustans (black homelands) were created, and all black South Africans were designated a citizen of one of these 10 areas. In theory, it was to give them more autonomy over their political rights, but it effectively only removed them from national politics.

And between 1961 and 1994, black people were stripped from rural locations, and the government sold their land to whites for next to nothing. It was systematic and sweeping, and meant to divide, cause mistrust, and fear.[18]

My father was white. The colour of his skin meant he had more privileges and could go where he wanted, when he wanted. He wanted out. By the time he was 20, he was working in the mines in Southern Rhodesia, present day Zimbabwe. At 25, he was travelling in Europe. And as he neared his thirties, his last stop was Canada before heading home. I've already told you what happened from there. But every step of the way was made easier because of the colour of his skin the day he was born.

I didn't know his stories from growing up in a fractured and violent environment; only that he had left to explore other lands and found a new home in Canada. Had he been disgusted, sympathetic, apathetic to it all? I don't know and am not sure if it makes much difference today. What I do know is that he wanted to see more of the world and would have seen a vastly different side of race relations outside of his homeland. It must have been eye opening. He certainly didn't race to return home. Whatever stories I heard from relatives were filtered through their own experiences, and time— he had been dead almost 20 years at that point. Ultimately though, the journey now was mine. And Port St. Johns provided the perfect backdrop to consider my father, my heritage, and a country whose blood ran through my own veins, however hard that seemed in quiet contemplation.

There was much to consider. The fact that I could afford to be there at all bore the mark of my privilege, but I tried to go further. I listened. I learned the history. I asked hard questions and struggled with my place in

---

[18] History.com Editors. (2020, March 3). Apartheid. History.com. https://www.history.com/topics/africa/apartheid.

those answers. But I also looked for the beauty in everything around me. From the land to the pastoral homes, and to the people who struggled to find a new footing in a world still teeming with changes. It was a learning curve for all.

As healing went on around me, the tranquility worked to recharge my tattered soul. I let go of hurts and embraced the simple act of journal writing and meditation. Fellow travellers mingled by candlelight around me. We let go of the hectic outside world in this simple, rustic place steeped in tradition. And most importantly, I discovered new life in a country working hard to remake its identity after so many years of apartheid and unrest. The very thing that separated the nation, was what unified my experience here— the people.

It wasn't all candlelit vigils though.

"I was talking to Pete," Miki said as we watched moonlight dance in the surrounding trees. "He offered to take us to the Mpande waterfall. It sounds cool! He'll drive us there, plus can arrange lunch at a local's house. You in?"

"Absolutely," I replied. "It sounds great!"

And it was. The falls, the exuberant area children who joined us for our swim, and the huge lunch of potatoes, tomatoes, onions, samp and noch (bean and corn mixture) all made for an incredible day. Even better though was that we met Michael, who would prove invaluable for our next excursion. He was a white South African, who just so happened to also love the Transkei.

"You have to see the country close up," he announced. "My cousin Tracey is here visiting from Canada as well. I'm planning on taking her on a

113

three-day hike along the Wild Coast Trail. It hugs the ocean through beautiful country and is incredibly pristine. It's not a hard hike, but you'll be sleeping under the stars. You are welcome to join us."

"That sounds amazing!" Miki gushed.

Of course, we were all in.

Two days later, we rose early and headed to town with Michael leading the way. We made our way to the taxi stand and let Michael do the hard work of trying to figure out which one of the decrepit kombis, overflowing bakkies, or packed buses would take us to Lusikisiki—the jumping off point for our trek. The raucous honking and shouting of passengers and drivers was intimidating to say the least, but our destination was over 40 kilometers away. As we didn't want to leave Arnie unattended in the middle of nowhere while we were hiking, we needed some other way to get to the start of the trail. Thankfully, Michael waded into the chaotic fray without fear.

"Come on," he said with a wave, as he threaded his way back through the crowd several minutes later. "I found someone who can take us straight to where we need to go for only a few Rand (ZAR) more."

"Sweet!"

Michael led us to a sleek minivan that not only had both headlights, but an intact, and working, slider door. Luxury, as compared to most of the other vans we strode past. Especially as Michael arranged for the van to be exclusively ours for the journey. No one hanging off the outside of the bus, or chickens crammed underfoot. Our privilege was showing, but in that moment, I was alright with it. We were off.

Bob Marley crooned, as our adventure began. The route meandered from paved highways to bumpy dirt paths. We were getting close.

"You can let us off here," Michael said to the driver.

"Where you go to?" he asked. "I can take you to the trail head."

"Thank you," Miki and I chimed in from the back.

"We'll have to give this bloke a fat tip," Brett chuckled. "He's alright!"

More hospitality to warm my heart and squash stereotypes that just didn't match with our experiences. Before we knew it though, our destination appeared. We scrambled out with our packs, as Michael handed over the agreed upon fare (plus a healthy tip).

"Thank you," we all called, as he did a cramped three-point turn in the narrow lane, then disappeared from sight. We turned from the dust cloud that dispersed in the distance. A waving grassland trembled around us. No buildings lay in sight.

"Okay then," Michael said. "Time to hike."

"Right on mate," Brett exclaimed. "Let's give at 'er." Michael consulted his compass, and we were off.

While we had left early, the sun was already inching higher into the sky. February was the height of summer, and it took nothing for us to soak through shirts and shorts. Taro tied a bandana around his head, while Miki wiped her brow with her own. The wind that gently blew through the grasses was welcome, but not as refreshing as I would have liked. Ocean breezes were still several hours away.

As the fields became craggier, we veered off course to skirt the dark chasms that plunged deep into the earth. We eventually needed to traverse the divide to make our way further north, but a suitable crossing had to be found first. In the interim, we jumped nimbly from boulders to rocks, and wading through the never-ending wavering fields of grass that rose to our waists. Distant rondavels dotted the horizon, but their inhabitants remained as remote as the view. And conversation was equally as sparse, as we focused on putting one foot in front of the other.

"Time to fill your water bottles," Michael croaked from dry lips, as a stream hove into sight.

"Really?" I asked uncertainly, as we got closer. "Is it safe to drink?"

"Can you see how clear it is?" Michael replied, as he dropped his pack to the ground. "That is the most pristine water you'll ever come across."

And to prove it, he crouched by the side of the stream and dunked in his baked head. With a sigh, he cupped his hands and sucked hungrily at the sparkling water. In an instant, we were at his side scrambling to reach the water ourselves. I looked over to see Miki slip off her backpack, followed by her runners. With a splash, she was in the water too. The rest of us were right behind her.

"Oh my God, that feels good," I cried.

"Bloody hell mate," Brett sighed. "I'm knackered. It's friggin' hot! This is alright though, then."

"C'mon Taro," Miki called out. "Where are you going? Jump in!"

He paused, as he pointed downstream. "We're not the only hot ones."

A group of boys splashed and paddled not far from where we bathed. Apparently, the lure of the stream was strong for anyone who came across it. These were the first people we had spied on our trek, and they looked just as happy to have found the river as we were. We playfully splashed and greedily gulped at the refreshing waters.

"We've still got a few more hours until we hit the coast," the Crazy Doc announced too soon, as he climbed back out of the stream. "Make sure to fill your water bottles and don't forget to check your legs for ticks before you put your socks and shoes back on."

We had named Michael the Crazy Doc, as he was a doctor, but also crazy about nature and all the perils surrounding us. He reminded me of Karel in that way, but like him, the warnings were warranted. Ticks could cause tick bite fever, causing a rash, muscle pain, severe headaches, and fevers. You might not feel them bite you, but if you didn't remove them right away, infection would set in within days.

Doc wore long socks that reached mid-calf; the better to protect himself. He also had plenty of bug spray, plus a stocked first aid kit. He might get a bit preachy at times, but I for one felt a little safer with him leading our troop.

With refilled water bottles and damp bandanas to keep us comfortable, we set off once more. Our spirits were buoyed by the break, so conversation resumed. Doc regaled us with new stories of snakes in the grass, cattle on the trails, and the beauty of the ocean ahead of us. What he hadn't mentioned before though, was his other plan.

The Indian Ocean finally snuck into our sightline and my excitement grew.

"With any luck, tonight we'll dine in style," Mike announced, as we carefully made our way down the rough, snaking pathway to the ocean below. A plateau greeted us with the ocean spraying up on one side and a waterfall serving as backdrop behind us. It was incredible and I was awed by the pristine beauty we had found. It felt like we were the first to discover it, tucked away as it was, but I knew better. Doc was already digging in his pack for something else he needed. Would it be a plaster for blisters, more sunscreen, or some kind of aloe to soothe baked lips?

In fact, it was a collapsible pot and a pocketknife. He wandered to a nearby tidal pool and peered into its crevices.

"Whatcha looking for?" I asked.

"Dinner," he answered, as he bent over and pried a shell off a rock.

"Mussels!" he declared triumphantly.

"Nice!" I cried.

Before long, he had scraped off a large collection of them and laid them aside. As the day waned, a fire was made, and our gourmet meal prepared. While Taro turned his nose up at the seafood, the rest of us tucked into the treat, along with other provisions from packs. Our bed that night was back up on the grassy hills, with our packs resting under our heads and the infinite stars to blanket us.

Could you call this heaven? It was a rustic traveller's version of it, to be sure. It seemed hard to believe that two short months previously, I had bumped into Miki in Johannesburg and my travel plans shifted so monumentally. I was grateful beyond belief for it all, especially in this moment of pure simplicity. If only we could have more of those moments everyday. But "real life" seemed to get in the way. And a measure of real life was waiting for us at the end of our hike the next day in the village of Mbotyi.

The next morning, I took advantage of the cool stream beside us to freshen up. Yesterday's sweat and dust were cleansed from me, and my steps lightened once more. I quickly jotted a few thoughts on the amazing adventure we were on in my journal before groans announced my fellow traveller's awakening. We stretched, tucked into breakfast, and cleaned the area of our traces. It was time to hike once more.

"A guide will meet us in Mbotyi," Michael said as we trekked along with the ocean on our left. More rocks and grasses covered our paths, but more rondavels popped into view too.

"There's a village about an hour and a half north of there." Doc continued. "He'll take us there and we'll spend the night with a local family." What I didn't fully realize yet though, was that this family lived in a rondavel, like the many huts we currently walked by. That would be where we slept that night. But first, the sleepy village of Mbotyi. Of course, the day we got there, it wasn't so sleepy!

I perched outside the store on a South Africa Brewery (SAB) container of Castle beer and sipped an orange soda. As we waited for our guide to arrive, I savoured the cold pop and watched locals mill about the shop. I had a bit of shell shock, coming from the pristine fields of the last two days, so welcomed my removed view. It was a veritable hive of activity.

People constantly went in and out of the shop. A man was carried outside and dumped in the dirt. My guess was that he was pissed out of his tree, but 15 minutes later, he stumbled back into the store for a taste of more. Young and old mingled in the local hub. A burst of shouts drew my attention to a bakkie that pulled up in the dirt parking lot.

"Ai, ai! Imamba[19]!"

People everywhere clamoured to get a look in the back of the truck. They pointed and shouted; words lost on me, but the gist clear. This was something to see. I stood on the packing crate to get a better look at what all the fuss was about and craned my neck to see.

"Oh my god!" I murmured. A huge dead snake was coiled in the back of the truck. It was as thick as my bicep and filled the bed.

"Black mamba," a man nearby stated. He mimicked the sign of a gun to indicate it had been shot.

I shuddered and mentally thanked my guardian angels—and our Crazy Doc—for not stumbling across any of these deadly snakes on our hike. One bite, and symptoms were upon you within 10 minutes. Without antivenom administered, you could die. But this one, wouldn't be bothering anyone anymore.

Shortly after the crowd dispersed, our guide arrived for the next part of our journey. And I for one, was glad to leave town behind once more. I couldn't wait for a closer look at one of the distant huts that had dotted the horizon over the last two days. Once again, this felt like a treat I was offered by the fates, and I relished every step that brough us closer to the hospitality of a local Xhosa family.

---

[19] imamba inyoka.

As we walked the final steps to the small collection of rondavels, I gazed in wonder around me. Chickens and mangy dogs scratched in the dirt. We had no common language, but the welcome felt genuine, nonetheless. We were ushered into the larger of the two huts and the obvious matriarch of the family bade us sit. I gratefully sank to the floor, shedding my pack against the nearby wall. No doors prevented the dogs or flies from entering, but they were shooed away, as dinner was served.

"Rice and samp[20]," our guide explained to us as rough plastic plates were handed round. "Mussels and fish, from ocean."

No cutlery was offered to help scoop up the samp, so fingers would have to do. After a long two days of hiking, I tucked in greedily though. It was delicious, but I couldn't help but notice that while we ate, and the other menfolk were offered food, the women and children lingered. It dawned on me that perhaps there weren't enough plates or bowls to go around, so I handed my plate back to the eager daughter. She was shy to meet our eyes but had her own plate of food soon enough. It suggested I had been right.

Once dinner was finished for all, our guests moved on to entertainment. They sang songs and attempted chitchat, but the language barrier proved difficult. Honestly though, we were exhausted, and I was happy to call it a day. We were ushered to the neighbouring rondavel where space was cleared on the dirt floor for our sleeping bags. It was all they had to offer, and that was alright. A roof overhead protected us from the elements, and that was alright.

Words were lost between us, but the welcome was not. We were guests in their home and respected that gift offered. There was no running water, no toilet, nor even doors to keep out the constant swarm of relentlessly

---

[20] dried corn kernels, coarsely chopped.

buzzing flies, but they willingly shared their space with us random strangers and even presented us with a bowl of water to wash up the next morning.

They had so little, but I was humbled regardless. Life wasn't measured in possessions. It was offered in time and companionship. How many people had truly learned those lessons? For me, it was perfect.

Appreciation for the simple things wasn't the only lesson I learned while in the Transkei though. I was also given a language lesson. It was perhaps the most poignant of all. I learned the Xhosa word 'enkosi'. It means thank you. And being able to explore this rich area and all it had to offer left me thankful indeed.

"Broken Peace"

For two weeks, we enjoyed the quiet peace and rural, rustic village life that Port St. Johns offered. We could have spent an eternity in this 'caught-in-time' community, but eventually the road called to us again. Out feet became itchy, as adventure called to us from the next bend in the road. As we moved on, Arnie still hugged the coastline, but our destination was like nothing we had come across thus far.

Durban was the urban capital of the newly created KwaZulu-Natal province. Not only was apartheid abolished and a black president elected, but in 1994, Natal and the KwaZulu Bantustan areas were merged to create a new province in southeast South Africa, with Durban at its centre. The busy beach town is the third largest city in South Africa and has the busiest port in Africa. That meant that wandering goats and stray dogs were replaced by traffic lights and high rises, surrounded by busy roads and the din of city life. We were as far away from Pondoland as we could get.

"Durban is supposed to have the best swells in South Africa," Brett announced in awe as we chugged toward the beachfront. "Some of the blokes I've met have warned me that competition is fierce, but say the waves are worth it."

As the Golden Mile came into view, he was like a kid in a candy store pointing out tubes, curls, and swells that had him gibbering in excitement. As the rest of us came from land-locked Ontario, the state of the surf was lost on us, but we appreciated that we had reached the surfing mecca of South Africa for Brett.

"Give at 'er mate," I called as Miki and I chose to walk the touristy Golden Mile while Brett strapped on his board to fight for his spot on a wave. He was so focused that he didn't even see us go.

After a brief wander, we returned to the warm Indian Ocean for some more leisurely swimming and sunning with Brett, while Taro wandered off to explore the city on his own. On the surface, it seemed ideal. It didn't take long for that feeling to subside though.

The multicultural community was a bit of a shell shock for us. Here, Blacks (mostly Zulus), Indians, and people of British descent mingled. Despite the holiday feel of the tourist destination, tensions seemed to be everywhere, including amongst our little band of travellers. As we had been in close quarters for a long stretch, we all needed some space. Durban offered plenty of places to disappear to though, so it was only a matter of time before we all went in opposite directions to explore this new metropolitan city.

For me, Durban was a stop to gather supplies and get housekeeping done. I stocked up on contact lenses, postcards, fresh music tapes, did some banking, and mailed souvenirs home. In between banal tasks, like buying a new towel, I marveled at the mixture of mosques, Indian cultural sites, and

Colonial heritage buildings. To my appraising eye, they seemed to mix reasonably well, unlike in other places we had visited. After soaking in the relative peace of the Transkei, I didn't think anything of aimlessly wandering Durban wherever my feet took me. Hence when that calm shattered, I was shaken to my core.

After my wanders about the city, I reclined in the airy courtyard of the Banana Backpackers hostel. I jotted paperwork details into my journal, before starting my next letter home, when a commotion caught my attention. A man stumbled in breathing heavily and seemingly dazed. A camera swung from his neck, as he weaved on his feet.

"Yoh man, what's wrong?" called a fellow backpacker.

When he staggered forward panting, someone yelled "Quick, someone help him." In an instant, he was surrounded by people who lowered him to the floor.

"He's bleeding!" someone yelled, as another traveller pushed into the growing circle of people around the injured man.

"Step back," he demanded as he dropped to the floor beside him. "Give him some air. And someone call an ambulance."

A hush fell over the courtyard, as we watched him expertly work on the injured man's wounds. He cut the bloody shirt away to reveal a stab wound to the man's shoulder. Undaunted, the traveller-come-medic used the scrap of cloth to staunch the wound that threatened to fill the courtyard with the injured man's life-force.

"What happened?" asked a friend of the injured traveller, as he took the camera that still clung around his neck.

"I was just out for a walk," he mumbled. "Snapped a few pictures, looked at the sites..." He winced as the Good Samaritan peeled the cloth back to look at the wound, before applying pressure again. "All of a sudden, this a guy attacked me. He knocked me down and started kicking me. I had no idea what was going on. I just tucked in and prayed, until I realized he was gone. Then I pulled myself up and limped home as fast as I could..."

He was a mere few blocks from the hostel in broad daylight. He didn't even realize he had been stabbed until blood began to seep across his shirt. And as horrible as the attack was, it was made all the worse by the fact that the attacker didn't even take the camera from his neck. If robbery was not the motive, then what was? Unease spread across the room, as we contemplated the reasoning behind the attack. No one had an answer as to why.

Forty-five minutes later an ambulance finally arrived to take over care of the fallen traveller. His departure didn't help to lighten the heavy spirits that settled on the hostel. The space where he had lain was conspicuously avoided; bad spirits still lingered in the air. And an uneasiness encroached on our little band of travellers.

"I saw two guys struggling in an alleyway yesterday," Miki noted. "One of them had a gun in his hand."

"Yeah, I saw two fights today too," Taro said. "And in both of them there was blood."

"Me too," Brett added. "And not just fighting for waves. I saw a couple of blokes scrapping downtown."

The illusion of peace and security we had brought with us from the Transkei was shattered. We were faced with the realities of violence that were commonplace in this struggling country. The horror stories which had been drilled into us by so many were now shoved at us with more examples than we desired to see. We could no longer ignore them or pooh-pooh the tales as paranoid delusions. The evidence was everywhere here.

Nervousness set in and we hurriedly listed the tasks that needed to get accomplished before we could move on. No one felt like extending our stay in Durban any longer than necessary. It was time to go. But before we could finalize our plans, a twist was thrown into our midst.

"Taro's not coming with us," Miki announced as we sat in the lounge.

Taro had come with us from Cape Town, but never entirely committed to our journey. He hadn't contributed to the purchase of the van (which wasn't a big deal but showed his reluctance to be part of our plans) and now opted to go no further with us. Between squabbles with his sister and the bad luck that plagued him along the way—a broken bike, lost camera, getting mugged, and bitten by a dog—I suppose I couldn't blame him. I could see how a change might be alluring to potentially sway his karma back to a more positive note. And the strain on his relationship with Miki seemed to be approaching a breaking point. But it was a big country to explore completely alone. And it worried all of us.

"I need to do this," he said. "I need to see the country for myself."

None of us could fault him for that. After all, we had all made our way to Africa alone, unsure of what it would hold. The tension never seemed to dissipate, only getting worse the longer we were together. So, before anger got the best of everyone, Taro decided to make his way on his own. He might have been Miki's little brother, but he was an adult capable of making his own decisions. And while this one pained Miki, we had to respect Taro's choice.

Our last supper together was bittersweet.

"I'm going to miss you," I said with a fierce hug. Taro had been my self-proclaimed protector when he wasn't falling into disasters of his own.

"Take care of yourself mate," Brett added with a clap on his shoulder. Even though the two of them had had their differences, I knew Brett would worry about him on his own.

But it was Miki that fought the biggest tears when we pulled away. Nothing could change his mind though and I could see his mental load visibly lighten once it had been made up.

The only thing that made the parting marginally easier was that a new hand helped waved goodbye as we drove away. Oliver now joined our midst. He was a German traveller we had met in Port St. Johns, and he agreed to join us to help with the driving.

Next stop Swaziland; a new country for us all.

"Swaziland"

"Good riddance South Africa. Bring on Swaziland!"

It was a sentiment held by all. Bad karma had been brewing and we needed a break from it. The hope was that Swaziland would be that difference. But we hadn't reached the border yet.

"The van won't start," Brett announced as we clamoured into Arnie.

"What?!" Miki and I exclaimed from the back seat.

"It won't turn over," he explained. "I'm getting nothing."

"But the radio is on," I said. Auto mechanics wasn't my thing, but I understood that the battery must be fine if Bob Marley could still jam. Our speedo had stopped working long before and a gas leak meant we couldn't fill the tank to the brim, but neither of these woes affected our present immobility.

"For pity's sake," I grumbled.

"I have an idea," Brett suggested. "Everyone out. Let's try giving it a push." I'm sure Oliver was less than impressed to have saddled himself with us at that point, but he gamely joined us at the back of the kombi. Lo and behold Arnie fired to life.

"Push start," Oliver joked. "That's fun."

"Hmph" I replied.

As the border approached, the thought didn't bring much comfort. We stopped to snap pictures of wildlife on the way without incidence, but when we stopped for gas, had to push once more. Apparently, this was our newest issue to contend with, but was sporadic for the moment.

"Don't stop when we get to the border," Miki suggested when we got closer. "Just idle so no one realizes there's a problem." Arnie complied while we handed over passports. And with a release of collectively held breath, we were Mbabane bound, no stalled engines in sight.

With South Africa behind us, we slipped into our own quiet worlds. The land outside our windows gradually rose, with gentle hills undulating into view. By the time Mbabane came into sight, the scenic Dlangeni Hills surrounded us. And while Mbabane was the capital, it was much smaller and a far more relaxed looking than the one we had left. The hope was that Durban's bad karma would disperse in this new terrain.

While we counted Swaziland as a new country, it's actually considered a kingdom (in 2018 it was renamed Eswatini, but that was long after we were there). Surrounded by South Africa on three sides, with Mozambique on the remaining edge, it is a land-locked country measuring 200 kilometers from north to south, and 130 kilometers from east to west. At just over 17,000 kilometres, it is one of the smallest countries in Africa, but was still a big part of our journey—it was where we needed to apply for visas to get into Mozambique.[21]

So, when Arnie slowly putted into Mbabane, struggling against the Highveld elevation of 1,200 metres, and the van's recent mechanical woes, we were happy to stop. Trading the high-energy glitz and tourism of Durban for the sleepy city of Mbabane was a welcome deal. No more surf boards and sun-kissed beaches. Brett had begrudgingly mailed his board home from Durban. Now, it was time for business.

"So, what does the Lonely Planet say Miki?" I asked. "Where do we rest our head tonight?"

"Hmm, there doesn't seem to be a lot of options. We either go high-end or a choice of two hostels."

"Eeny, meeny, miny, moe..." She read the descriptions and we picked one to steer towards it. Vacancy wasn't an issue, so we moved into

---

[21] Masson, J. R. (n.d.). Eswatini. Encyclopædia Britannica. https://www.britannica.com/place/Eswatini.

our next home away from home for a few days. You could tell already that we had stepped off the popular tourist trail.

While Swaziland has plenty of hills and forests to admire, they weren't a priority for us either. Sure, they were nice and a welcome change in scenery, but Swaziland held the closest Mozambique Embassy. We all required visas to visit the former Portuguese colony. The next closest embassy was in Johannesburg, which was several hundred kilometers, and days, out of our way. Swaziland it was.

"Let's deal with our visas first," Brett suggested.

With passports in hand, we headed to the out-of-the-way government office. After quietly shuffling through long, slow-moving lines, with nothing to look at but dingy, drab walls, we finally handed over our applications and emerged from the dreary consulate. Our time inside the stale embassy had felt oppressive and never-ending, but surprisingly there was still plenty of day left.

"What do we want to do now?" Miki asked as we blinked in the bright sun.

"Whatever we do, it has to be close," Oliver remarked. The consulate had kept our passports until the visas were processed.

"Let's check out the city," Miki suggested.

"Ok," I replied.

"I've had enough of cities," Brett remarked. "I'm heading for the hills."

"Count me in," Oliver added. And with that, we drifted apart. Brett and Oliver disappeared into the nearby hills, while Miki and I wandered the small city. It didn't take long.

"Do you want to see a movie?" Miki half-heartedly asked.

"Meh," I replied. I didn't want to do much of anything. "I might just write a few letters…" I just wanted to be alone. It was hard being an introvert surrounded by people all day and some days I just needed to decompress. When we had the luxury of separating, I took advantage.

The next day, I continued my solitary state and picked a new direction to wander in. I spied a church/community centre and poked my nose in the door. A TV blared in the corner with a handful of people scattered at random tables.

"Sawubona."

A man approached the doorway where I hovered. "Hello. Come in! All are welcome here."

"Thank you," I said, as I tentatively stepped over the threshold.

"What brings you to Mbabane?" the man asked. It was obvious I wasn't from around these parts.

I chitchatted about my travels, then asked about Swaziland.

"Swaziland is beautiful, but you are lucky you weren't here a month ago," he said. "The country was in a bad way. There was a massive strike. No water, electricity, nor phones lines. It lasted eight days and practically shut down the country."

I had heard of the strike and the violence that came with it, but not the cause; maternity leave and back pay for nurses, amongst other reasons.

"Nurses were owed eight million Lilangeni (equivalent to rand)," he added.

"Wow," I exclaimed wide-eyed.

I had no way to verify his claims but was thankful that we were there a month after the fray. And hoped that the strikes and efforts of the labour unions would make a difference.

"Politics moves slowly," he said. "The monarchy doesn't help."

Apparently, it took shutting down an entire country to make those changes. Although I had no way of knowing if the changes would stick. I was glad we had missed it regardless.[22]

It made our own woes seem petty by comparison; Miki's worries about her brother, a scuffle for Brett back in Durban that left bruises, but no broken bones, malaria pills left behind by me, and the kombi which seemed to develop a new problem every time we stopped. But they were our problems and ones that travelled with us. I didn't want any heavier cross to bear than my own.

I prayed that once we collected our passports, better roads would fill our future. I couldn't shake a sense of foreboding though. Mozambique was our next destination and it had only come out of its own conflicts three years previous. The country had spent 10 years battling for independence

---

[22] Mutume, G. (1997, February 5). SWAZILAND-POLITICS: The Struggle for Democracy Continues. AfricaFocus. http://www.africafocus.org/docs97/swaz9702.php.

from Portugal, then another 15 years in internal civil wars. I worried about what we would find when we crossed the border.

We would soon find out.

*****

MOZAMBIQUE

"A New Land"

"Right, time to pick up our passports…"

They couldn't be ready soon enough. Scowling government officials handed them over, still uncertain about this ragtag group of miscreants, but we were free to hit the road again. Swaziland served its purpose and now it was on to the next country.

"I can't wait to see Mozambique!" Miki exclaimed.

"Bloody van better not break down at the border, is all," Brett grumbled from the driver's seat.

He was our primary driver, so I understood his concerns. Arnie was a stick shift and Miki and I only knew how to drive automatic. We had the will, but not the ability to tackle the roads. Hence the importance of adding Oliver to our midst, although he didn't have the same vested interest in the vehicle as we did. I'm sure the responsibility weighed heavier on Brett, but it couldn't be helped. Onward and upward.

It was the better part of two hours to the border, so we settled in for the drive. We drove through sparsely populated regions punctuated by dry, mountainous hills and scrubby valleys. As the border drew nearer, our elevation steadily dropped. Where Mbabane sat at an elevation of 1243 metres, by the time we reached Maputo, we would be sitting at a mere 47 metres. Going from cool mountains to a hot, semi-arid ocean climate would make a difference as well. What other differences would we find?

Before we got to the coast, we would have to cross the border though. Our brand-new entry visas were ready. Whether Arnie was ready, remained to be seen though. It was doubtful that the border guards at Naamacha would look kindly at us pushing our vehicle across an international border. And Arnie's track record had slowly been going downhill. To our delight, he sputtered to life once our visas were stamped. It was worth celebrating, but we did our best not to show it as we slowly entered Mozambique.

"My fifth country in Africa!" I noted once the border lay safely behind us.

"Number three for me," Miki added.

"Me too," echoed Brett. "Bring on the ocean!"

Only 80 kilometers to go.

Mozambique is on the Southeastern edge of the African continent. It is bordered by Swaziland (which we just left), the Indian Ocean (which we headed towards), Zimbabwe (where we planned to go next), South Africa (spent plenty of time there already), Malawi, Tanzania, and Zambia. That's a lot of borders. It was a Portuguese colony from 1505 to 1975, so not surprising that the official language was Portuguese. We hoped to find people who spoke English but expected to hear many other local dialects as well, such as Swahili, Sena, Makhuwa, Ndau, and Shangaan.[23] Whether we heard any of them or not, I can only speculate, but we managed fine in English.

The closer we got to the coast, the worse the roads became.

---

[23] Penvenne, J. M. (n.d.). Mozambique. Encyclopædia Britannica. https://www.britannica.com/place/Mozambique.

"Looks like their taxes are in arrears," Oliver remarked, as the edges of the roads began to crumble.

"Either that, or they've got more important things than roads to spend their budgets on," Brett answered.

"Or maybe no one cares," I quietly added. In comparison, Swaziland and South African roads had been clean and maintained. Here, potholes littered the highway. We were on the main thoroughfare from the border to the capital city of Maputo. It wasn't promising. And as we neared the city, our progress slowed even more due to the dilapidated streets. Soon, the city came into view.

"Surely, these are the outer city limit slums," I speculated, as an increase in debris littered the roadway.

The further we drove, the less likely that became. A shocked silence filled the van. Burnt out vehicles sat on makeshift blocks with not a scrap of rubber on the warped rims, glass in the windows, nor paint on the frames. Empty lots filled with rubble were interspersed by small businesses and sketchy homes.

And the potholes grew bigger.

As I stared wide-eyed out my window, I caught glimpses of the city's former grandeur amongst the wreckage. Ornate buildings crumbled at the seams. Grand hotels stood obviously empty and abandoned. You could see the prosperity that existed before the Portuguese fled for their lives with their money in tow. Maputo seemed to cry out that it had been the 'belle-of-the-ball' in its hey-day; back when the city had gone by Lourenço Marques. Those days had disappeared 20 years before though and the subsequent civil wars had left the capital on its knees, both structurally and economically.

This was where we would spend the night.

"Jeez, it's rough looking," Brett whistled with a shake of his head. "Where are we headed to Miko?"

She consulted the Lonely Planet guide in her lap. Budget was what we were looking for and that was exactly what she found for us.

"The Pensao Nini[24]," she replied, when we pulled up to the drab building on a busy road. "Home sweet home."

It had vacancies, so would do. We took two rooms: one for Miki and me, the other for Brett and Oliver. We lugged our packs up to our adjacent rooms to settle in, before heading out to see what the city had on offer.

"Ugh, gross cockroaches. Faak!" I cried, as the fleet insects scurried into the filthy corners of the room when I opened our door. "Miki, is this the best we can do? God, I don't want to even lie on the beds!"

"You've got your own sleeping bag to crawl into, mate," Brett chuckled as he stepped into his own matching room across the hall. "They won't come anywhere near you if you let one of your bloody breezers go."

"Thanks," I said, as I rolled my eyes. "My hero."

Hopefully, no creepy crawlies would tag along with us when we left. Which I hoped would be sooner rather than later.

---

[24] guest house.

"Why don't we grab a bier and make a plan," Oliver suggested. "Decide what we want to do and see."

"Great idea," Miki said.

I was more than happy to get out of our divey room. We dumped our backpacks and left the pensao nini[25] in search of a few cervezas. Anything to distract from the overwhelming destruction we were steeped in. Of course, my travel companions didn't see it that way.

"Should be cool checking out the city tomorrow," Brett remarked as he took a long haul off his drink.

"Yeah, we should find a market," Miki replied. "Stock up on supplies and see what's around. There looks like there's some cool buildings."

Hadn't they noticed the potholes and paupers that seemed to be everywhere? Was I the only one who had misgivings about being in such a derelict place? I listened to them excitedly make plans and couldn't fathom what they saw.

Maybe it isn't as bad as it looks, I grudgingly thought. *Perhaps I would be pleasantly surprised if I aimed for a positive outlook?* I mostly sipped my beer in silence, as they planned.

"Right then," Brett said finally. "Time to call it a night. Big day ahead tomorrow."

Our first night in Mozambique came quietly to a close. We returned to the pensao where Brett and Oliver retired to their room, and Miki and I to

---

[25] guest house.

ours. I hoped that perhaps the world would look a little brighter in the morning. But that wasn't to be.

"A Grain of Sand"

I went through my ablutions in preparation for bed; teeth, hands, face, eyes - check! I donned PJs and looked forward to an early night in bed; the better to dim the initial rocky introduction to Mozambique.

Knock, knock, knock...

"Hey mate, does anyone have an ibuprofen?" Brett asked. "I've got a bloody stitch in me side that's kickin' the shit out of me."

His face was pale and drawn. Miki and I dug in our packs to see what was in our personal pharmacies. Miki handed over Advil, while I held up a bottle of Tylenol.

"Maybe we should find a doctor," Miki suggested.

"Naw, I'll be a'right once the meds kick in," Brett said.

"You do look kind of shitty," I offered.

"Thanks mate," he remarked with a limp smile, before leaning forward in another spasm of pain.

"Are you sure," Miki asked as we both watched on helplessly until he straightened again.

He took a couple of deep breaths before he straightened up again. "I'm sure I'll be right as rain in the morning, but if not, we'll see what we can find then."

He swallowed a handful of painkillers, then headed back to bed. A peaceful night was not to be though. The pills did nothing. Brett tossed and flip-flopped on his bed, but the pain only got worse. A mere 10 minutes after we turned out the light, Brett was at our door again. He was ashen.

"It's worse," Brett said through gritted teeth. "I think we need to find the hospital—now..."

Oliver stood behind him in the doorway and nodded. "I'll drive," he said.

We scrambled back into our clothes and rushed downstairs. Oliver turned the ignition with no response. As Brett stoically sat grim faced behind the wheel, Miki, Oliver, and I pushed the stubborn van down the street. Arnie refused to cooperate. The van would not turn over at all. We ran half-way down the street and back, huffing and puffing all the way. With every new spasm, Brett writhed in agony in the driver's seat, but our efforts were for naught. When we were at our most desperate, Arnie refused to come to our aid.

"What's going on," asked a passerby curious about the commotion. While I explained that our friend was in pain and the van's starter motor didn't work, Miki flagged down a motorist. They agreed to help, and she hastily scooped Brett out of one vehicle and into the other.

And then they were gone. Oliver and I were left behind to tend to our broken-down vehicle.

"We can give you a push," said one of the youths who now surrounded us.

"Umm," I thought out loud, trying to formulate a plan.

Too late. Before we knew it, a mob of street kids helped push Arnie back to the motel for the night.

"Thanks," we offered. "We appreciate it."

But they lingered in an expectant way. They wanted more than just our gratitude. They expected to be paid for their assistance.

"Oh Jesus," I grumbled. "What do you have Oliver?"

We scrounged up R10 and 50,000 Metical. Really, 5,000 to 10,000 MT should have been sufficient, but they wanted more. Highway robbery in the middle of the night! It might have been a pittance for us in the grand scheme of things—and their idea of fair wages—but Oliver wouldn't let it go and argued the fee. I took the opportunity and sprinted off to the hospital in search of my friends.

Need I remind you that we had just arrived in Maputo that afternoon? While we had wandered around our pensao a bit, I was far from familiar with the city. Hence racing through it after dark probably wasn't the smartest thing to do. My vision was clouded with tortured images of Brett in agony though. I didn't think about the fact that I was a solitary, white female running through a dark, run-down metropolis. In hindsight, that was probably for the best.

Somehow, I managed to stumble upon the hospital. I found Brett tucked into a crisp, white bed with Miki at his side. A doctor stood at the end of the bed with a clipboard in hand.

"Have you... figured out... what's wrong?" I panted as I glanced at the IV that slowly dripped into his arm.

"It looks like your friend has kidney stones," the doctor explained. "His recent hike in the mountains probably dehydrated him. Dehydration is a common cause of kidney stones."

"What exactly are they?" Miki asked. As the doctor set about administering medicine through Brett's drip, he explained.

"Kidney stones are usually calcium-based, crystal-like materials which form in the kidneys or urinary tract. They are often small—about the size of a grain of sand—but can get much larger. What your friend can attest to is that as they pass through the urethra, they are incredibly painful. In fact, they are one of the most painful things one can go through. Giving birth, having a heart attack, and kidney stones are your three most painful experiences."

Miki and I exchanged a shocked glance.

"What do you do for them?" I asked.

"Most times the only thing that needs to be done for someone suffering from kidney stones is to hydrate them to help the stones pass more freely. We are administering something for the pain, but the IV will rehydrate Brett as well. Ultimately, the stone needs to pass on its own and that requires time."

"How much time?" Miki asked anxiously.

"We'll keep you in hospital overnight to rehydrate you and monitor your pain levels," the doctor said addressing Brett. He turned back to Miki and me. "You should be able to collect your friend in the morning."

There was nothing more we could do. Brett was in capable hands and had found a measure of comfort via their welcome medication. It was time for Miki and me to find a measure of sleep and comfort ourselves. We promised to return in the morning and stumbled home to our pensao.

"Alms"

Another grubby hand snaked out in front of me.

"Five Rand (ZAR), sistah!" a voice rang out. "1,000 Meticals (MZN)—enough for bread… Please! I am so hungry missus," he added with imploring eyes, as his fingers danced towards me.

I turned away and mumbled, "sorry..."

My heart broke a little more for this ailing nation. While coins jangled in my pocket, it wasn't enough. I couldn't fix the country with spare change. Too many people pleaded for hand-outs, and I couldn't feed them all. This boy was just one soul in a vast sea of need.

It was overwhelming to see poverty on such a level. Everywhere you turned dirty palms were jammed in your face. Only that morning a boy stopped in front of me as we wandered in a market. He didn't say a word, only pointed to his mouth. Whether he could speak or not, I don't know, but his mouth was a misshapen gash. I had no idea whether it was a birth defect from insufficient prenatal care or a misadventure with a land mine, but it

143

made no difference. He was horribly deformed and trying to capitalize on it. I likened the image to a macabre jack-o-lantern or horror movie makeup, but the boy stood flesh and blood in front of me demanding sympathy.

I quickly turned away, unable to face yet another stark reminder of the poverty in Mozambique. His errant few teeth and broken lips were yet another example of the horrors this country attempted to survive through. It sickened me. How could life have turned so wrong on such a large scale? This deformed child screamed of a whole nation contorted by the ugliness of war, greed, and misuse. How could one person, one handful of change make a difference? It could not.

As I turned away, I suspected only the passage of time would help heal the wounds so prevalent here. Aid organizations offered what they could, but at times only seemed to beget more issues. There was need, so groups swooped in with help. When items were distributed, people were grateful, but then some thought they could just sit back and have money handed to them without effort. The issues ran much deeper than that, but faced with the massive scale of poverty, destitution, and begging, I was hard pressed to see beyond the ragged clothes and snapshot of the moment.

My white skin felt like a beacon of prosperity that proclaimed my affluence. Many of the aid workers shared the colour of my skin, linking me to their alms. I couldn't help but note the discrepancy between my idea of riches and theirs. I walked with all my possessions on my back, but still had more wealth than most of these people would ever see in a lifetime. My plane ticket home was equivalent to freedom, tantamount to innumerable fortunes in their world.

It was doubtful the mutilated boy would ever experience half of the privileges I was honoured with. But his presence was a gift I would never forget. His wretchedness served to remind me of the wealth I had, whether it was a few coins in my pocket, the clothes on my back, or a plane ticket which could take me away. I was blessed.

While the phenomenal poverty at every turn was a struggle to process, we did what we could to give back in this suffering land. Our alms came in the form of food. As compared to those around us, we had plenty to give. One group of children was offered leftover rice. A man who sold Miki a batik got our remaining rice salad. Another group of children were offered slightly stale bread, improved with a bit of jam. And our small kindnesses were met with broad smiles.

"Asante sana! Obrigado[26]! Thank you!" they shouted. It was so little, but their heartfelt appreciation helped to take some of the chill from my aching heart.

More than the inherent hunger gave me pause though. We skirted monstrous potholes, which gaped six feet deep and wide at times. Tattered tarps and scrap lumber held together market stalls. Many people's outfits were equally ill-held together. These images screamed of a social and economic system which was broken, perhaps nonexistent. It broke my heart. Canada might as well have been another planet, for the comparisons I could make.

I processed what I could and took strength from my travelling companions. Brett's recent trip to the hospital was forgotten, as he strode along with a smile on his face. He appeared to enjoy himself immensely, as did Oliver and Miki. They seemed to take the experience in stride and focus more on the positives they could find. So, I looked harder. I sought their faith in the world and their hope for this country, which was actively ridding itself

---

[26] thanks.

of landmines, war, and yesterday's ugliness. Their optimism that life would get better and continue stirred me. It was a balm I used to survive the ugliness that surrounded us.

A proverb struck me as we skimmed across a world not our own: "Give a man a fish and feed him for a day. Teach a man to fish and feed him for a lifetime."

These people had fish but were only just learning how to catch them again. We could feed them today but had to have faith that they would learn how take over tomorrow. I prayed that would be the case for this poor, besotted country. And tried to make peace with the divide in the interim.

"Coastal Magic"

"I've tried really hard to be open and as non-judgemental as I can of Maputo. But I can't take it anymore guys," I said to my fellow travellers a few days later. "It's too much. We've explored and seen as much as I care to see. Can we please move on?"

I would never forget the visions of the children who struggled to survive in a world of abject poverty. While life wasn't perfect back home in Canada, we weren't subjected to the horrors of civil war, rampant diseases, and the utter destitution which seemed to be everywhere here. I knew only too well that I was blessed to have the choice to leave. And after spending several nights in Maputo, I felt that it was time to go. Thankfully, my travelling companions agreed.

Even as we drove away from the capital city, I knew Maputo's children would remain in my mind's eye. I couldn't shake the wretched images of Mozambique that plagued me, nor the hopelessness I felt at not being able to do anything about this once proud country. I prayed a change in scenery might also bring about a change of heart. As we headed north hugging the coast though, I refused to look back.

We chugged into Xai Xai and set up tents in a small campground beside the Indian Ocean. Its presence was large as life beside us and helped me to breathe again now that the city was behind us. A white sand beach stretched before us, huts and small business enterprises scattered here and there, and little market stalls were plentiful. Clad in brightly coloured sarongs, women stood behind piles of bananas and miniature tomatoes. Loosely knit groups of men lazed in the shade of nearby trees, as innocuous cartons of beer were passed around with plenty of well-worn stories. Children were the glue between these groups as they ran laughing, heedless of the heat. It was like nothing I had seen in Canada, but felt comfortable, nonetheless.

"This isn't so bad," I mused as we settled into our new home in Xai Xai. There was a bar in the campground, as well as clean running water. It was a different face of Mozambique, a quieter and more welcome environment.

"It's too quiet," a woman I met that night at the camp bar remarked. She had recently emigrated from Namibia and wasn't impressed. "There's nothing to do here; no night clubs or shopping, nothing at all. I'm bored."

While I could relate to her need for entertainment, as I had been in a similar state of mind when I first arrived in Africa, I far preferred this village to our last stop in Maputo. The sleepy community where children's smiles bloomed large, and life seemed to be full of simple things was more my speed at that point.

"Don't they have someplace where they play music at night?" I asked. "Could you go to Maputo or maybe back home for a visit?" The idea of returning to Maputo gave me the shivers, but I could understand the draw of city living. I had been to a nightclub or two in my day and enjoyed the thrill of it. As for me though, the handful of days we had been in the present sleepy community helped me to let go of my jaded images of Mozambique. And that was exactly what I needed. I finally began to enjoy the country and its beauty.

We spent a few nights in Xai Xai, then moved on to Praia de Tofo. Here is where the blues of the ocean stole my heart. The pure white sand beach beckoned to me, and I could not resist. I battled the scorching heat of the silky sands to plunge into the salty waters of the ocean. It was heavenly to gently paddle in the warm waves which ebbed in and out. It was too hot to sit in the direct sunlight, but I refused to leave the ocean's side. Instead, I laid my towel in the shade to soak up the pristine beauty of Mozambique's coastline.

How could there be so much suffering in such a beautiful place, I wondered. *Was it the heat which made people's demeanours turn hostile? Did my colder clime make the people more prone to huddle together and therefore more temperate in nature?* I scribbled my thoughts into the journal in front of me, occasionally looking up to soak in the view.

The next time I looked up, a boy stood in front of me, watching me write. He did nothing, but stare. He appeared tiny, but his vast eyes were huge. They seemed to hold all that Mozambique represented and more, and the moment imprinted on me pedagogically. His silence reminded me that I did not know his language or experiences, but he was beautiful, nonetheless. We didn't live in the same world but inhabited this same moment.

A man materialized behind the boy and smiled shyly at me.

"Habari," he said.

"Hello," I returned. "Is this your son?"

"Si," he said. "Yes, he is."

"Beautiful. Very petite though," I remarked as I dramatically dropped my hand to the boy's height to get my point across. I knew almost no Swahili and the man obviously struggled in English. "How old is he?" I asked pointing to the boy. I held up several fingers trying to make him understand my question. "3, 4, 5, 8? Me 22," I added pointing back at myself, then pointed to the boy again.

"Four," he replied holding up four fingers. Our sign language caught Miki's attention from across the beach and she joined us.

"Would you like some fish?" she asked mouthing invisible food. "Barracuda?" Our leftovers from the previous night's dinner. We already recognized that even on our thin budget, we often had more than those we travelled amongst. He was no different.

"Si[27]," he said nodding his head. "Yes, please. Asante sana[28]."

They gladly took the food we offered. I couldn't help but wonder how regular their meals were. And wondered if perhaps that contributed to the diminutive size of the children we had seen. This boy was tiny and the children we had come across in Xai Xai were no better. Those children had claimed to be between 12 and 16 but looked more like between six and 12. I

---

[27] yes.
[28] thank you very much.

pondered again what it was that made these people who they were. Did lack of vitamins and proper nutrition stunt the children's growth so much, or did the atmosphere of war factor in as well?

I could suppose and guess but would never truly know the answers. I had not lived, breathed, or grown up there. I could only conjecture at their lives' paths. And to be honest, a piece of me wondered whether I could handle their truth even if I knew it. In that moment of time, perhaps it was best I knew as little as I did.

*****

After the man and his son left, I packed up my towel and wandered to the village square. The tiny settlement didn't hold much, aside from the makeshift market, so my adventure was short-lived. What I longed to explore though was the beautiful old hotel, which served as a backdrop to the village. Prudence made leery.

As I gazed at the decrepit building, I imagined its former glory. Halls that exuded grandeur, sweeping staircases, and decadent suites, where the rich once frolicked at this seaside town. That was far from the case now though. It was obvious the hotel had been abandoned long ago. Broken windows and crumbling walls disintegrated in more than one spot, leaving the building eerily unsafe. As much as I craved a peek inside, I couldn't chance another hospital trip. A decided lack of medical care made the risk too great. All I could do was gaze longingly from afar and dream of its former opulence. Its broken beauty was like so many other pieces of Mozambique— forgotten to the world. And I too turned away with a sad sigh...

Instead, I opted to support the local economy.

"Uma cerveja por favor[29]," I requested from a nearby dilapidated stand. I opted for bottled beer over the popular local, Chibuku. I just couldn't bring myself to try beer from a warm cardboard carton. "Obrigado," I replied, as I toted the cold beer back to my spot on the beach. It was a luxury on another sweltering day.

I took a long pull off the cold bottle, then returned to my writing. My thoughts strayed back to the man and his son, whom I had met earlier. As if I had summoned him with my thoughts, a shadow fell across my page. I looked up to see the father in front of me once more.

"Habari," I said with a smile.

He nodded and his eyes flashed to the beer which glistened in front of me. I looked from the bottle to the man, and back to the beer again. He was thirsty. I could see the longing in his eyes. I wondered how long it had been since he had been able to afford a real beer versus the prevalent Chibuku Shake Shake, which I distained. What would it hurt to share a swallow?

"Would you like a sip," I asked as I held the bottle towards him. He accepted the bottle with a nod, then turned and walked away. "What?!"

I sat up and frowned at his retreating figure. He was leaving! He had taken my almost full beer and left. While I was willing to share, I still wanted more. My thirst was far from quenched.

"Shit," I mumbled. I knew it wasn't worth chasing after him to retrieve it. "I guess he needed it more than I did. Lesson learned..."

---

[29] a beer if you please.

I mused on what had just happened. Perhaps when you gave something to someone there, they kept it until their needs were sated, then they too passed it along. I had no basis to pin that on but chalked it up to a hands-on cultural lesson for me; different lands hold different customs. I returned to my journal once more, only to be interrupted anew. The man was on his way back again. And this time, he carried a pail.

"Maji," he said as he mimicked drinking. "Water." I knew it would be fresh, clean, and fit to drink. He was returning the good deed I had unknowingly offered him—fish and beer for potable water. One good turn deserves another…

As we hadn't camped at a formal campground, we had to walk to the village to get our water like everyone else in the village, at a communal tap. It was a fair walk. Not a huge problem, but not having taps handy to instantly access water was a foreign concept for us. The man's gift of water was worth far more than the humble beer I had given him. I was uplifted by his simple act of sharing and a humanity I had not expected. I felt small in light of his act of kindness but awed by the generosity of it. Here was a spirit of compassion and community. Items were freely shared amongst people, and it was an understood thing amongst everyone. And I was now part of that community.

The beauty of Mozambique lifted to the top of my destinations in this simple, yet unforgettable moment. I was in love.

"Off the Grid"

I wished peace with all my heart to the beautiful people I met in Praia de Tofo and cherished the lessons I learned there, but it was time to hit the road once more. The further north we travelled though, the worse the road became. We weaved across its surface avoiding gaping potholes which threatened to rip axles, wheels, or whatever it could snatch, right off.

There was no other road to choose from though.

Eventually, we found shelter in Vilanculos. We pulled into a compound by the ocean and decided to call it home for a few days. The outdoor shower in the middle of the walled compound might have helped in the decision too. We hadn't seen a shower in days and a good scrubbing was due us all.

"You might want to save your showers for the afternoon," the man who toured us around the compound remarked. "We fill the shower from the well in the village every morning. As the day progresses, the water in the drum warms up. A morning shower can be pretty bracing. Depending upon where you are in the queue, at least you'll get a chance to wash the sand out of your skivvies though." As he turned to continue the tour, he said over his shoulder, "Your call. You're free to use it whenever you fancy..."

For a chance at warm water to cleanse body and soul, I was happy to wait. We had enough tasks to tackle beforehand anyway, which would make us dirty all over again; putting up tents usually added a layer of fresh grime.

To be honest, I was grateful for both the shower and the handy toilets. As much as we had done our due diligence in boiling all the water we drank and cooked with before using it, my body was suffering a little. It wasn't nearly as bad as when I first arrived, but my bowels had taken on an unpleasant squishiness that I was having a hard time shaking. The joys of travelling in the rough.

But man, my turn at the shower was heavenly! You stepped into a giant corrugated metal surround. There was a large steel tank above your

153

head with an attached faucet. The tank was filled by hand every morning from the water tap outside of the campground, and as the gentleman had noted earlier, as the day progressed, the water warmed up. If you wanted refreshing, you went earlier. All you had to do was turn on the tap and gravity did the rest. There is nothing quite like an open-air shower on a hot day to make you appreciate living, let me tell you.

Unfortunately, the shower didn't help everyone. Once we cleaned up, we wandered around the new village where we had pitched up. The locals were warm and friendly, with ready smiles wherever we went. Another beautiful beach dotted with fishing boats was on our doorstep. A small market was tucked in between, where we could pick up essentials, like tomatoes and bread. Mozambique's simple pleasures continued to charm me, but Brett grew paler every step we took. It appeared his stones were back. We hurried back to camp.

"Shit," he moaned, as he writhed in pain.

"Advil? Midol?"

"They don't do anything," he choked through clenched teeth. They were useless against the kidney stones which again savagely worked their way out of Brett, wreaking havoc as they went. It was obvious he needed medical attention, but none could be had at that time of day. All we could do was sit vigil for the night.

Miki and I set out at first light to see what we could find.

"Our friend has kidney stones," we implored at the small clinic in the village. The barren building offered little help.

"You need bigger hospital. Maputo," the overworked nurses suggested with a sympathetic shrug. They had little more than bandages and frayed compassion to offer anyone, regardless of their ailment. Not even a telephone was available to call for help. The closest phone was in Inhambane; a full day's drive back the way we had come. Miki and I fled the clinic in despair.

"There," she pointed as we scoured the tiny community. A small airstrip clung to the edge of town. Our fragile hopes soared, as we scurried inside.

"We need a flight to Maputo," Miki exclaimed. "As soon as possible."

"There is one today," the agent replied. "Oh, Samahani," she quickly added. "So sorry. It is sold out… But wait. There is a charter to Johannesburg with seats available. Shall I book it for you?"

"Yes," Miki exclaimed eagerly. "Oh, thank God!" Our excitement was short-lived.

"That will be $1,500 USD," the agent said. "Cash only."

And with that our hopes were dashed. Neither Brett, nor all of us combined had that kind of money. As we couldn't call Brett's health insurance company—again, a lack of a phone rendered that impossible—there was no way to have them arrange payment for the flight. We were back to square one.

By the time we returned, Brett was weakening noticeably. He could barely stand and had trouble catching his breath.

"We have to do something," Miki cried. The question was what. We could drive him back in the van or put him on a bus back to Maputo, where he could catch a flight to Johannesburg.

"I'll take the bus," Brett insisted. "There's no point ruining everyone's trip. They'll take care of me in Jo'burg."

"Are you sure," Miki asked. "Someone could go with you..."

"No," Brett replied through gritted teeth.

He had no extra breath to spare, so we resigned ourselves to his departure. Miki and I scraped together what money we could spare and pressed it into his hands. We prayed the journey would be bearable, but knew it was out of our hands. Fate was now his companion and guide.

A few hours later, the bus rumbled into view from where we stood on the side of the highway. It should be no surprise to you that there was no bus depot.

"We'll meet in Harare, Zimbabwe once you're recovered. Say in one and a half to two weeks?"

"Right," he managed to spit out, as he shuffled up the steps and disappeared inside.

He was gone.

In the meantime, Miki, Oliver, and I would make our way north. We added Rob to our midst, another Aussie who could drive stick. It made Miki and I a little anxious, but there was nothing to be done about it. It wasn't fair to ask Oliver to tackle the dreaded highway to Beira alone. And Rob was heading into Zimbabwe as well, so he was happy for the ride. It was the best we could do until we got Brett back.

In the interim, we waited. While there were no luxuries, like today's cell phones or internet to check on his progress, we held on to blind faith that we would see him again. And blissfully, that faith provided us with distraction.

"Long time no see," a voice cut through our gloomy fog. As was the way of the enchanted world of travelling, a couple we had met in Tofo strolled up to where we sat at the compound.

"Hey," I cried. Their presence was exactly what was needed. We caught up on our happenings since we had seen each other last, and chit chatted about plans.

"We are going over to Magaruque. We're renting a dhow for the day to see the island. Why don't you join us?"

"That sounds perfect!" But as much as the day sounded enchanting, expectations don't always live up to reality. Not this day anyway.

A dhow is one of the local sailboats. You see them everywhere on the coast. They are a common form of transportation, so we thought nothing of hiring one. Of course, the dhow we happened to hire was ancient and *very* tippy. More than one of us clutched onto the thick sides of the boat, as we lurched across the short crossing. Our guide grunted and pushed us along with his long pole with an unsteady gait that reminded me we were at both his and the ocean's mercy. Thankfully, we eventually made solid ground and we quickly scurried away to explore; our guide's parting message lost on the breeze.

"It's gorgeous," I murmured as we wandered along the stunning white sand beach.

"No," remarked Rob grumpily. "It's hot. Way too hot. I need shade." He might have had a bad attitude, but he was right. While the day was sunny and beautiful, it was far too hot for casually exploring the island. Both our skin and feet were getting baked to a crisp by the scorching heat.

"Look, umbrellas," Miki said as she pointed towards colourful bastions of shade. No sooner had we gratefully sunk down underneath them though when an angry hotel employee appeared.

"No, no, no! You cannot sit," he exclaimed wildly waving his arms. "For hotel guests only!"

"Okay, okay. We're leaving," we said as we reluctantly walked away from the blissful shade.

"How about snorkelling?"

"This is better," I remarked, as I carefully crept into the comparatively cooler ocean. "Ouch!"

I stumbled on my next step down on a jagged rock. Every step forward found another one. So, while the water offered a welcome reprieve from the sun's rays, the ocean bottom was murder on the feet.

"Crikey, this is murder," Rob grumbled.

By the time we returned to our dhow captains, we sported several new cuts and scrapes from the treacherous coral. Not to mention a slight bit of dehydration. Water everywhere, but none to drink. Their cross faces didn't offer much welcome either.

"You late," they snapped. "Suppose be back 13:00."

"What?" Rob shot back.

"You said 3:00 p.m.," Oliver added.

"No," the man proclaimed, "you late!" Yet another communication faux pas chalked up for the day.

"Like anyone is on time anywhere around here," I mumbled to Miki under my breath. But we allowed ourselves to be quickly ushered back into the dhows, as the angry captains roughly pushed us back to the mainland. Enough was enough.

The only saving grace to the day was that welcome afternoon shower. We had one last sleep, before we said goodbye to Mozambique, but a rough road lay ahead of us before the border would be in sight. The next leg of our journey wouldn't be pretty, but it was the only way to get back to Brett. So northward ho, we would go!

"Where the Road Ends…"

By the dim light of a new day, we packed our gear, ate a quick breakfast, and prepared for the road ahead of us. We had heard several horror stories of what lay ahead, but plenty of rough patches of road lay behind us already. How bad could this next stretch be? We would find out soon enough.

"I'll take the first stretch of road," announced Rob, the newest addition to our van.

Again, Miki and I were at the mercy of others when it came to driving. Despite a few practice sessions in Xai-Xai, we knew that manipulating Arnie along a questionable stretch of road was out of the question. Until we met back up with Brett, we had to accept favours from wherever they were offered and hope they were tolerable.

Miki handed over the keys.

"Don't forget to get petrol at the last station before you hit the road," called out Richard before we left. "And get a jerry can filled while you're there as well!"

The warnings were enough to make us paranoid, but we made a point of heeding them when the gas station peeked into sight. The jerry can was dutifully filled to the brim as well. Stories of buses and transport trucks getting stuck on the road, falling off the road, or simply running out of gas along the road, were numerous and swam in the back of our minds as we checked the map for the route ahead of us. No dots for towns or villages appeared until the end of Highway 1 and even with the van and extra gas can filled up, it would be a tight squeeze to get to the next petrol station. There were no other roads to take though and there was no way any of us wanted to get stuck on this road, so a few prayers went out to the gas gods of Mozambique and the kombi kings of Africa. Whatever it took to get us through to the other side.

"Your turn to drive mate," announced Rob as he slipped out of the driver's seat.

"Don't be shy on giving a push then," replied Oliver as he made his way to the driver's side. We all had to push, but point noted. Oliver would get the first leg of the road from hell. We had a full tank and shaky confidence. Time to conquer the divide.

Wider, deeper, and more frequent potholes dominated the morning, but the road steadily kept getting worse. Soon we found ourselves swerving all over the road to avoid the ever-growing potholes. Whole sections of pavement slid deep into gullies. Our speed dropped, as we feared the unknown gaps in the road ahead. At points we crawled to a slither, to bump into and through more manageable obstructions.

"There's another one on the right," I chimed in from the back seat.

"Maybe try to go around it on the left," Rob suggested.

"You might as well just go straight through," Miki advised, as yet another pothole loomed in front of us.

This was the extent of our conversation. The only thing on our minds was how to maneuver the road. Windows were cracked to dispel the heavy breath in the van. Dust filled our lungs instead. Just when we thought the road could get no worse, we eased to a stop.

"Oh my god," breathed Miki.

We had just finagled a particularly nasty stretch which saw us careen from one side of the road to the other. We had also managed to scrape our exhaust pipe in the process of avoiding especially deep drops in the roadway. Now, as we surveyed the road ahead of us, it dawned on us why the warnings had been so numerous and dire. A mere metre in front of the van, the road ceased to exist. The asphalt road just stopped. The path that lay in front of us was no more than two ruts in the mud. There was no tarmac as far as the eye could see.

This was the main highway. The only highway that led from the capital to Beira; the second largest city in Mozambique. We would have to descend into this trench if we were to get to the other side.

I was speechless.

"Scheiße[30]," Oliver muttered as he stared at the road in front of us. If we met another vehicle on this road, we would be buggered. There was only one set of muddy tire tracks bordered by a steep precipice on one side and craggy hillside on the other. There was no other route to take.

"Onward?" Oliver looked to Miki beside him, then to me and Rob in the back seat.

I glanced at Miki. We owned the vehicle. Rob and Oliver were just along for the ride. It was ultimately our call, but there wasn't much call to make, if we wanted to get to the Zimbabwe border.

I released a deep sigh.

"Onward," I replied. "It's our only choice."

Not much of a choice, but there was no point in dwelling on our grim situation.

"Hold tight," Oliver said as he slowly inched Arnie into the tire tracks that would take us out of this country. If we made it to the other end…

*****

---

[30] shit.

Conversation stopped. The road engulfed us. We held our breath and scanned for the reappearance of pavement. Our search was in vain.

As much as I tried not to, I could not prevent my eyes from scanning our surroundings. I had heard tell of the mishaps of travellers before us. I did not want to see the shattered vehicles, but my brain wouldn't stop repeating the stories of rain-drenched tracks which sucked overland trucks and transports deep into the mire. Tales of vehicles that collided when there was no other path to avoid impact filled my thoughts as well. There was nothing to distract me from the images that played on auto-repeat as we rumbled along. And closing my eyes was no help.

The ruts in the road grew steadily deeper. Scraping noises now accompanied our path, as we laboured forward over the broken terrain. My heart beat a little harder, even as my breath slipped from me in whispers.

The minutes turned into hours and still the road before us lay as a scathing reminder of a country nowhere near healed from the gaping wounds it had been forced to endure. I was horrified at the appalling state of something which I took for granted back home; a simple roadway to take me from point A to B. This thoroughfare was the main artery to get goods from the capitol and its harbour to the rest of the country. This road linked the two biggest cities in Mozambique. It was broken beyond any reasonable expectation of repair and yet was still imperative and heavily utilized. I sat in shock, unable to comprehend this failure of a system.

"We need to refuel," Oliver broke the tense silence.

The needle on our gas gauge had slowly inched away from the large F, as the miles had dragged behind us at a painstakingly slow pace. Now Arnie was gently eased to a halt.

"Don't turn it off," Rob said.

Normally one would stop a vehicle, turn it off, open the gas cap, refuel, replace the gas cap, pay for the fuel, then restart the vehicle and be on your merry little way. Unfortunately, we had a couple of very distinct issues with normal that day. For one, Arnie pretty much refused to start by the simple action of a key turned in the ignition. No, in general our vehicle relied heavily on good old muscle power to give it a big push to get it on its way again. Only with enough momentum built would Arnie's engine fire to life.

Stopped in the still-muddy rut, from a rainstorm far from anyone's memory, we pondered what to do.

"We can't fill the van up while it's running," I cried, remembering my driver's ed training from year's past.

"There's no way in hell we'll get it running again if we turn it off," Rob said. "And we can't push it in this fucking mud."

He was right of course, but how safe was it to refuel a running vehicle? At that point, our choices were slim. We might not be able to get moving again regardless of whether the engine was running or not, but at least we had a better chance. We were stuck between a rock and a hard place. Quite literally, it was more like between sludge and suicide.

"I don't think we have a choice," Miki added resignedly.

So, half of our precious petrol was poured into the still running van. No explosions ensued and no push was required on this pit stop. We would not be so lucky further down the road.

The road was not kind to our van or spirits. We clung to our prayers that the lowly van would stick to the road. At points, our prayers were literally answered, and we were required to jump out and push poor Arnie back into motion again from its mired home. We jogged to catch back up to our caked kombi, heedless of the mud on ourselves, as we continued our journey of hell. Another roadside fill-up was imminent, but it was in fate's hands now. And still the trek pushed on.

"That's the last of our petrol," Rob declared, as the last of our jerry can was emptied into Arnie's hold on our next stop.

Now the search for a break in the tire tracks of mud was on in earnest. The light of the day waned, and we wondered if perhaps we had pushed our luck too far this day. I forced myself to not think about what would happen if we ran out of fuel in these road ruts. It just could not happen. My hands throbbed as I clenched them ever tighter. The needle on the gas gauge bobbed closer to "**E**". Panic pushed us as a tailwind.

"Do you hear that?" asked Rob. It was more like what we couldn't hear though. The incessant scraping from under the van seemed less pronounced. As we craned our ears to listen, it gradually stopped. The ruts grew shallower.

"Oh my God," I thought. I didn't want to jinx it, but my heart couldn't help but speed up. "We're going to make it!" Before we had a chance to react, the van scraped heavily on a lip of asphalt, and we were suddenly back on solid land.

"Yes!" we all cheered as one. High fives were slapped all around and the breath we had collectively been holding was released.

We weren't out of the woods yet though. The gas gauge still mocked our triumph and threatened to squash it. The T-junction lay ahead and hopefully the promised gas station. Speed seemed of the essence, as we raced towards the finish line—a petrol sign. Would we make it in time? The needle inched ever closer to "E". There was no denying it. "E" was for empty and that was where the needle was buried. Not certain how long we could fly on fumes, we began to glide down any hills we came upon.

"Look," I cried, as a little village hove into site. We slowed to a crawl craning to see the gas station. Our search was in vain though, as a stop sign halted our flight. We had made it to the T-junction.

"Which way do we go?" Rob asked from behind the wheel.

We had no idea.

"Right takes us towards Beira," Miki announced. "And left towards the border."

"But which way would the gas station be in?" Rob growled.

As we sat there idling, the question hung in the air. Should we turn left or right? No signs pointed the way and there was nothing in sight to answer our question. A wrong guess could leave us stranded at the side of the road in the middle of nowhere. But without a clear answer, our only choice was to guess. A light began to slowly seep red on the dash.

"Why don't we try right," I suggested. "It makes sense that they would put it in the direction of Beira. It's the second biggest city in Mozambique. Wouldn't most people go in that direction?" My logic failed us though. After a scant few miles of spying nothing, the gas gauge forced our hand.

"I don't see anything," exclaimed Rob with annoyance. "We should have gone the other way." He pulled a U-turn and jammed his foot down as we headed in the other direction. We coasted down hills and instinctively leaned our bodies into the inclines.

"Where the fuck is it?" muttered Rob, as the miles clicked past and still nothing came into view. Sweat trickled into my bra, as stress level reached insurmountable heights in our battered van. With a red light blazing on the dash, we slowly pushed up yet another hill, certain it would be our last.

At the crest of the hill though, a beautiful sight finally appeared. The sign we had been so desperately searching for—GAS. And even though the sun had sunk on another day, the station was still open. We drifted towards our salvation on fumes and stopped beside the pump. Laughter, hugs, and relief swamped us in a crazy celebration of triumph. We had battled and won the challenge of the worst road in Africa.

*****

ZIMBABWE

"A Piece of Heaven"

The clink of ice in my glass set the tone, as I reflected on recent days. The whisky burned sweet, and I savoured the simple luxury in aptly named Heaven Lodge. It felt like a piece of heaven, compared to some of the places we had recently been. Zimbabwe was a new country. Chimanimani, a start to new adventures. Or so I hoped.

Mozambique lay behind us. It felt like a surreal dream, with curves so far removed from any realities I had known before as to be unreal. Poverty, landmines, potholes, and pristine beaches—they were peppered with images of desperate beggars and remarkably friendly souls who went out of their way to help when they could. Mozambique was a lesson in appreciation for the simple things in life; medical care, safe shelter, clean water, a full belly, and the ability to get my creature comforts met on a whim. Those simple pleasures and necessities were not always so easy to attain in East Africa, whether you had the monetary means to get them or not. The lesson was not lost on me. I lifted my glass once more and recalled my last moments in Mozambique.

With precious petrol in the tank once more, we headed for the border only to find it closed for the night. It made a dent in our high of triumph over vanquishing the 'Road from Hell' but could not be helped.

"I guess we sleep in the van for the night," Oliver noted.

Our options were limited, so we hunkered down as best we could. The next morning, a passing gentleman pointed out a nearby hostel that we hadn't noticed the night before, where we could refresh ourselves and perhaps rest our heads for a spell, but a new country awaited. We thanked him for his help but left Mozambique behind. A new appreciation of the beautiful nation remained; one that coloured everything I now saw or felt. Not enough to keep me there a moment longer though.

Zimbabwe beckoned. It held much promise; especially that of HOT, running water. Five hours after crossing the border, we found that and more at Ann Bruce's (Backpacker) House. It was amazing to me how I hadn't appreciated this luxury before. Back home, I had a roof over my head, hot and cold running water, food in the cupboards, and more within the fridge. I never had to worry about how far I had to go to find water and whether or not it might cause me stomach discomforts. This was the mark between the haves and have nots. The difference between privilege and poverty. No matter the number of coins in my pocket, just by dint of me arriving in Africa, I had more wealth than most of the people I would come across in my journeys. That wealth felt richer now in comparison.

Showers and meditation couldn't occupy all my hours though. Africa held so much beauty and intrigue, not the least of which were its abundant game parks. And Zimbabwe had plenty. So, game viewing it was. We spied rhinoceros, giraffes, eland, and ostrich, plus a magnificent sunset to round out the day. Brett was still in the back of our minds though. "I think we've got time for a detour," Oliver said as we pulled out the map to reference our next route. "Some backpackers were talking about a park not far from here that has great hiking trails. It's called Chimanimani National Park."

Oliver was just as keen to meet back up with Brett as Miki and me, but he was right. By the distance on the map and our roughly expected arrival in Harare, there was enough time for some backcountry hiking.

"Let's do it," Miki cried excitedly.

I'm never one to turn down adventure so before I knew it, a trek into Chimanimani National Park was planned. We hammered out details, then I was left to my journal and whisky. I bent to my writing, until a voice broke through my reverie.

"We could use a fourth for euchre." I have a weakness for cards and seldom turn down the opportunity to play. That night was no different.

"Alright," I replied as shut my journal and I picked up my drink to join them. I failed to mention that I came from a long line of card players. My grandfather taught me how to play when I was young, ostensibly to teach me how to count, but realistically so that there were more faces around the card table.

As soon as I snapped the deck through a few shuffles, they knew they had a player worth their salt amongst them. In no time, we were fast friends. A friendly card game can do that. The world and its troubles were left behind as we counted trump and learned new playing partners. I have to admit, though, that after a night full of laughs, cards, and a drink or two, the mountains had their revenge.

"The Mountain's Revenge"

Beep, beep, beep…

Dawn had not yet broken, but I felt certain that I was. Broken that is. A glance at the bottle on my bedside table made my head pulse.

"Ohhh," I moaned. "So, not a good sign..."

The level in it was dangerously low. Whiskey still coursed through my veins. A massive hangover was sure to arrive imminently. The fact that I retired relatively early wouldn't prevent it. And 5:00 a.m. seemed an extraordinary punishment for a fun night of cards with friends.

No matter, it was rise and shine. The alarm screeched at me to face the day and get ready for the hike ahead of us. Our plan was to hike into Chimanimani National Park and spend two nights camping in the wilds. A wet coating of rye and gingers on my brain muted yesterday's enthusiasm.

Maybe a shower will make me feel more human, I thickly mused.

It didn't hurt, but only served to make me more presentable on the outside. Inside, I dreamt of spending the day camped beside a toilet bowl. To be fair, none of us were too chipper though after an evening on the piss. Such was the life of a traveller. We were still game for adventure.

"Don't forget to fill up your water bottle Katherine," one of cardplayers from the night before said with a laugh when he saw me packing. "It looks like you're down a pint."

"Piss off," I mumbled, as I dutifully filled up before joining the others in the vehicle waiting to head to the park. I concentrated on breathing during the drive over.

A thick registry met us at the park.

"Fill in your name, country of origin, and length of time you plan to be in the park," the Warden instructed. "If you're late returning, we send out a search party to look for you."

We glanced at each other nervously. *What were we getting into?*

"People get into trouble in the hills—with falls, animals, getting lost, etc.—so we treat it seriously when anyone is gone longer than their estimated time. We've called in rescue searchers more times than I care to count."

"Just two nights," we advised them. And hoped we wouldn't be proven wrong by stern park wardens plucking us from trouble later.

With waivers signed, we continued on foot from there. No vehicles were allowed in the park, so we bid adieu to our driver. It was time for the trek to begin.

Our rag-taggle group included me, Oliver, Rob, Miki, plus three other travellers from the lodge; Allen, Cindy, and Hubert. Allen fashioned himself our leader and led the route into the hills. I happily fell further back in the pack, swigging regularly off my precious water bottle to stave off the shakes.

It was a beautiful day. The early sun lit the cool path, as we wandered beside crystal clear streams and lush vegetation. Conversation floated easily on the well-worn path, but it didn't take long for the trail to gather a steeper pitch. I lagged further and further behind, as words disappeared from my lips. Stories of my mother's asthma attacks filled my head, as my lungs began to ache. Had I miraculously developed this affliction during my attempt on the mountain?

Monte Binga, the highest peak in the 50-kilometre range, measured in at 2,437 m or 7,993 ft. It was no Everest but might as well have been. Not that we planned to climb those heights anyway, but the foothills we traversed still burned in my chest. I seriously doubted that I would make it.

"Allen says the water is safe to drink," Miki offered as I walked up to her at a serene pool where she rested. I was the last to arrive, and others had already started to move off.

"Awesome," I gasped, as I bent at the waist with sweaty palms on knees. She waited with me as I caught my breath, then matched my stride as we set out together. My lungs burned in protest. My liver reprimanded me—"rye isn't to be trusted in future, no matter its cajoling nature." Not helpful in the moment. The last of my travelling companions pushed on ahead and disappeared, as I struggled on by myself.

"Nice easy hike," I panted. "Pfft, yeah right." All I wanted to do was stop. Perhaps lay down and die, or something to that effect. Apparently, I was too stubborn for that though. And there was no going back. I was miles from base camp and alone in the universe, but for the buzzards that swung lazily over my head.

Christ, I'm going to die... My thoughts, as I found myself clinging to a rock wall. *How the hell did I get here?* My fingers sought hidden niches in the craggy face of boulders. My laden backpack threatened to tear me off the wall and drop me into the abyss. *Not today,* I thought, as with a final burst of shaky determination I heaved myself up onto a ledge with a gasp.

I shakily pulled myself to standing and stood panting above the world. I cursed my body, the mountains, and my place in them, before my gaze flicked to the realm below. My fellow hikers lay far beneath me in a relatively flat valley, patiently waiting beside a boulder.

"Seriously?" I gasped, before bursting into hysterical laughter. "Unbelievable…" The mountain had forced more out of me than I thought I had. But I survived. "Screw you Binga," I muttered in triumph. The weight in my chest disappeared, as did the worst of my hangover. I won. I waved to my friends far below. The rest of the climb would be fine.

When I finally made my way down to them, Rob asked, "Where've you been?"

"Oh, you know," I said. "Hanging around..." The only smug note I had was that I had taken the more challenging path. Not that that was worth bragging about.

They allowed me a quick break, and then I fell into line as we set off once more. We found ourselves pushing through chest-high grasses on a level plateau. The rock cairns, which up to this point had directed the path up the mountain, disappeared into the waving meadows, leaving the route a little dicier. Somehow, we managed. The stiff reeds scraped at our burning legs and arms, but there was no choice. No other path presented, so we pushed through.

"There," he said. Allen finally pointed into the distance.

"Where?" I asked, bewildered. All I could see was the start of another mound of rocks far ahead of us.

"The cave?" Oliver asked in confusion. And then I spied a subtle rocky path leading up to the yawning mouth of a cave.

"Home for the next two nights," Allen stated matter-of-factly.

"Huh," I exclaimed. "Cool." Honestly, we couldn't have asked for a better one. We pushed through the last of the fields, excited to explore. Everyone shed their heavy packs around the lip of the cave, as we eagerly scrambled into the crevasse.

"This is awesome," Miki said.

The little ledge opened to a dark cavern. Walls were roughened by time and the ceiling stretched high enough to walk upright inside. At the mouth of the cave, evidence bore the marks from previous travellers. Grass was clumped about for bedding and a makeshift fire pit was hemmed in by rough stones. Further back in the cave, the sound of trickling water led me to discover a perfectly placed stream. We had all the comforts of home we could ask for—shelter, water, fire. After an exhausting day of climbing, it was definitely appreciated.

Dinner was a simple affair—canned goods warmed over the fire— but that was alright. This experience wasn't about the food, rather the place. And, as I fell asleep under the sky that night, I counted my lucky stars that we had found it.

The next two days were full of incredible bliss. Days broke cool and misty. Silence was softened by the soft trickle of water from the back of the cave. The occasional bird circled lazily high overhead.

There was no place we had to be—other than the present. I luxuriated in that. From my sleeping bag, I could take in the waving grasses and rocky hills that encircled us. No buildings, people, cars, or other visible signs of humanity were in sight. The biggest task of the day was to rekindle the fire that had burned low from the previous evening.

"Coffee?" Miki asked as she joined me at my spot near the mouth of the cave.

I shuffled to a sitting position and gladly accepted the mug of steaming instant java.

"It's beautiful, isn't it?" she remarked as we quietly stared out into the pristine beauty of Chimanimani Park.

"Mmmm," I answered.

Nothing more needed to be said.

By mid-morning, the sun had burnt off the mist. We headed out to explore more of our surroundings. The air was fresh and pure, and fuelled our curiosity. Aside from the occasional piles of rocks to mark the paths, there was no sign of civilization. We were alone with nature. It stole our hearts and words in its beauty. After wandering for a few hours, beauty began to lack the ability to fuel our strides though.

"Anyone else hungry?" Miki asked.

"Me!" I chimed in.

"Ja," Oliver added.

We returned to the cave and rummaged around our packs to pull together the makings of a feast. A pile of canned potatoes, tomatoes, brown beans, and veggies were added to udon noodles and a handful of rice. Curry seasoning topped off the makings of our communal meal. Chef Miki took the helm stirring together our concoction; an offering, as we broke bread together in our version of God's country. It was solemn and joyful, and a day like no other. Another starry night graced our sleep, with the moon as night light, rocks for a pillow, and the fresh outside air my goodnight kiss from Mother Earth.

Another misty morning woke us, but it was time to go.

"I could stay here forever," I lamented from the comfort of my sleeping bag.

"Don't want the rangers to come looking for us," Oliver joked as he finished rolling up his sleeping bag and repacked his belongings.

With a groan, I too began the day. It was time to bid farewell to this magical place. We left behind the grassy beds we had found, the firewood collected, but unburned, and footprints from our brief visit. The memories, we took with us.

The arduous trek down the mountain failed to break the spell I was under. I stopped to drink from crystal clears streams and was again enraptured by the pristine beauty of this African park we were privileged to call home for a few scant nights. The way might have been hard, and I might have felt broken, but Chimanimani put me back together again. I couldn't have been happier.

"The Reunion"

Heaven Lodge welcomed us back, but our second stop was just long enough to wash away the sweat from our trek through Chimanimani National Park. Nothing could wash away memories of star-filled nights unblighted by city's illuminations and I wouldn't want to lose them anyway. It was time to refuel for our trip to Harare though. Brett was waiting.

In the days before smart phones and instant communication, our means of getting a hold of people were limited. We had no address for Brett to send a letter and carrier pigeons weren't in the budget. We had no way of knowing if Brett would be in Harare or not, so had to rely on faith. Haste was our best bet to get answers met, so we hightailed it as quickly as we could. Our rush was well met.

"How's ya bum for grubs?" remarked Brett when we arrived.

"What?!"

"It means 'how're you going?'" Miki translated for me, as she grabbed him for a bear hug.

"Me next," I cried. "Ya fucking weirdo…"

"C'mere, Bush Woman," he said as he pulled me in next.

Dear Brettski was alive and well.

"What happened?"

"Are you alright?"

"Details man, we want details," Oliver chimed in.

"Yes!" Miki and I exclaimed together.

Rob inconspicuously faded away. He had only met Brett briefly and knew that his space in the kombi had now been usurped. Brett was part owner of Arnie after all, and Rob had just taken advantage of getting a lift from Mozambique into Zimbabwe. With Harare attained, he would go his own way once more. In our excitement to see Brett, the rest of us barely noticed his departure. With a laugh, Brett shared his adventure.

"The bus ride south was agony, cramped seats, hoards of people and the like. When I got down to Maputo, the doctors sent me straightaway to Jo'burg. It was real good, like, as I talked to my insurance carrier, and they were right helpful. They paid for a flight to Johannesburg, no questions asked. I went straight to hospital, but x-rays suggested I'd probably already passed the stones. Figure that! All for nothing. Anyway, I spent a few days there, then made my way north here to meet up with you lot. You took your bloody time getting here, too!"

His smile alone was proof that he was indeed feeling better. His colour was good, his laugh goofy, and essentially, he looked no worse for wear. We were more than grateful. In fact, Brett had been in Harare two or three nights already. He had started to see the sights and even poked around in a dark corner or two, as was his way. Our reunion was a cause for celebration. First stop, shopping.

We played the tourist card and went curio shopping at a local open-air artisan market. I bought soap stone carvings, a sarong, a crocheted vest, and t-shirts for family back home. The rest of the gang picked up their own souvenirs to remember our time spent in the far reaches of this universe. It was a far cry from the supermalls back home, and we loved it all the more for that.

A new outfit is only as exciting as the place you wear it, which brought us to the second part of our celebrations. We needed to toast Brett's recovery as well! The worthy cause deserved a decadent meal, so we decked out in our finest and went to Rani's, a local Indian restaurant. As worldly sophisticates, we traipsed in like this was an excursion we made every day (Miki and I even put on makeup for the occasion!). And for their part, they treated us with all the geniality we sought.

This was our night on the town, and we dressed the part. Never mind that we normally lived out of backpacks stuffed with the bare minimum; in my case six pairs of underwear, two t-shirts, three tank tops, one sweater, one pair of jeans, two long-sleeved shirts, three pairs of shorts, a sarong (newly purchased!), a dress, a skirt, a pair of pajamas, and one towel (or something like that). On this night, we daintily held our forks as we discussed the state of the world, glorying in this break from our reality. Whether other patrons could see through our threadbare veneers was a point none of us cared about. We stuffed ourselves silly and revelled in the evening, aware that we would be on the road soon enough and back to peanut butter and banana sandwiches once more.

"I think I'll call home," I announced as we waddled out of the restaurant, stuffed to burst. "It's been ages since I talked to anyone from home. Heck, it's been ages since we've been close to a phone!"

"You wouldn't believe the road we just travelled," I exclaimed when my sister picked up the phone, thousands of miles away. "What's new with everyone at home?"

It felt good to reconnect and let the miles between us disappear, even if only for a moment. Life was good. She had a job, but my stepfather did not. Mom was fine, as was the cat. Life continued on the same as it always had, despite the adventures I flitted through on the other side of the world. The phone card never lasted long enough though, and I had to call Cape Town too, so I rang off after a few minutes.

"Hello, from Harare!" I cried, once Uncle Jock picked up. "How are you?"

"We're healthy and well, and happy to hear you are too," remarked Uncle Jock.

"You be safe," Aunt Elsa called from the background. "We worry about you travelling through some of those places."

After giving brief updates about my trip through Mozambique, Uncle Jock passed Aunt Elsa the phone so she could say a few words too.

"Oh, before I forget, you've received some letters," she added. "We'll forward them along to your next stop en route."

By then, the timer was counting down on my card, so I quickly said goodbye and promised to call again soon. It was good talking to family, both new and old. Even their well-meaning worry was welcome after being away from everyone for so long. And hearing tell that I would have letters waiting at our next stop was kind of exciting too.

As I wandered back to our hostel, my heart was full. I had a full belly, a roof over my head that night, and had talked to many of the people I loved. It gave Harare a nice glow in my books and left me wondering if I would see it again once we left.

"Great Zimbabwe"

"Right, my turn behind the wheel," Brett announced as we packed up city life and headed to the country.

History was calling and Zimbabwe had plenty of it to explore. We were ready to step back in time. Our first destination was Masvingo. The ancient ruins of Great Zimbabwe lay there, the former capitol of the Kingdom of Zimbabwe. It was now but a dusty memory.

Having toured Europe the previous year, my sense of history had grown in scale. Back home in Canada, old houses were 80-150 years old, but massive trees easily beat out any man-made historical sites around. Not so in Europe, where many buildings have stood for hundreds, if not thousands of years. Trees were scarce, but plenty of the individual buildings had seen a wide array of unique uses throughout their lifetime. One building I toured through had been a brothel, church, school, torture chamber, and most recently a museum. Hard to imagine, but remarkable! A quiet respect had filled me, as I walked through solid rock structures that had seen members of the Roman Empire walk those selfsame rooms. History became tangible and reachable in ways I had never experienced before.

Africa was a different story though. Not many old structures crossed my path there. Hence my excitement at our next stop. Typically, Africa's history was recorded in people's songs and stories. Most buildings were modern contrivances, with histories that only rivaled the lifespan of elephants. And while some of the world's oldest human remains have been found on the African continent, the people typically were groups of hunters and gatherers. That equated to temporary mud and grass huts that were frequently abandoned to follow herds of migrating animals, or to escape times of drought. Mother Nature quickly took her land back once men moved on.

So, while the rondavels might have looked decrepit and old, in the grand scheme of things, they held little historical value. They spoke of the way people lived today, and in recent history, but ancient history disappeared with the wind.

Great Zimbabwe was different though. Here was a landmark which began construction in the 11th century. Built entirely of stone, no mortar or other binding agents existed here. It grew, thrived, and then was abandoned once the surrounding land was stripped of its resources. All between the country's Late Iron Age—1100 and 1450 AD. Crumbling ruins were all that was left of this once great empire. As we wandered through the stone structures, a view emerged of an organized people, where upwards of 18,000 people may have lived in its day.

"Can you imagine what it would have looked like back in the day," I marvelled. "Towers there and there," I pointed into the now blank space. "Living quarters and communal areas…"

"Don't forget the rooms for the reigning chiefs and foreign dignitaries," Miki added.

"Yeah. Like us," Brett laughed. "We would get that area over there where the walls are crumbling."

"Or one of the 'ritual areas'," Oliver said deadpan. All of us exploded with laughter.

"Yup, that would be about right. Ritual sacrifices…"

Displays helped us envision Chinese and Persian travellers coming far afar to trade spices for beads. Considering the length of time that had passed since its abandonment, it was amazing how much was still intact. The impressive Conical Tower still towered over the area at 18 feet in diameter and 30 feet high.

The Shona people ruled here long before white faces invaded the lands. Skill and an advanced level of craftsmanship were in evidence in the 1,800 acres that spanned a 100- to 200-mile radius. It was hard not to be impressed by this ancient civilization. Even more so when one noted it was a black civilization in a land where whites still wielded their superiority, despite the relatively recent end to apartheid in South Africa. The colour barrier was still very much present in the many communities we wandered through. But this monument was proof that the tenets behind apartheid were baseless. These people were far from simple or inferior.

Of course, we were not in South Africa anymore. Racial tensions had eased somewhat when we crossed the border. They were still in evidence though. And a day spent wandering along walled passages and ducking under ancient stone lintels was an interesting experience that gave another snapshot of history in this land that held more trees and rocks, than historical sites.

Exploring the area around Masvingo on horse-back later in the day gave the historical perspective more depth. It was like stepping back in time. As the wind whipped mine and Miki's faces, it took little imagination to picture what the ancient people in the area might have seen—grassy savannah, with occasional kopjes and baobabs to break up the flat terrain. No vehicles. Few people. It would have been a very different world in some respects, even as pieces of that ancient way of life flitted in the margins.

At the end of the day though, we returned to modern times and amenities. A home-cooked meal greeted us at Clovelly Lodge. Mosquito nets protected us as we slept. And hot, running water was available at the twist of a tap.

As I drifted off to sleep that night, I surmised that this must be how the other half lived—good food, great friends, exciting adventures galore. It had been a glorious day in Africa. I couldn't help but be filled up knowing how sweet the gift of this time was.

"Birthday Surprise!"

"Happy Birthday, dear Brettski. Happy Birthday to you!!!"

Brett blew out the candles on the flaming cake and looked round at the small circle of faces around him. Miki, Oliver, and I beamed back, sipping champagne, and noshing on birthday cake. We were in the middle of Matopos National Park; an ideal place to ring in one's 25th birthday. But not without its challenges.

A few days earlier, we had left Masvingo behind, as well as our long-time travelling companion Oliver. It was now the end of March and Oliver had joined us way back in February when we left Durban. While only a month, it seemed like a lifetime. Such was the way of friendships on the road; friends were made fast, and bonds seemed stronger for forming on the excitement of the road. Parting was always sweet sorrow, made with promises of reconnecting further down the line. The hope was to at least send a letter or two.

But Oliver had a different path from ours, so we bid him adieu when we left Clovelly Lodge. Our destination—a game park for Brett's birthday. Who can resist singing "Happy Birthday" with backup vocals from monkeys, lions, and hyenas?

"Brett, you go see if you can find something to quiet our muffler, so we don't scare away all the animals in Matopos," Miki suggested when we arrived in town. "Katherine and I will pick up groceries." While groceries were certainly on the list, we also sought accoutrements for a surprise party for three.

"We need a cake, card, and candles," she said.

"And a bottle of champagne?" I added with a grin.

"Of course!"

We hid our birthday treats amongst the general supplies, so as to surprise Brett, before rejoining him to head to the park. Regardless of our clandestine activities, we were just as excited for another game drive and couldn't wait to hit the park roads.

*****

"Rise and shine my little maties," Brett called quietly, as he shook us awake early the next morning. "The early bird catches the lion!"

"Happy Birthday," I mumbled, as I quickly pulled on clothes.

I don't think I ever got used to the pre-dawn wake-up calls for game drives, despite the enthusiasm that spurred them on. Sure, we got to see animals, but getting up before the sun always hurt. Like every time. But on that day, the birthday boy was treated to a rare treat to mark his special day.

We quietly pushed Arnie into life and left the campground for the game park. Mother Nature was generous. We spied warthogs and impalas, kudus, and giraffes, but more was yet to come. The coup of the day was seeing the elusive member of the Big Five—black rhino. Not just one either; we saw *six* of them! Nothing says happy birthday like a six-pack of gray, horned battering rams grazing on clumps of dry grass.

"Hoo, boy!" Brett whistled, as he snapped pictures. He was in his glory, rightfully so. As the sun rose and the heat of the day started in, it was time to head back to camp though. By the time we hit camp for a belated breakfast, we were wide awake and ready to face the day.

"The Rhodes Memorial is not far," Miki read as we sipped at the last of our coffees. "We should check that out too."

It claimed to be the "View of the World". And yes, it was a pretty darn nice view. But I couldn't help but feel disillusioned by this monument. It felt very unlike our recent trip into Great Zimbabwe. That historical site was a monument to a great people who built up an empire with ingenuity and hard work. This memorial was clouded by the knowledge that Cecil Rhodes was a racist tyrant (from all I had read about him). His place in the history of South Africa and Zimbabwe (Rhodesia back in his day) could not be denied though and his mark was still felt in the country.[31] Because of that, this view left me less than impressed. After reading historical plaques and exploring what there was to see, we left headed back to camp.

"How are we going to do this," I whispered to Miki when we got back to camp. Brett crawled into the tent, as her and I huddled together to scheme. "I swear he's trying to peek. He went to 'fix' his bed just now."

"That's where the cake is!" she exclaimed.

"I know," I replied.

"I think I'll go for a bit of a walkabout," Brett announced as he re-emerged from the tent. "Anyone want to go with?"

"Nah, I think I'll catch up on my journal," I casually replied.

"I've got letters to write too," Miki chimed in quickly.

---

[31] Parkinson, J. (2015, April 1). Why is Cecil Rhodes such a controversial figure? BBC News. https://www.bbc.com/news/magazine-32131829.

"Right then. I'll be back in a bit." Cheeky bugger was probably playing us, but we took advantage, nonetheless. We hastily set the table with our goodies, laying out glasses and cake, then sat back to await his return.

"There he is," Miki squeaked a short while later.

He strolled back towards our site with a barely concealed smirk on his face. He had been gone just long enough. Like he had planned it or something. No matter.

"Surprise!" we yelled in unison. And no, he didn't look surprised in the least. But he was pleased.

"Let's get the cork out of that bottle and get this party started then," he laughed.

"Do you have enough to share with a fourth?" a voice asked. To our surprise, there was Oliver, casually walking up to camp like he had just done a short walkabout too.

"I couldn't miss out on Brett's birthday," he announced with a grin.

We were a party of four again and it was the best darn 25th surprise party that anyone had ever planned in the back countries of Zimbabwe.

"The Voice of Africa"

Ah, Bob Marley. The voice of Africa. Everywhere we went, Bob Marley blasted from tinny ghetto blasters. Arnie's stereo was no better. The same two tapes were on heavy rotation in the van. It was everywhere—a soundtrack to our journey.

For a break, I would occasionally slip into the arms of Robert Smith from The Cure or delve into melancholy with John Waite as he sang about "Missing You" on my Walkman. They were indulgences that reminded me of faraway friends. Most days I was content to hum along with Bob Marley though, as the miles passed under our wheels in the pursuit of life and adventure.

With time, the tapes began to show wear and tear, as did Arnie. In Masvingo, we patched the hole ripped in the muffler from the road from hell in Mozambique. It was a temporary fix, and as the miles stretched out ahead of us again, the putty didn't hold its muster. That was just one complaint though. Other signs emerged pointing to the fact that Arnie was done with our constant pilgrimage as well. Our starter motor was now completely pooched. Fuel efficiency slowly slipped. It also didn't help that there was a hole at the top of the tank, which meant we couldn't fill it all the way anyway. The slider door no longer sealed easily, often needing multiple heaves to shut it tight. Yes, it was almost time to say goodbye.

Goodbyes loomed large for more than just the van though. In a week's time, Fate's gift from way back at the Johannesburg airport, would drift away from me; from us. It was time for Miki to go home. In a mere week and a half, she would be back in Canada, far from the dry landscape of Zimbabwe. Oliver would go his own way again as well. Brett and I would have to decide how much further we could push Arnie, before we propped a 'For Sale' in his window, ending this portion of our adventure.

We hadn't reached that day yet though. Twisty, turny roads still unfolded in front of us. Making it to another petrol station was always a celebration. New points on the map were still the goal. Bulawayo was next up and another taste of city life.

The roads got shorter though and Bob's voice more poignant, as I stared at my travelling companion's heads in the front seat. There wouldn't be many more days like this. Tomorrow was just a day away.

Sing it Bob…'No woman, no cry.'

"Miki's Last Game Park"

"There it is! Hwange National Park!" Miki exclaimed. It is the largest game reserve in Zimbabwe. It was also her last game park before leaving Africa. That bittersweet fact was not lost on us. The promise of spying a plethora of animals pushed us onward though.

"Time to set up camp," Brett announced as Arnie slid into our camp site. "Early start in the morning for the lot of us."

"Hopefully, Arnie doesn't scare all the animals away," I added, as I noisily eased the slider door open.

In addition to our lack of speedometer, the putty we slathered on the muffler did little to abate Arnie's noise complaints. Scratches decorated Arnie's sides—trophies from previous game parks—and the beginnings of rust bubbled fenders from salty ocean-side drives. The starter motor was a distant memory, and a steady gas leak meant even more frequent petrol stops. Our most recent woes were a decided lack of get-up-and-go when you stomped on the gas, and intermittent glitches with the slider door. It had to be slammed two, three times, or more before it would seal. It was irritating at best, but Arnie still managed to get us where we needed to go.

"I'm off to bed," Oliver announced shortly after dinner.

"Don't forget to set your alarms." he added, pointedly looking at Miki then myself.

As we all knew, game viewing at dawn is best. An early evening maximized our potential to see animals the next day. With over 105 different mammals in the park, plus 400+ bird species swinging through, there was plenty to look for. And not enough hours in the day to see them all. My check list was handy, ready to tick off new species spied, in addition to other species seen elsewhere. Anticipation made sleep more difficult, but eventually I drifted off to the sounds of the savannah around us.

The sun had not quite hit the horizon when quiet rustling noises roused me from sleep. I reflexively squeezed my eyes tighter together, not yet ready for the new day. But the day held game viewing, so I dared a peek at the world. Darkness bathed the tent, but Miki's eyes peered back at me.

Neither of us were great morning people (heck, it was still dark!), so words were conspicuously absent. The sounds came from outside our tent—the sounds of Brett and Oliver preparing to leave. I pulled the blankets up over my head in protest but deigned to stretch in anticipation. I could see Miki do likewise.

The scrape from one of Arnie's doors jolted me from my blanket cocoon though.

"What are they doing?" Miki exclaimed.

We both stared at each other. It was painfully obvious exactly what they were doing. The soft crunch of Arnie's tires on the earth let us know that the van was in motion. Brett and Oliver were quietly pushing it away from camp.

"They're leaving us!" I said in shock. Miki scrambled with the zipper on the tent, but it was too late. Arnie's engine sputtered to life. She watched them drive away from the doorway, then turned to stare at me.

"What the hell!" I cried. "It's your last park!"

"I can't believe they left without us!" she sputtered. "I seriously cannot believe they just drove away…"

The problem was, we could. It had been brewing for a while. The boys were of the early to bed, early to rise variety. Miki and I on the other hand could stretch an evening out to all hours and luxuriated in leisurely mornings. But this was different. This was Miki's last park before leaving Africa.

"Bastards!" I spat. "How could they do that? Now of all times! Fuck."

I turned to Miki, "what do we do?"

"I'll tell you what we're going to do," she said with a fierce determination. "How do you feel about a little road trip of our own?" And a plan was hatched.

By the time Brett and Oliver returned, Miki and I were up and dressed, stuffed packs sitting beside us. There was no mistaking our displeasure.

"We're leaving," Miki stated as they stepped out of the van.

"What!" Brett cried. "You can't leave."

"You left us," I said.

"You were still sleeping." Oliver said, trying to shift blame. "We couldn't wait. We figured you would have taken too long to get ready…"

"I'm sorry mate," Brett beseeched. "Look, we'll go for a drive now."

"Yes," Oliver added. "We can go now."

"We need a break," Miki said flatly. "We all do. We have been cooped up with each other for too long. Katherine and I are going to go to Victoria Falls."

"We'll meet back up with you in a few days," I added. "There is a bus we can catch that takes us straight there. We can do our thing and you can do yours. I think we need it."

"We do," Miki said. And they knew it. But it pained Brett nonetheless that we planned to go.

"Ok," he finally relented. "But we should still go on a game drive now before you go."

We acquiesced but needn't have bothered. Mid-day is a notoriously shitty time to spy animals in Africa. It's too hot for man or beast, especially the closer you get to the Equator. My checklist didn't grow in the least. Funny enough, conversation didn't either.

"Okay, time for us to go," Miki announced, when we got back to camp.

The boys knew there was no point in arguing. Before the day was done, Miki and I were on a bus to Victoria Falls. Our last great game park adventure together was a bust.

"The Mighty Zambezi"

"Bring on Vic Falls!" I cried as we settled into the bus. "You are going to love it, Miki. There is so much to do! Do you want to go white water rafting? I loved it last time I was there. There's bungee jumping. We could fly over the falls in a helicopter. I'm sure there is tonnes of other cools things we can check out too. Maybe some other kind of paddling adventure…"

"It all sounds cool. Do you want to do something you haven't done yet though?"

"I'd be happy with anything really, but something new is always good."

That something ended up being a two-day getaway to a lodge just outside of town. This time we were above the falls though. The trip included game drives, canoeing on the upper Zambezi, sleeping in a luxurious tent with our very own outdoor shower, and plenty of home cooked meals. It was the perfect compromise after our missed game drive at Hwange.

"Welcome to Victoria Falls," our guide said with a smile as Miki and I arrived at the Shearwater Headquarters. "My name is Peter and this is Luxor. We'll be your guides into camp. Feel free to stow your packs, but make sure to keep your cameras ready. We'll be sure to see zebra, impalas, elephants, and more along the way."

He wasn't kidding. We happily scrambled into the waiting jeep and headed out of the busy town. Soon enough, we crossed into the surrounding countryside and entered Zambezi National Park. Our pace slowed considerably. It is kind of hard to go at a decent clip when baboons blocked the road. They lay idly picking lice off fellow apes, heedless of anyone passing by. We also had to pause to let stately elephants slowly amble across the plains in front of us. And it wasn't a hardship to stop and gaze at giraffes nibbling leaves from nearby trees. Nor to slow down so as not to disturb herds of skittish impalas grazing on grasses.

"This is incredible," Miki exclaimed. "All we see at home are squirrels, birds, and maybe daring raccoons and skunks rummaging through garbage cans."

"Nothing like this," she said in awe with a sweep of her hand at the grunting buffalos we paused beside. She was so right, and I too admired the view as much as her. Before we knew it though, we arrived at the mighty Zambezi.

"Leave your bags," Peter said as the jeep came to a stop beside the river. "Magic here will make sure they get to your tent. I will show you where the bathroom is to freshen up, but don't get too comfortable. We are on to the river next. Okay?"

"Perfect," I said.

"You must earn your bed with a paddle on the river," Luxor said when Miki and I returned. "Come now. Get your life jackets and we go." He ushered us into canoes for the second half of our journey. The rest of the way to camp was by river. Little did we know it would take the rest of the day to get there.

"This just gets better and better," Miki said as we pushed away from shore.

"How close are we to the falls," I asked with a hint of trepidation. I remembered vividly the Class IV rapids that had drenched me the last time I was at Victoria Falls.

"Nothing to worry about," Luxor replied. "There are a few small rapids, but nothing like downriver. Nyami Nyami[32] should be kind to us."

"Who's Nyami Nyami," I asked with a worried look at him over my shoulder.

"Nyami Nyami is the River God of the Zambezi," Luxor said. "The Tonga people say he controls life in and on the river. If he is pleased, life is good. If not, his wrath makes the river run red. I am sure that he is in good spirits today though," he added with a twinkle in his eye.

He was right. While a few ripples gave us little thrills, the magic was in the scenery. Warm waters buoyed us along on the easy paddle. We spied a myriad of birds and other animals on the riverbank while the sun kissed our smiling faces. Miki and I thrilled to be alive in this incredible place. No thoughts drifted to the ailing van or our missing travelling companions. We were present and soaked up every moment spent on the glorious Zambezi. Our paddle down the river held nothing but joy.

By late in the day, after a midday picnic on the riverbank, we finally reached our camp on the Zambezi's edge. "Welcome to your home for the night," Luxor cried, as he pointed out a small encampment. Several large tents clustered on the water's edge. They were a far cry from our small tents we had left with the boys.

---

[32] VictoriaFalls24. (2014, March 21). The Legend of Nyami Nyami. https://victoriafalls24.com/blog/2014/03/21/the-legend-of-nyami-nyami/.

"Help yourself to a shower missus," Magic offered, as he carried our bags to one of the tents. Two twin beds filled the tent, including mosquito nets, down pillows and comforters, scatter rugs, and bedside tables. The showers were just as luxurious, with a huge vat of warm water available to wash away the day's toils. "Dinner will be about one hour, so relax and get refreshed."

The hearty meal was welcome after a long day's paddle, and the roaring campfire afterwards was a perfect end to the magnificent day. We sipped beverages and chatted around the glow of the fire. And I'm fairly sure Nyami Nyami approved.

*****

Sometimes a break is the best remedy for strained relationships. Such was the case for us. Our three-day hiatus was the perfect time period to rekindle our slipping ties. We all knew it.

"Welcome back," Oliver said as Miki and I stepped out of the jeep, upon our return from our canoe safari.

"Missed you," Miki said as she hugged Brett. "I'm sorry things got so out of hand."

"Me too," I added. "But I know how we can best kiss and makeup. How about a booze cruise!"

"Now you're talking, matie," Brett laughed as he grabbed me for a hug too. "Where to?"

"We get to slip into Zambia for it. New country!"

"Excellent," Brett remarked.

"Passport ready," Oliver added, as he lifted his from his money belt. "We just have to stow our bags."

And with that, we were off. As so many people crossed the Zimbabwe/Zambia border for day trips, the crossing was easy. Even better, it was only a short walk, so no one had to drive. We made our way to the boat launch on the other side, paid the fare and set out to watch the sun go down on another glorious day in Africa.

"Cheers," Brett laughed, as he handed Oliver a drink once the boat pushed off. "Get it in ya, Ollie! No one has to fight over the keys tonight."

"Cheers," I cried as we all clinked glasses. "To being together once more and to a beautiful evening on the Zambezi River."

And a beautiful evening it was. The sunset was stunning. Birds flocked the water's edge with crocodiles lurking just below the surface. If you looked, you could see the distant cloud of mist that permanently hung over the falls. But after a drink or two, it all became a bit of a blur.

The thing with the sunset cruise, was that it also had free booze. Which is great in theory, but dangerous too. By the time the boat docked, we were feeling no pain. Poor Miki stumbled and weaved along as we wended our way back across the bridge to Zimbabwe. I'm sure the border guards hated the many partygoers who crisscrossed the bridge in search of the sunset cruises. Cleanup duty must be a bitch but think of the economy! It benefited, if not our livers.

"Come on Miko," Brett coaxed, as we stumbled back to our campsite. "We're almost home." Home was less than inviting though. We might have had our tent once more, but a lamppost blazed above us, bright as day. We tossed and turned until three am, then gave up.

"Are you feeling any better Miki," I whispered.

"I'd feel better, if I could sleep," she replied.

"Nah," Brett chuckled. "This is brilliant. I've got me mates back. I'm chuffed. Honestly though," he added. "I am right sorry about Hwange. I still feel like an ass."

"Forget it," Miki said. "We needed the break. We were all at each other's heads and it was getting nasty."

"And you missed out on some excellent game viewing anyway," I snickered. We passed stories back and forth on our adventures during our short absence from each other, but by 5:00 a.m. managed to drift off to sleep.

"I'm going to catch the sunrise at the falls," Brett stated, as mine and Miki's eyes fluttered shut.

"Mmmph," I replied. The falls would be there once I got some sleep into me.

Miki and I got our fill of the magnificent views later the next afternoon. The spray from the mighty Zambezi washed away the last of the cobwebs, even as it marked the last of our hours together.

"So, there's no way you would consider extending your trip a little more? Maybe heading into Botswana, or Namibia?" I asked, as we gazed into the abyss.

"I promised I would be home for Easter," she said. "I miss Pops and Taro. I'm ready."

It was time. This was our coup de grâce for a journey that spanned more than three months. She was bound for Johannesburg the next day. And while I was sad to see her go, I would be forever grateful that fate had thrown her onto my path in the first place. My journey wouldn't have been the same without her, by a long shot.

A year earlier, my plan had been to meet relatives and explore South Africa a little bit for a few months. I hoped to see some animals, bond with cousins, and come home slightly more well-rounded than I had left. Instead, I bought a kombi, threw caution to the wind, and backpacked across the African continent with someone I barely knew from high school, an Aussie bloke, and a variety of other travellers whom we happened across. Miki helped me get comfortable in my backpack's straps. She also gave me the confidence to strike out on my own. And for that I will be forever grateful.

With a heavy heart I wished her well, but knew that when she left the next evening, I would wipe away my tears, then turn to the next bend in the road on my African Adventure. That is what she would have done in my place. The only way to go, was forward...

*****

ARNIE'S LAST DAYS

"To Chobe We Go"

With Miki gone, we knew our time in Arnie was slowly winding to a close. The little blue kombi had been good to us but was sorely battered and bruised. Miki was part owner and with her now gone, her investment sat tenuously in our hands. It left us more consciously aware of how nasty we were to the poor van. Any new ailments that befell Arnie, cut into Miki's share of the vehicle too. But our travels weren't done yet though.

Brett turned to me as the bus drove off. "I know we said we'd head to Harare to sell Arnie, but…do you think you have one last trip in you for good measure?"

I paused, as I contemplated the offer. What was one more trip in the van, after all the miles already in? It wouldn't add too many more miles or time. Would that affect the resale value? Nope.

"Definitely," I replied with a grin, as I turned to him. "Time to hit Chobe."

"I'm in," Oliver added, despite his own plans to leave us. Plans were only as good as the moment they happened, and that was alright.

"Let's go!"

Chobe National Park is only 70 kilometers from Victoria Falls. It is Botswana's second largest game park and a must see for anyone visiting the area. I, of course, had travelled through Chobe during my overland trip in December, but the game viewing was so magnificent I couldn't resist another trip. I knew it would be worthwhile. I said goodbye to friends in Victoria Falls and we pulled out passports to enter a new country.

Botswana was a relatively poor neighbour to Zimbabwe but seemed comfortable in its own skin. Scenes of poverty did not slap you in the face and the tourist trappings of Victoria Falls were gone. We were guests in a proud nation that seemed to take care of itself in a way we had not seen thus far. A feeling of peace filled me as we drove towards the park entrance. I smiled at the dry landscape we passed and the beautiful people in their simply constructed rondavel homes. This was the Africa of my dreams.

While Chobe National Park is not Botswana's largest park, it does hold some of the biggest concentrations of game. There are massive herds of elephants. Hippos laze on riverbanks or slowly drift downriver from multitudes of hungry crocodiles. Assorted deer species such as impala, sable, kudu, eland, bushbuck, and waterbuck live within the park's borders, as well as many of the 'Big Five' (leopard, Cape Buffalo, elephants, rhinoceros, and lion). Odds were good that we would see plenty of animals while we traversed the relatively flat country.

"Oh my God, look," I cried. Impalas and giraffes ambled in the midday sun. We passed baboons and warthogs, buffalo and zebras, and that was before we even got into the park.

"Bloody right," Brett laughed. "There are heaps of animals. We don't even have to look for 'em! They're everywhere!"

"Let's setup camp, so we can go for a proper game drive tonight," Oliver said. "If there are this many animals during the day, think about how many we will see during peak hours."

He was right of course. Game viewing is best between six and nine in the morning, or four to six in the evening. Most animals sleep during the worst heat of the day. After setting up camp, we did too. It was the best way to escape the hot, dry heat. Once the sun passed its zenith though, we stirred in anticipation of our evening game drive.

"Maybe we'll see even more s'arvo[33]," Brett giddily said.

Maybe we would…

*****

Rustling outside the tent was always a dead giveaway that it was just about time to go. Oliver was itching to leave, as per usual. A twinge of sadness briefly swept me, as I remembered Miki and the last time we were supposed to go game viewing together. The boys had left us behind that day, but not today. I tucked my journal away with a sigh and crawled into the afternoon sunshine.

"Hello matie," Brett said with a smile. "Ready to get at er?"

"Yup," I replied, as I smiled at my remaining travelling companions. "Should we have a quick snack before we go, to tide us over until dinner?" Oliver frowned but nodded. Dinner wouldn't be until closer to seven or later; whenever we got back from our evening game drive. No need to scare the animals away with growls from empty tummies.

"Gut[34]," Oliver said, as he brushed crumbs from his shorts shortly thereafter. "Let's go!"

---

[33] this afternoon.
[34] good.

"Right then," I responded. "Good to go."

I pushed with as much vigour as the boys, as we set off for the vast flat plains of Chobe National Park. Arnie fired to life with a roar, and we chugged off to the main park entrance with hopes of spying lions, cheetahs, jackals, or perhaps even a leopard!

A few hours later, we returned to camp dejected. Yes, we had seen the magnificent Botswana landscape and driven along breathtaking dirt roads that skirted the river. Sure, we saw animals, impalas being the most prevalent. They were so abundant that we became inured to their presence though. They were a far cry from hyenas, leopards, or lions. The most exciting moment of our drive was when we spied baboons grooming each other in the middle of the road. It wasn't enough though. We were thirsty for something more. Our cameras longed to shoot the big game. We were denied.

"No worries," Brett remarked when we returned. "I'm sure we'll see something in the morning."

But our game drive the next morning was just as disappointing. We searched high and low for sights of a fresh kill being eaten by vultures, a crocodile attacking a zebra too slow at the water hole, or even something, anything more exotic than the by now prolific impala. We were jaded and pooh-poohed the beautiful antelope with its warmly coloured reddish-brown coat, white underbelly and thin dark line that ran down its back and stretched down each hind leg. It could be found everywhere from South Africa to Mozambique, throughout Zimbabwe, Zambia, and Botswana, even upwards to Tanzania, Uganda, and Kenya. We weren't interested in impalas. We wanted blood.

"Tonight," Oliver said. "We will go again tonight."

It would be our last chance…

"Maybe head towards the river where we've seen most of the animals," I suggested once we slammed Arnie's doors tight that afternoon.

I gazed out the side window and thought about what the future held. Brett and I aimed to sell the van after this trip. Where would I go from there? Back to Cape Town and family? I looked up when the van slowed to a crawl.

"What is it," I asked from the back seat. "Can you see something?"

"No," Brett began to reply, but Oliver's hand shot out.

"There," he cried in excitement.

Sport utility vehicles (SUV) parked haphazardly about. I sat up to see what the commotion was about. Oliver scrambled to grab his camera from the floor of the van. Brett's eyes grew in excitement, as he steered closer. The closer we got, the more SUVs I counted. Obviously, something exciting was nearby.

"Oh ho," Brett cried. "Check out the buffalo!"

Hundreds of Cape Buffalo slowly migrated towards the Chobe River. The mighty bovines mooed placidly as they nibbled grass and made their way to the river for a last drink before settling down for the night.

"Halt, stop," Oliver hissed.

"What about Arnie…" I started. "Oh, screw it. Let's watch for a bit."

The buffalos were incredible to behold, but something even more exciting was in the air and we were keen to find out exactly what. The sound of Arnie's engine died away.

"Grab my camera mate," Brett squealed. "There, there behind the seat... Oh shit, there's hundreds of them!"

I handed his camera up to him, as Oliver snapped picture after picture. A palpable hum filled the air, electric in its presence. We could hear people in nearby vehicles chattering excitedly in hushed tones. But the source of the drama was still a mystery. When Brett finally managed to get his lens in place and leaned out the window to get a better angle, someone from a nearby SUV called over to us.

"Oi! Careful how far out you go. Look there!" We followed the man's finger and suddenly noticed all his passengers focused on the bushes behind us. That's when we realized what all the fuss was really over.

"Lions!" Oliver cried.

"More than one it looks like too," Brett said. "How many do ya reckon there are? I see one, two, three, four..."

"There's another one there," I added.

"Ya, mein Gott[35]," Oliver mumbled as the largest of them rose and slowly sauntered out of the bush. "Die mutterlast[36]."

---

[35] my god.
[36] the mother's burden.

In fact, there were seven in total, and they paid no mind to the vehicles and humans strewn about. Their focus was the buffalo. Dinner was on their minds and the menu was obvious.

Over the next hour, we watched as the lions stealthily made their way closer and closer to the ever-drifting buffalo herd. The sun made its way across the sky, but still the lions stalked their prey apparently unnoticed by the lumbering bovines. Other vehicles stopped to take in this awe-inspiring sight, as a festive feel filled the air.

"Open the slider Katherine," Brett said.

"What?" I exclaimed.

"To get a better view," he said. "I'll switch spots with you. I want to grab more snaps."

I reluctantly slid the resistant door open and stepped out of the way so he could capture the hunt in process. I couldn't help but feel nervous but was as rapt as anyone watching the slow pursuit across the savannah.

The lions fanned out around us. They kept low in the scrub, communicating silently amongst themselves. The herd was in their sight— the stragglers in the crosshairs. Old, weak, and the young typically make for the best targets. I assumed that was where they would focus their assault. They inched closer and closer to the shuffling buffaloes, heedless of the human spectators desperately capturing every moment on film.

And then the wind shifted.

The lions were maybe ten feet from the herd. We sat a few hundred yards further away with lenses clicking and flashes lighting up the late afternoon sky. Even from a distance, we could tell something had shifted though. Some of the larger dominant buffaloes moved out of formation and tossed their heads aggressively looking around the herd and the surrounding landscape.

"They've smelled them," I whispered.

"Scheiße[37]," Oliver grumbled. He jostled in his seat to get a better look at the change in action. The lions sat frozen waiting to see what the buffaloes would do. No one breathed. But the gig was up.

One of the buffaloes snorted the alarm and the next thing we knew four or five of the bulls broke off from the herd. Alarmed, the rest of the bovines began to trot faster; some running to put distance between them and the perceived threats behind them.

"Oh my," I said, as the bulls charged the defeated pride.

"Dinner has been cancelled for tonight," Brett chided as the angry Cape Buffaloes swung their massive horns at the retreating lions.

The lions knew they were beat and also knew it wasn't worthwhile to take on the thousand-pound cows with thick and deadly horns. They skulked off from the menace of the approaching bulls. Despite poor eyesight, the massive horns on the buffalo's heads made for an effective deterrent for most beasts debating an attack.

"Holy shit," Brett exclaimed. "That was incredible!"

"Yea," I agreed. "Even despite them not getting dinner."

---

[37] shit.

Just then, I noticed a new sound beginning to fill the air. It was the sound of engines starting. As the lions retreated back toward the bushes from where they originally emerged, people realized the show was over and prepared to leave. There were still a few more pictures to snap, as the big cats slunk away from their spoiled dinner plans, but for many it was time to go.

"Oh," I exclaimed as a thought occurred to me. We were in the path that led the lions back to where the action had started in the first place.

For many, it was an opportunity for spectacular close-ups, but for me my brain scrambled to react. The slider door where I sat was open and seven hungry predators were headed in my direction; right after they had missed out on a potential meal. The puny sides of our little tin can would be no match for their razor-sharp claws, but it would be even easier to snatch a quick bite with nothing in the way of a snack but a few articles of clothes.

"Shit," I cried, as I quickly pulled my legs back into the van and scrambled to my knees. I grabbed the handle of the slider door and reefed on it to pull it closed. It slid across, bumped into the side of the frame, and bounced back.

The door did not seal.

"Fuck," I squealed. "Oh, shit! Brett, the door! It didn't close! Brett!!!"

He looked up from frantically snapping photos of the approaching lions.

"What?"

"The door," I cried. "It didn't catch. It's not closed. I can't close it!"

Panic rose in me, as I peered through the crack in the door frame. My hands began to tremble, as I watched the lead lioness sprawl three feet from our front bumper. Another lay down behind us. Still more plunked down just to our left behind us. My knuckles turned white on the handle of the door and my heart tripped into overtime. I could not open the slider to chance slamming it shut again. What if it didn't seal and all I accomplished was gaining the attention of the hungry felines that surrounded us? Not an option.

A whimper escaped me, as I clung to the handle.

"Just relax," Brett said as he continued snapping pictures of the massive beasts lying outside our door.

"Relax! There's a fucking lion right there! I can see it's yellow eye through the crack in the door..."

There was no way I was going to relax.

We could not start the van and drive away, as so many of the other vehicles now did. The starter had not worked on the van in months. Arnie required a push start before he would acquiesce and spring to life. There was no way that Brett and Oliver could jump out of the van to push the vehicle far enough to have it fire to life. There were lions on either side of the front wheels!

"There are two males in the bush there," a passing driver announced as he pointed just beyond us as well.

"Wicked," Oliver exclaimed, as he swung his camera in a new direction.

Good Christ, my mind screamed. *What are we going to do?!*

"How strong are you feeling Katherine," Oliver laughed.

"Fuck you," I muttered. Needless to say, their humour did not lift my spirits.

The sun sank steadily towards the western horizon. It would be dark soon. Most of the other vehicles were gone, as all vehicles were supposed to be out of the park by 6:30 p.m., and it quickly worked its way towards 7:00 p.m. Brett called over to one of the last SUVs that still lingered to inform them of our dilemma.

"Mind giving us a push," Brett shouted. "In a bit of a tricky spot and the kombi's a push start at present."

"I don't know," the driver replied. "It'll wreck your bumper..." Not to mention possibly damaging his own. And the plan to sell the van for top dollar once we left the park might be affected as well.

"We're not in a position to do much else, I'm afraid," Brett said. "We have to risk it."

"All right then," he said. "If you're sure. I'll slowly push you with the bush bar. Hopefully, we'll get you fired to life."

I couldn't stop shaking. I wanted life. So, so badly. Screw the van and whatever might happen to it. A crumpled bumper was far preferable to becoming dinner.

"Look," Oliver exclaimed as a lion slowly stood up and sauntered away. From around us, the rest of them took that as a cue. The ladies rose and walked off a pace.

"Right, go!" Brett shouted. He and Oliver jumped out and sprinted for all they were worth, pushing Arnie down the trail. Mercifully, he sprang to life.

As we sputtered into gear, I pulled the door back and swung it closed with a monstrous clang. As the sweet sound of that life-affirming click rang in my ears, I sank back trembling. It was closed. I took a ragged breath and felt adrenaline course through me.

"Crikey, that was excellent," Brett exclaimed.

"Truly," Oliver agreed.

My hands were still shaking, and I hadn't finished processing that I wouldn't be a lion steak that night. But yes, that was an experience I would never forget. And it made for a pretty wicked tale to tell.

"The Last Journey"

And with that, more goodbyes were at hand. When we left Chobe, we left Botswana. We also left Oliver too. For good this time.

Brett and I were now solo and on our last journey in Arnie. It was time for us to shed our metal companion and set out on foot. We crossed back into Zimbabwe, then headed south to Bulawayo. It was a just a pitstop on the way to Harare and our final stop in Arnie. But Bulawayo was comfortable and a good place to enjoy some of the comforts from home.

"Care to go for a coffee?" Trix asked. "I found a cafe that serves real coffee, not that chicory garbage."

Brett and I had picked up Trix and Jim in Victoria Falls. We had bumped into them several times in our travels. They needed a lift in the direction we were headed, so we effectively traded Oliver for them on the journey south. New companions were always welcome for the conversation as much as to share gas money for a spell. Over coffee that evening, Jim suggested heading to the post office to inquire about selling the van.

"They might be able to direct you on where to sell it," Jim offered. "Give you an idea on price too."

It was a good idea, but the answers we got the next day left us with a new dilemma. In order to sell a South African van outside of South Africa, there was an awful lot of paperwork. Not to mention we had to go to the border regardless, to get a police check on the vehicle. There didn't seem much point to go to the border for paperwork, then turn around and head back to Harare to sell Arnie.

"Bollocks," Brett exclaimed. "We've got to go back to South Africa. I'd rather not make the drive, but the paperwork isn't worth it to save a few kilometers."

"I know," I sighed. "It's ridiculous, but there's nothing we can do. At least it's only 500 clicks. What is that? Half a day's drive?"

"Ya, roundabout that," he agreed.

"There's no point in leaving today," Trix said when she heard about our change in plans over coffee again. "Do you want to catch a flick?"

"Sure," I said. "Might as well. I haven't seen a movie in ages. What's playing?"

"Let's find out," she said brightly.

There were a couple of options, but we settled on *Babe*, a movie about a talking pig turned sheepherder. We bought extravagant vats of popcorn and settled into some of the lumpiest theatre seats I had ever had the pleasure of easing into. But then the lights dimmed, and I left Africa behind for a few mesmerizing hours. Despite the family rating, I was transported by the sights, sounds, and familiar feel of the movie. And it was exactly what we needed.

"I almost forgot we were in Africa," I murmured as we blinked in the light of the African sun when the movie ended.

Only days before, we had watched a pride of lions stalk a herd of buffalos across the dusty plains of Botswana. And yet I had just had a two-hour taste of North American life. Canada and home were over six thousand miles away. God only knew how many months it would be until I saw my native soil again, but the familiarity of city life transported me as we walked back to our hostel. I felt closer to home than I had in a long while.

But home was still a long way away. What awaited me when I returned? I still had no answer. What would I do when I returned home? Where would I live? What would life look like? Africa faded around me, as 'real life' threatened.

I'm not ready, I thought to myself. *Be present. I'm still in Africa. I'm on an adventure of a lifetime with people at my side who are more real than any questions my mind might conjure.*

I was in Bulawayo. Every mile under my belt and every African breath I took transformed me. There was no return to what life used to look like. What life used to be. I had seen too much, touched too many, let go of outmoded ways of thinking that I could no longer justify.

We were about to sell the van, a vital part of our travels. I had no idea what that would mean for my journey, nor what direction it might send me in. Further North? Back South? Somewhere else entirely?

For the time being, I let my musings go and mentally rejoined the people around me as we walked through Zimbabwe's second largest city streets. For now, I was exactly where I needed to be.

"Arnie's Goodbye"

"Welcome to Pietersburg," Brett said as we passed the welcome sign.

There wasn't much to see. Pietersburg was a town. It had the same amenities you would find in most small towns across North America; bank, grocery store, gas station. Nothing special. No terribly interesting tourist sites to explore. No handy game parks to scour for ferocious animals. No real reason to go there except for our explicit purpose—to sell the van.

"Last stop, Arnie," I added.

We had crossed the border back into South Africa a few hours earlier. This was the closest place to part ways with our final travel companion, Arnie. Pietersburg was convenient—close to the border—and big enough to hopefully sell the van. It wasn't beautiful or intriguing, but that was fine. All we needed was a quick sale before starting the next leg of our journeys.

"There's a campground on the edge of town," a man at the petrol station told us.

"Perfect," I said. "Let's set up camp, then pick up supplies."

"We can't go crazy," Brett cautioned. "We'll be carrying everything shortly, with any luck. I do want to ship some curios mind you…"

It was time to empty the van. Souvenirs, extra clothes, books, and more were dead weight. We needed our camp gear until the van sold, but it too would go. My sleeping bag would stay with me, but the tent was a luxury neither of us wanted to carry. It all had to go.

"Time to finally become a full-fledged backpacker," I remarked as I restuffed my considerably thinner pack.

"Right on matie," Brett laughed. "Ship everything but a couple pair of skivvies."

"Ha, not quite!" I said. "But there is plenty to get rid of. And after that, we should clean Arnie, so he shows his best."

"Good idea," Brett said. "Maybe get a few more bucks for him."

We set to wiping windows, the dash, and anything that still held several months worth of dust. It was a celebration, as much as a goodbye. There were many fond memories created in our time along Arnie's roads. Some good, some bracing, but all worthy of note.

"That's a right fine kombi," he said. "Did I see you pushing it earlier though?" A neighbour in the campground stopped to admire our work that afternoon.

"Ya," Brett replied. "The starter is buggered."

"Oush," the burly South African said. "Let's take a look then. See if there's anything that can be done about that." After popping the hood, poking through the engine, and under the dash, a simple solution was presented. "Ack, man. I don't think it is your starter at all. Your ignition is the problem. We can go round it altogether. Give me a minute and I'll hook something up."

I shrugged, as Brett agreed. Within five minutes, he had hooked up a simple button that once pushed, started the van with ease. No pushing, shoving, or grunting required.

"Oh my god," I exclaimed. "That was so easy. Thank you so much!"

"That is going to add a few bucks to our asking price too," Brett added. "Excellent mate! We can't thank you enough. Now, would you happen to know where we might go to sell it?"

"There's a carpark just on the edge of town," our new best friend said. "People park their cars there. Just pop a for sale sign in the dash and you'll be good to go."

It was as good a plan as any. The van was too old to try to sell to a dealership, especially without buying a new vehicle in trade. It might not have seemed fair to Arnie, but we needed the money. He would probably be turned into an overstuffed taxi transporting hordes of people, but it couldn't be helped. It was past time to part ways. We needed the money and that was what Arnie represented now.

"Some kaffir[38] will buy that up right quick."

I paused. My view of our new friend took a decided turn in my eyes. Brett and I exchanged looks. The South African man's help was entirely due to the colour of our skin—Brett and I were as white as could be. That help would not have been offered, if we had been anything other than white. Racial tensions were alive and well once more. Oh, South Africa. Why did you have to be such a disappointment every time I thought better of you?

"Thank you again," I hurriedly said, as Brett's jaw tensed. I steered him towards the driver's seat. "Time to find our carpark!"

"What an arse," Brett exploded once we had safely driven away—without the push that had been our mainstay for the last two months.

"I know," I said. "It sucks. And it's everywhere. Whites are afraid and intolerant of blacks. Blacks don't trust whites. Their world has been broken for too long and they aren't ready to let go of their prejudices. They aren't all evil though. He would have given us the shirt off his back!"

"Only because we were the right colour," Brett grumbled.

"We don't have to agree with them," I said. "Let it go. Be thankful he fixed the van. And changed the spark plugs to boot."

"I am so sick of their asinine prejudices. Arnie can't sell soon enough…" Brett's ugly mood coloured our last trip in Arnie, but at least the

---

[38] an insulting term for a black African.

van looked better than it had ever looked when we dropped it off near the highway.

"Let's grab a box of wine to celebrate," I said as we walked away. "And something for an Easter dinner." Instant noodle soup and tomatoes with none of the trimmings. A feast we were thankful for none the less.

As the evening wore on, the wine and conversation flowed until the thread was lost. I couldn't tell you what we talked about, but could guess we rehashed adventures, philosophized about social politics, and roughly planned our next steps. At some point, my bladder roused me from a sleep I don't remember falling into. The sky was just beginning to lighten, as I crawled out of the tent. It was going to be a long day. I was quite sure it was not going to be a good one either.

"How you feeling, matie?" Brett asked as I crawled back into my sleeping bag. "Reckon you'll make it?"

"Drunk," I replied with a groan. "Ugh, I think I'm going to die once my hangover kicks in."

"Do you remember getting up in the middle of the night?" he chuckled.

"I don't want to know. Please…" I begged. "I just want to lie here until I can move again and not feel like I'm going to throw up."

"So, no coffee then?"

My stomach lurched. I scrambled out of the tent, as quickly as I could manage to hang my head into the bushes. For the first time, but not the last that morning. At least the hangover made the idle hours waiting for the van to sell tick by. It seemed cruel that something so fun one moment could hurt so much the next day. As the day progressed, I crawled from shade patch to shade patch. Occasionally, I made the longer trek across the campsite for water. My god it hurt though.

"You should eat something," Brett said mid-day. Food might have saved me, but the thought made my stomach clench anew. How was it that I never learned? The near empty wine box didn't help.

"We right killed it, I reckon," Brett said as he sloshed the remaining scant bit of liquid around.

"Give at er," I muttered. "All yours. I can't believe we almost drank the whole thing…"

No amount of swearing off booze would save that day, but blissfully the sun eventually sank back into the horizon again. I would survive. My prayers and dreams for that night centered on a speedy sale of the van, so that we could leave Pietersburg and its rowdy memories behind.

"Epitaph"

Arnie
1972 VW Kombi Van

January 8th, 1995 - April 13th, 1996

He served us well
and always came through
in times of need

- Left Cape Town Jan 15/95
- Filled up at 31 km
- Discovered gas leak, speedo stopped at 81 km
- Got bolt stuck in tire – R10 fix
  - Lost starter motor between Durban and Swaziland (near False Bay); later to discover that it was the ignition that was giving us grief all along
  - Gashed hole in exhaust in Mozambique between Vilanculos and Beira (see "The worst Road in Africa"); muffler sealant applied later in Masvingo with little effect
- Various scratches from several game parks
- Some new rust from ocean-side journeys (and a distinct lack of washing)
- Door slider started to go around Hwange
  - Lost power on the way to Hwange, revved high, popped out of first gear; equated to tempers running high and popping for the occupants of Arnie as well
- Survived it all!
- Chugged into Pietersburg
- Sold Arnie April 13th, 1996

*****

TRAVELS FOR TWO

"Show a Little Leg"

As I settled back into the familiar setting of Sable Lodge in Harare, I reflected on the last few days. I lazed poolside thinking about where we had been and what direction life would spin from there. Arnie was gone; sold to the highest bidder. Transportation now wasn't nearly as comfortable or secure. The thrill of new adventures whetted our appetite for life on the road again though. And that road was an entirely different thing.

"Why do I have to stand here alone, while you hang back not even in sight," I called to Brett.

"Blokes aren't going to want to pick up two people," he replied. "Show a little leg Sheila. She'll be aright. We'll get a ride yet."

"Sexist pig," I grumbled, but flirtatiously waved the hem of my skirt a little higher. "How's this?"

"Aces!"

"Lord help me," I laughed. "You are incorrigible!"

Yes, hitchhiking was our new mode of transport. I was the pawn to attract a ride. Not surprisingly, it worked. A sweet ride picked us up in Pietersburg and took us 100 kilometers north to Louis Trichardt. There, we bumped into another traveller we had met in Pietersberg.

"Hey Deon," Brett called out. "Where you heading?"

"Pointed north my friends," he replied with a smile.

"Us too," I added.

"Do you mind if I join you, then?" he asked.

"It might make catching a ride a little trickier," Brett said. "Folks will be leery of picking up three hitchhikers. Unless you can work your magic again, Katherine."

"Yes, do!" Deon added.

"Bah!" I fumed in mock exasperation. But I knew they were right. "Fine…"

When a truck finally stopped for us, the driver insisted I get the luxury of the front seat of the bakkie. The boys both got the back of the pickup, and for their efforts had to don every sweater they owned and tuck into sleeping bags to keep warm. Only fair, as I did all the work. Or something like that.

Our driver's arm stretched across the back of my seat, as he asked. "So, those lads friends of yours?"

"Oh yes," I replied as I shrank towards the passenger door. "Brett is my boyfriend. We have been travelling together for months!"

"Really," Alex murmured as his hand dropped to shift gears and brushed my knee.

"He's a great guy. Sometimes a little jealous of other blokes, but right decent to me."

I recrossed my legs to keep Alex's hand from inching further up my leg. *Maybe this seat wasn't quite as good as it seemed,* I thought. But one look back at the freezing boys and I figured I could hold my own in the warmth of the cab. It took effort but was worth the trip all the way into Harare.

"Thanks again for the ride, Alex," I said, as I quickly attached myself to Brett's frozen side once we finally arrived.

Brett and Deon's teeth chattered, as they pulled their packs out of the back of the bakkie, but they managed thanks too. As Alex drove off, Deon turned to us.

"You must crash at my flat tonight. It is too late to find anything else."

Brett was too cold, and I was too tired, to disagree. He even cooked us steak and eggs for breakfast; a rare treat for us poor lot who had subsisted on dry noodle soup and peanut butter for the last while.

"Come back and have dinner with us tonight too," Deon insisted when we finally left for Sable Lodge. "You can meet my roommate. Watch a little TV too!"

"Excellent!" Brett said. "Count us in."

The Simpsons was a luxury we couldn't resist. There was plenty of time to figure out where we would head next.

"What's a Single Girl to Do?"

"Thanks for nothing, Deon," I muttered as I scribbled away in my journal.

I should have known his false promises and Cheshire grins were not to be trusted. Did I really fall for that? Did my heart deceive me by contemplating the hollow words whispered by a blatant player? My loneliness apparently made me desperate.

At least I played coy long enough for him to move on to the next backpacker, I thought to myself.

My heart wasn't really bruised though. He was just one of an array of men who seemed to gravitate to me in Harare. I had a hard time keeping up.

"One, two, three," I murmured as I counted the roses in a cup. They coincided with the number of guys who had spun into and out of my world in the last few days. "Four, five, six, seven, eight, nine."

That didn't include the one I lost, the one I gave away, the one that wilted too soon, and the red one without a stem that I pressed between the pages of my journal. I hadn't had that much attention in a long time. And truth be told, I was flattered by it all. Especially as Harare was where Jack's letter finally caught up to me.

The letter. The letter I had been waiting for since New Year's. The one that was supposed to explain everything. But didn't. It was cold and short. But three months on, my anger matched it; I flared, then faded. As I suspected, he needed a suitor better in tune with his musical side. I didn't fit the bill. I didn't fit the bill on a few fronts, but truth be told, neither did he. This trip was proof of that. I couldn't lie in someone's shadow and expect to flourish. The attention I had so recently received proved that there was no reason why I shouldn't move on. I might not always attract the ideal mate, but I had options and I had to remember that. The reminder of our two years together still hurt, but I couldn't linger any longer.

I sniffed the delicate blooms once more and returned to the present. Brett had been by my side since January. Despite the opportunity, no romance complicated our travels. We were just friends enjoying the open road together. I cherished the safety of that. The blooms reminded me that I had something more going for me though.

"What's a single girl to do?" I smiled to myself, as I thought about the attention that had been showered upon me.

The roses came from Eddy, Barry, Ian, Adam, and of course Deon. To be fair, my wounded ego from breaking up with Jack and a dearth of attention over the last few months were reason enough to warm up to the idea of someone taking a fancy to me. He was charming, to a fault. The only problem was that his lines were the same for every lady that walked in the front door of his father's hostel. He had the pick of a proverbially rotating litter. I was simply happy that I hadn't succumbed too soon.

"Is he really any worse than Ian though?" I mused.

Ian was a whole other kettle of fish. They both did nothing more than 'talk shit', as the local guys liked to say. I met him through friends of Deon's and as soon as he saw me, the charm was flowing fast and furious. It made my head swoon. Would it hurt to flirt a little?

"Did you have to agree to be his 'woman' though," I sighed to myself. "I'm leaving tomorrow! What exactly is the point in that? Will I ever even see him again? Whatever..."

It was an unrealistic vow that was part of the game, a game played by young fools and itinerant travellers. The lure of romance, the excitement of bars, and the overall experience of city life shaped into a chimera of bliss. It became a blur. And I luxuriated in it, even if only for a little while.

Of course, it wasn't all parties and nightlife. Harare also presented time for shopping, sending mail, and arranging visas to cut through Mozambique to get to Malawi. Malawi was the next destination on the map. I had finally decided that I would head a little further north with Brett before returning to South Africa and home.

The only problem was that our passports came back at different times. Once Brett picked his up, he was itching to get out of Harare.

"Right, let's grab a feast before I take off," Brett suggested as he repacked his backpack.

Harare was the perfect place to splurge on things like that. We decided on The Manchurian Restaurant, an all-you-can-eat Mongolian restaurant that was nothing if not decadent. And it certainly beat out any of the food we had eaten recently.

"Oh my god this is good," I declared after my umpteenth plate of food. "I am going to burst! Thank god for stretchy waistbands."

"Right you are," Brett agreed as he popped the top button on his shorts. "I am done with dinner and done with city life. I can't wait to go walkabout tomorrow."

"What am I going to do without you?" I mock pouted.

"Ha," he snorted. "You've got plenty of blokes to keep you company. You'll be on the road in a few days yerself too though."

"Not for three days though! Who's going to protect me from them?"

"You'll do alright mate. Just don't do anything I wouldn't do…"

"Hah!"

The trick was to keep myself out of harm's way until then. And I mostly did. By Tuesday I followed in Brett's wake on the 14-hour bus ride from Harare to Blantyre, Malawi.

Romance and Zimbabwe were left behind in diesel-fumed dreams of memory.

"A Culinary Excursion"

Brett sat at a table with a ridiculously huge grin on his face and a cold beer in front of him.

"Hey Matie!" he exclaimed, as he weaved his way to stand and gave me a hug. "Good ta see ya! Grab a pint and play catchup. I've been to the Carlsberg Brewery." The crooked smile on his face was proof that the tour had been a good one.

"I guess I will," I laughed.

I ordered a beer and sank into the chair across from him to hear what he had been up to since I saw him last a few days previous. The 14-hour bus ride slowly slipped from my shoulders as I watched him giggle and titter. He was pretty soused and very willing to talk. Not sure if it was his silly grin or just being off the bus in general, but I had to admit that his good mood was infectious.

"…and then I jumped up on a chair and was just grabbing handfuls of 'em. The other bloke was waving a net around and catching mittfuls of 'em! It was awesome!" he spluttered.

"Grasshoppers?" I queried. "Why? What were they going to do with them?"

"Why, eat 'em o' course!" Brett exclaimed. He cackled and slapped his knee. It seemed everything was especially funny.

"Ew," I said with a grimace.

Brett went on to explain. "They come across the lake this time of year and people go bananas! It is a feast for everyone. They scrape the little buggers off the walls, and floors, and wherever, then toss them into a little oil to fry 'em up."

"Blech!" I exclaimed, as he shook with laughter again. "How many did you catch?"

"Hundreds of 'em, mate!" he said. "They were everywhere! It was excellent fun." I shook my head. I couldn't help but smile at his enthusiasm though. "Tomorrow, I'll take you to the market so you can try some," he said.

I wasn't so sure I was interested in trying grasshoppers but replied "we'll see," to appease him. We sat in the bar until Brett's stories became illegible and I had a pleasant glow on. He rambled on about this and that until I could take no more, then we packed up to head back to the hostel.

"Nah, mate. You HAVE to try them! They're awesome!"

"Okay, okay," I dutifully promised as we weaved our way to our newest home. "I'll try them!" I doubted they would be anything like the manna from heaven that he described, but I am always up for trying new foods. At least once. Sometimes, that is enough. And I suspected that might be the case with Brett's grasshoppers.

The next day Brett and I made our way to the market, despite my hopes that he would forget the wild stories he had regaled me with the previous evening. Not a chance. He sought out a stall as soon as we got there.

"A funnel for the lady," he announced to the seller.

"Couldn't I just try one?" I countered. "I don't think I can eat a whole funnel's worth."

Apparently, my miming of just one didn't cut it though. The man didn't speak English and my Chichewa was rusty. I watched him toss grasshoppers in a beaten-up wok over a homemade hibachi. My anticipation was closer to dread than Brett's excitement, but I put on my game face. Once the grasshoppers were sufficiently fried, the market chef deftly wrapped newspapers into a cone and shook his delicacy in. The greasy package was then handed to me, bulging with its contents of small, deep-fried insects.

Whether I liked it or not, I was committed. In for a penny, in for a pound! I tentatively pulled a crispy critter out of its paper container and inspected it warily.

"They're getting cold mate," Brett exclaimed. "Get it in ya!"

That was the least of my worries. I tried to feign polite for the humble cook, but how was I possibly going to put one those disgusting creatures in my mouth? My spit seemed to evaporate at the thought of it. The pressure mounted. The helpful vendor mimed for me to pull it apart. The more I could discard the better I figured.

"I take off the wings?" I asked doubtfully, as I pointed at the little body. Brett just stood laughing, as I squirmed and stalled.

What they both failed to mention though, was that I should have also pulled off the legs. I daresay that might have improved my enjoyment of this Malawian delicacy, but it is doubtful. As it was, I couldn't get beyond the feel of little feet 'walking' down my throat. I still gag a little now remembering this failed haute cuisine. But I pulled it together and swallowed and didn't even throw up on myself. Of course, if I had done so, I would have aimed at Brett in retaliation.

To be fair though, if you are in Malawi when the grasshoppers swarm across the lake, you should try this local delicacy. Residents love them, as do some travellers, plus they are a great source of protein. And you never know. You just might find you like them.

Blah...

"The Magic of Lake Malawi"

Culinary adventures aside, Blantyre wasn't the draw of Malawi. Brett and I had our sights set on the lake we had heard so much about. Cape Maclear was our next destination, and I was excited to be near the water again. And as Malawi was a land-locked country, Lake Malawi was a hub for the small, sub-tropical nation. It was a thoroughfare, source of food, drinking water, and entertainment. Also known as Lake Nyasa, it runs three quarters of the length of Malawi; 587 kilometers (365 miles) long and 84 kilometers (52 miles) wide. Truly beautiful to behold for anyone who gets the pleasure to view her.

The magic of Malawi settled over me as we arrived on the shores of this pristine lake. The lure was palpable. Its soft waves were forever within hearing distance, if not in sight. The people were friendly with a simple air about them that lent an alluring quality. It was probably the poorest nation I had visited, perhaps barring parts of Mozambique, but the people were amongst the richest in attitude. Was it the sunshine? The proximity to soothing waters? Or was it the lack of aid organizations that brought with them handouts, which in turn seemed to transform people into beggars. Here people were happy with their lot in life, and it showed in their eyes, which sparkled despite lack of material wealth. Their peace was infectious.

"I was gabbing with a few locals," Brett said, after coming back from a reconnaissance mission of our new locale. "Whatcha reckon we row out to Pemba Island tomorrow, Bush Woman? They promised sun, snorkelling, and snackies!"

"Awesome," I said. "Sign us up! I can't wait to get on the water. You're always so good to find us the coolest adventures, Brettski. Sweet!"

This was an adventure that couldn't be beat. We made our way to the beach next morning and found our polers waiting for us beside their mokoros. These dug-out canoes were narrower than the mokoros I had lazed in on the Okavango Delta, but still a marvel. We perched on the lip of the boat, with our feet and whatever belongings we had, stowed underneath us.

"The water is so blue," I remarked as we slowly pushed along.

"Clear too," Brett added. "The better to see loads of fish."

"Speaking of, when do we jump in to see them up close?" Brett asked our guide with swimming motions. We got quite adept at makeshift sign language when language was a barrier, and most people were happy to communicate however they could. Our guide picked up a mask and pointed to the island we made our way towards.

"Just about there it looks like," I said.

The wait was worth it. Once the boats were beached, we slipped on flippers and masks and dove in. We paddled behind colourful fish amongst the shoals, swimming this way and that. I felt like we were in a National Geographic explorer show, as the warm waters teemed with life around us.

By the time we stepped back onto land, a feast was waiting for us. Our guides had caught fish while we swam and they cooked it with rice, potatoes, and tomatoes for a simple, but delicious meal on the beach. Aalon's special banana cake finished it off and tripped us over the moon. It was a brilliant way to top off a perfect day soaking up the beauty of Malawi.

On the last of our three nights in Cape Maclear, a young man from Blantyre asked me to join him at 'Ba'blue'. We walked to the small local bar, where locals sat around sipping drinks and playing an intriguing game.

"What's that?" I asked. "What game are they playing?"

"You don't know bao?" he replied. "It is a good game. They move their markers—beans—around the board and collect/steal beans as you go."

We watched a few men play on the homemade wooden boards. They scooped beans out of dugout holes and plunked them down rapidly around and around the board. It was a version of mancala, but I had never seen it before. Here though, everyone seemed to play, and I watched intently, earnest to pick up the rules. The point was to collect all the beans from your opponent; you each had a series of dugout holes and if you finished your beans across from where an opponent held markers, you could collect theirs too, leaving them sparse. My competitive edge had me yearning to steal people's beans too!

"Like this?" I asked, when a space opened up for me at one of the many game tables.

"No, no," my friend said with a laugh. "They have to have beans available or else your turn is over."

"Oh," I said, as I puzzled over the new game. Before long though, I was holding my own.

"Gotcha!" I cried, as I scooped a deep pile of beans out of an opponent's hole. I was hooked. And before we left for the capital, Lilongwe, I had my very own bao game board stuffed into my backpack.

"Bartered Goods"

I played another game in Malawi that I felt equally ill-prepared for—bartering. This time for curios. I had my heart set on a Chief's Chair and the only place to get one was at market. So off I strolled.

As I wound my way through the stalls of yet another market, a cacophony of sound filled my ears. People called out as you passed, hawking their wares. Dogs snuffled in the dirt, looking for dropped treats. Music blared from ancient boom boxes. And skinny chickens clucked in the dirt, as they waited their turn to be plucked and stuffed into giant woks, then served with nsima (the local version of cornmeal porridge).

I had eaten enough nsima to find it palatable, as long as it came with the ever-present tomato and onion sauce that was found everywhere in southern Africa. Thank God, I liked tomatoes, as the small fruits were one of the few staples that were prevalent at every outdoor market I had come across in Africa. Onions and eggplants were also readily available in little triangular hills on top of rickety wooden stalls, or worse, balanced precariously on a piece of plywood resting atop an over-turned bucket. Whomever said that people were starving in Africa hadn't wandered any of the markets I went through, apparently. Mixed with rice, and the luxury of salt and pepper, a tomato feast could be had any night.

As far as protein went, though, that was a different story. You could find live chickens stuffed inside innumerable totes or underfoot at most markets. There was never any question as to its freshness. Beef, on the other hand, was always tough, and pork non-existent (not kosher or halal). Beans and peanut butter usually filled my 'meat and alternates' quotient. A rare treat of fresh fish infused my vegetarian style diet, but I still grew lumpy on the starchy staples that were my main fare. It supplied good enough reason to dive into Lake Malawi to swim off a meal or two though.

So, while I did pick up a few staples, this particular shopping trip centered on a more cultural note. I fought through the throngs of people, the greasy food stands, and discarded piles of glass coke bottles. My aim—wood carvings. And this market was a veritable treasure trove. There were wooden carved bowls, figures of men, elaborate tables, and, of course, the famous Chief's Chairs. They were exquisite, and I wanted all of them.

"Sistah, sistah!" curio sellers called as I sauntered down the long line of carvers' stalls.

I glanced at the wares but did my best not to stop. If you did, the vendor would spring into action, and then it was impossible to move on. I wanted to see what was available before I settled on anything. I nodded and smiled as I passed.

Intricately detailed facial features peered out at me from dark hardwood pieces. Elephants, zebras, and various other animals adorned yet more. I had no idea how I would be able to narrow down my search for the perfect curio, but the first challenge was to not look interested. My white face was already enough to drive the prices up, let alone being an easy mark by looking too keen. Buying a curio was a complex task that required a discerning eye, excellent bargaining prowess, and restraint enough to not get sucked into buying too much. I wasn't confident I had enough of any of those skills.

"Chief's Chairs! Solid ebony. Nice chairs just for you!"

"I have chairs too sistah! Come look! Bowls too. Come see!" I smiled as I strolled past but tried not to get sucked in just yet. There were too many stalls to see; too many items to choose from. The many wares were lined up in the dirt but were not marred by the setting in the least. My eyes flicked from intricately carved women balancing parcels on their heads, to ferocious lions snarling threats. Which image represented Africa the most to me? What did I want to bring home? What to choose?

Ok, Katherine, I thought to myself. *Be strong. You know that as soon as you stop, they will pounce. Are you ready? You want a table. Nothing more. You got this.*

Bartering was part of the business and I braced myself to drive a hard bargain. Who was I kidding though? I screamed easy mark. I had no willpower and couldn't turn down the high-power sales tactics that were part of the game. If I paused too long, a young man would have a giraffe in my hand and be chanting prices in my ear. While I listened to his spiel, he would be maneuvering me into one of the enormous Chief's Chairs to rest my feet for a moment. Just to see how comfortable it was.

"Be strong," I chanted to myself again. "You want a table."

Not just any table though. I had fallen in love with the delicate three-legged tables; legs carved from a single piece of wood but still entwined in the middle. The legs served as a tripod for a flat, round top. The surface held ornately carved images, both top and bottom. Those images spoke to me of what Africa was all about. I had to have one.

I walked up and down the stalls, lingered here, or smiled at a seller's antics there, before I finally returned to a little stall that had called to me. The smell of money was strong on me, but nothing would have changed that.

"How much for the tables?" I casually asked. "That one there with the elephants."

"Nice choice, Mama," my wily salesman replied as he looked at the table with elephants encircling the perimeter of its surface. "This one 1,000 kwacha."

"Oh!" I cried in mock surprise, "that much…" I hesitated and wandered down the line of wooden items, pretending to think over whether I wanted the table. Was he fooled?

"See the details?" he said. "Did you look at the other side? Rhinos too! Very nice piece. Very nice price."

"Mmm," I murmured.

"What about that one with the woman?" I asked pointing to another table.

"More work. She holding pitcher. She smiling. Bigger price," he hesitated. "How about I give you Chief's Chair too. Make deal…" He pulled a small two-piece chair from the row and placed it beside the rhino table. "Everyone need Chief's Chair."

He wasn't wrong. I did want one of them as well. And as much as I was trying to be nonchalant, I would have paid the first price he threw out there if I didn't think I would offend him. Bartering was a part of the process. And now that I had started the process, I was in it for the long haul.

"How about 500," I offered back.

"Oh, missus!" he cried. "No, no, no. See the legs? All carved from one piece of beautiful mahogany. You can't get this anywhere else." He thrust the legs into my hands, as he talked.

"800 kwacha. No lower. All hand carved!" It was killing me, but Brett told me I had to go back and forth several times before we agreed on a price. I just wanted to say yes and throw my money at him, but I demurred.

"The chair is nice I guess, but I don't know how to get it home."

"Easy!" the young man cried. "I will wrap, so you can mail."

"I don't know," I hesitated. "Maybe I will look a little more…"

"Oi, okay! 600 kwacha. Final price. Och, I am giving away!" he shook his head in mock dismay, as he threw his hands up.

"Okay," I replied, then beamed. I had a beautiful new tripod table, plus a small Chief's Chair to boot. I figured the chair would make a wonderful souvenir for my cousin back home, but the table was all mine. I counted out 600 Kwacha (the equivalent of about $60 CAD at the time), while the seller gathered up cardboard to package my purchases in.

"Very nice missus. You like." Oh, I liked. I just hoped it would make it to Canada in one piece, so that I could enjoy my souvenirs once I returned home myself. The umpteen forms and double-checked packaging looked alright, but I had my doubts. Supposedly they would take three to six months to ship. My plane ticket said I was supposed to fly home in three weeks. Would I beat them? Or would the road tempt me to stay longer, leaving family to unpack my wares back home? How reliable was the postal service in Malawi anyway?

"Mwaya Beach"

"Sheets," I exclaimed. "Look, there are actual sheets on the beds! And mosquito nets too," I added, as I fingered the delicate gauzy material that hung from the roof of the thatch hut.

"Pretty sweet, mate," Brett nodded as he dropped his pack onto the matching twin bed on his side of the hut. A man materialized at the door with lemonade.

"Thanks Joey," I said as he placed the tray on a sturdy wooden table and set two tall glasses down.

"Can I get you anything else?" he politely asked yet again. We had been in Mwaya Beach for only a handful of minutes, yet Joey had already taken our dinner orders, retrieved pillows for our luxurious looking beds, and shown us every courtesy he could. For 50 Kwacha a night (at the time 16 Kwacha was the equivalent of $1 USD), this would be the best money ever spent.

After he double-checked yet again that we had everything we needed, Joey bowed low, then quietly retreated to the kitchen across the sandy courtyard. I caught sight of the swish of a colourful sarong, but its owner disappeared before I could see anything more of her. My curiosity piqued, but I turned back to our room for the time being.

"This is going to be bloody awesome," Brett declared as he bounced on the bed with a laugh. "What should we get up to first, ya reckon?"

"I need to jump in the lake," I declared. The sparkling lake beckoned just a stone's throw from our hut.

"Right then. Get your bathers on," Brett said as he stepped onto the porch. "Rattle your dags[39]!" he called over his shoulder, as he walked away.

"Keep your pants on, dude," I said as I emerged with a sarong wrapped around my waist. "The lake's not going anywhere."

But I was plenty ready for it anyway. And the best part was that we had it all to ourselves. No one else wandered along our small section of private beach where I dropped my towel, sunglasses, journal, and pen.

---

[39] hurry; 'dags' are pieces of dried waste on the tail of a sheep that make a rattling noise if the sheep runs.

"Last one in's a rotten egg," I yelled as I splashed in up to my thighs, before diving headlong into the warm waters of Lake Malawi. "Oh," I moaned as I burst to the water's surface. "This is perfect!"

I swam a few strokes, before flipping to my back to drift aimlessly in the serene waters, my face to the clear Malawian sky. The sandy beach lay behind me with its cluster of neat huts tucked amongst waving palm trees. Further out, men in mokoros cast nets in hopes of ensnaring a generous bounty of fish. If anyone else touched my sphere, I was blissfully unawares. I was lost in this luxuriant moment.

There was no place I had to go. Nothing pressing I had to do. I didn't even have to worry about dinner, as Joey had promised seafood crepes for our evening meal. It would be delivered across the sandy expanse from the kitchen to our hut by his competent hands; homemade cuisine nestled under a gleaming silver platter. And a comforting reassurance that our wish was his command. He repeatedly promised to provide anything we desired. All I wanted though was to breathe in this precious moment of serenity. Oh, to have that moment live forever!

When I eventually returned to my towel on the beach, Brett was up and ready to go with his camera slung around his neck.

"I'm off to go walkabout," he said. "Care to join?"

"Nah, I just want to chill. Scribble in my journal. Catch you up at dinner."

"Right then. See ya!"

I watched him wander down the beach for a moment, then pulled open my journal to capture this magical place. It was beautiful and a luxury I hadn't experienced in too long. Sheets! I smiled to myself once more.

"We might even have to dress up for the occasion," I mumbled to myself with a smile. "Crepes are pretty fancy..." A few hours later, I discovered that they really were.

"Cheers," we declared as we bit into our delicate crepes with gusto. Candles glimmered between us and threw an ethereal light to our dinner.

"So good," I groaned with pleasure between mouthfuls. "Oh my God..."

"Right?" Brett replied. "Better than grasshoppers even!"

"WAY better!" I snorted. "So, what did you get up to this aft while I lounged on the beach?"

"The kids swarmed me," he laughed. "They followed after me and begged me to take their pics. They were manic, jumping, posing, and the like. A right sight to behold. Pretty sure they hadn't seen the likes of me before."

I had seen it myself. When he finally ambled back up the beach, he had an entourage of tittering boys in tow. They had stopped at my towel and were a sight to behold. The gregarious boys laughed and ran in circles around us. Shy girls, on the other hand, clung quietly to the outskirts of the circle: a part of the fray, but by their meek nature, removed. A select few daring girls came over to feel my blonde hair and white skin, to see if it felt any different from their own black counterparts. I held my arms out in encouragement, these docile girls restricted by their patriarchal culture.

242

"Go ahead," I encouraged with a smile. "I like your hair. So pretty!" I said to a young girl pointing to her intricate braids. "Yours too," I added, turning my gaze to another shy girl hiding behind their self-appointed leader. She giggled, then snaked out her hand to touch my thin, flat hair, so different than her own curly mane.

I was glad that Brett had trailed them back to me, but the afternoon wasn't all idyllic. While the children were happy and friendly, their poverty was all too apparent. They were dressed in nothing more than rags. Excessive wear had robbed their clothes of any colour they once may have sported. The contrast between their childish glee and obvious poverty was starkly punctuated by their drab monotonous colour palette. While it did not dampen their enthusiasm, it did diminish our joy.

"Did you see the boy without a crotch in his pants?" I asked Brett as we lingered over a glass of wine, the last light of day fading. "He was heartbreaking! He didn't even seem to notice." His little 'chaps' spoke volumes of the standard of living that was so disparate from my own, so far away.

"He probably has another pair for school," he countered. It didn't make me feel much better.

"I wouldn't keep those for rags back home, but here they run around in public like that," I lamented. Far from a prude, his tattered clothes hurt my heart and soul. "What do you think we'll see tomorrow?" I asked.

Brett had arranged for us to visit a local school in the morning. It was the last day of the term for the students at Mwaya Beach Primary School. A couple of boys from the beach had invited us to tag along with them to hear test results and tour their classrooms.

"It'll be interesting anyway," he guessed. "We'll see if they do have 'good' clothes." I watched the full moon rise into the sky before the mosquito nets beckoned for us to avoid the mozzie hordes that descended. Our date at the chalkboards called.

The next day, a contingent of children gathered at the beach to escort Brett and I to school. "Come missus, come mistah," they called. "We going to school. You come to school with us today…"

They led the way, laughing and shouting as we went. Our entourage grew from a straggler or two, to a much larger contingent by the time we neared the school. I couldn't help but notice that our suspicions were correct; overall, they dressed better and not quite as ragged and torn as the day before. By the time we reached Mwaya Beach Public School, our group merged with other students and began to disperse. Before they all went off to join their friends, a few of the bolder students brought us to the office though. And that is where we met the Deputy Headmaster.

"Welcome," he said. "You've come on a special day. Today is the last day of term. The students receive their marks today. But first, we must show you our humble school. Come, let's see the classrooms."

We didn't have far to go. While the office appeared to be tiny, the number of classrooms explained the size. There was a mere handful spread across a dusty clearing. At the first classroom, the Deputy Headmaster walked into the sparse room. A chalk board hung in the simple rectangular room. No chairs or desks were present.

"You can see we don't have much," the Deputy Headmaster explained. "We don't have many supplies, some books, but no workbooks, pencils, or paper. We rarely have chalk either, but the teachers often take their classes outside anyway." Maybe it was more comfortable outside, except on rainy days. And how many students showed up on those days anyway?

"Class sizes range upwards of several hundred students," the Deputy Headmaster continued, "but many of them don't show up regularly, so it is not as bad as it sounds." I was shocked. How could one person effectively teach a class of over 300 pupils? Why would they want to when the pay was poor and, from all accounts, usually late? This was nothing like the schooling I received back in Canada, where class sizes ranged from 15 to 30 children. Comparatively, the Canadian compatriots had nothing to complain about.

"Let me show you our book collection in the office," our tour guide announced after the brief tour of the sparse classrooms. As we walked across the courtyard, he asked "Where are you from?"

"Australia," Brett announced.

"I'm from Canada," I chimed in as he opened the office door.

"Canada!" he exclaimed. "My friend, you are a special guest. Look here!" He handed me a book with the cover open from a small stack of tomes on the floor. Inside, a stamp proclaimed that the textbook was a donation from the Canadian government. Several texts and workbooks were in the collection. While I was proud to see the donation, I dismally knew it was just a drop in the bucket. Stacks of books sat on the floor and on shelves, but for the numbers of pupils, it was ridiculously insufficient. There were 1,096 registered students at Mwaya Beach, but the books possibly numbered close to a hundred in the cramped office: probably less.

"We should go now," the Deputy Headmaster announced. "The assembly is about to begin." He steered us back out to the clearing where hundreds of people now sat. Students leaned on trees, sat pressed up against other pupils, or lingered on the fringes of the group, barely there.

"You must sit here," he said, as he steered me towards the head table with the school's 12 teachers and Headmaster. Before I could protest, Brett disappeared into the sea of children, swamped by hordes of little boys fawning over him and the magical camera slung around his neck.

"Please, sit," said a teacher near the end of the table. I glanced back out to the sea of little black faces, then back to the smiling gentleman. I awkwardly smiled back and sank into the proffered chair with a weak thanks.

"Welcome," said the headmaster as he stood up at his place at the table. "Thank you all for coming today." He glanced my way with a smile, then continued in Chichewa. While the rest of his words were lost to me, the teacher beside me picked up in English where the headmaster left off.

"He is explaining how new testing formats were rolled out this semester," he said. "It was very difficult for many students. Their marks reflect that. Extremely poor overall, unfortunately." The teachers went down the table and stood to read out their pupils' grades. As names were called, it become obvious that the new teaching methods had been lost on the children. Nervous students stood to receive their marks and just as quickly sat back down again, disheartened. Most of them failed. Over and over again, names were called, and the grades fell far below passing standards. While I was embarrassed for them hearing the dismal results aloud in front of their peers, I remembered the lack of supplies; there was no paper to write down individual student's marks. If they didn't have paper for learning, how could they spare it for report cards?

Once the last teacher finished reading their marks, the Deputy Headmaster stood to make further announcements. My translator leaned in to give me a synopsis of the speeches once more. "A new Junior Primary School is to be opened next term," he said. "It will only be for Standards One through Three, but it will reduce the distance the children have to walk. Maybe more of them will come to school then. They hope to expand it later, as funds allow." I nodded in approval, trying to be considerate of the ongoing speeches.

"Some of the students walk very far to come to school; upwards of four-and-a-half kilometers every day."

"Really?" I asked in shock.

"Many do not bother," he added. "It is too far. And when they don't come, they fall behind, so don't want to come even more." It was a vicious cycle that was easy to understand. A new more accessible school could make all the difference.

The headmaster took over again and spoke of the ills of 'chamba'—marijuana. I looked out at the children in front of me, as I heard the gist of the speech. A great way to escape reality, but they seemed too young to need the release. Another teacher rose and spoke against the practice of early marriages.

"Many families marry their girls off young," my interpreter said. "Fewer mouths to feed. The problem though is that they begin new families and then there are many more young mouths to feed. When children have babies at 14 or 15 though, there is much time to have too many babies."

My head swam with his words. This was the real picture of life in Malawi. The smiling faces in front of me held such promise, but the odds of success in a struggling school system and imperfect cycle of life were bleak. A few of these children would make it to high school. Many would not. Even less would attend post-secondary training to help lift them out of their cycle of poverty.

A tug on my skirt distracted me from the overwhelming statistics. A young girl smiled up at me and reached out to touch my hand. I melted. As much as this community faced adversity, they held a beautiful spirit that felt pure in its earnestness. I might not be able to change their realities, but I would always remember the lessons these genuine people offered. The warm heart of Africa had stolen mine.

*****

The next day, my eyes fluttered open to take in another beautiful day in Malawi; blue skies with drifts of lacy clouds slipping down the inviting beach. The comfortable bed that enclosed me was a luxury I had almost forgotten. I stretched and swung my legs to the floor, as I pushed the mosquito net aside.

"Morning, sleepy head," Brett called from the porch. Of course, he was up already. He was always up with the sun, off to chase down adventure.

Joey materialized a moment later with a glass of freshly squeezed orange juice. "Would you be liking breakfast? We have freshly baked scones, fruit, eggs."

"The eggs are bang up," Brett added between mouthfuls of eggs and toast.

"Oh Joey, that sounds wonderful," I replied. "I would love all of that."

"Very good," he replied with a bow as he retreated to the kitchen hut.

"How did you sleep mate?" Brett asked. "That must have been the best sleep I've had in ages!"

"Oh my god," I said. "The bed was so comfortable! I could have stayed in it forever."

"What else is new," he scoffed as he wiped the last of his egg yolk into his mouth with his crust of bread.

"Shut up," I laughed. "So, what's the plan for today? I think I want to catch up my journal. Maybe have a lazy day on the beach."

"Right. I might join you for a bit, but there are a few more nooks I wanted to scout out. You be alright if I wander?"

"Perfectly fine," I replied. I relished the idea of a quiet day alone on the beach. It was exactly what I craved after the busy day at school the day before.

Once Joey cleared breakfast, Brett went one way and I headed to the beach with a towel and my journal in tow. I knew the day would heat up, so I staked out a patch of shade where I laid my handful of possessions. First things first though, the gentle lake called to wash my soul clean for another perfect day in Malawi. I dashed across the already hot sand and dove into the inviting waters that glittered steps from my towel. After gliding underwater for as long as I could, I popped up with the intent to strike out for the distant shore.

Who was I kidding? After several strong strokes, I paused to tread water and look around. Small, colourful fish darted away from my foreign intrusion, but the wind came to kiss my cheeks. Closer to shore, the breeze danced with stately palms. I caught sight of the housekeeper, as she wandered over to clean our hut. I still hadn't managed to see much of her shy figure, except from a distance. It seemed that was the way with women there.

I rolled onto my back and lazily kicked my feet, as I traced cloud shapes in the Malawian sky. A bird flew overhead and glided towards shore, but I remained in the present. Life was idyllic in this moment, and I wanted it to last forever. My sun-warmed smile filled the universe, and I was at peace.

"This couldn't be any more perfect," I murmured to myself. "Except for my wrinkled fingers, I suppose. Perhaps time to dry off for a bit…" Nothing my towel and a minute in the sun wouldn't fix. I leisurely swam back to shore and made my way to my towel. I closed my eyes to allow the water to evaporate, but it only took a moment. I wanted to capture the recent experiences from our days in Mwaya Beach before they unwound from me. It wasn't hard. My pen flew across the page, as I recounted our trip to the school the day before.

Movement caught the corner of my eye, and I looked up to see a man walking by. I nodded in greeting.

"Jambo," he said. "Hello."

"Hello," I replied. "Beautiful day." I noticed the net thrown over his shoulder. "Are you going fishing," I asked. He looked confused, so I pointed to the stringy bundle on his back. "Your net? You are a fisherman?"

"No, no" he said, finally understanding. "I work at the Matete post office. This is my towel." His towel was nothing more than a few threads loosely strung together. "My towel very worn," he replied. "Washed many times. Do you have towel you give me?"

My heart lurched. "Oh, I'm sorry," I said. "This is my only one. I kind of need it. I still have a long journey in front of me."

Which may or may not have been true, but I felt called out, nonetheless. While I could probably afford to buy a new one, I was on a tight budget. I knew I was rich in their eyes, just by my presence alone. Handing them anything and everything would do little good though. I had seen how aid organizations in Mozambique created a beggar society by abundantly handing out alms. People came to expect and rely on it. I loathed the thought of the friendly people of Malawi following in those same footsteps.

"Have a good day," he said with a smile, as he wandered off to enjoy his bath in the lake.

I was left to contemplate the economics of wealth in a continent largely unfamiliar with it. Back home, I had clothes and towels aplenty. More than enough to spare and share. I knew that hand-outs took their toll in pride though. I offered my good-will and that was enough for the day. I prayed that the warm heart of Africa could keep its special nature, and perhaps one day be able to proudly have more wealth to share with its people. Today though, it shared what it was able, and I was grateful for all that Malawi was.

The question was, would I remember all the stark lessons that seemed to overwhelm me on a regular basis? They felt so strong and visceral, how could I not?

*****

GOING IT ALONE

"A Ghost on Board"

Bodies littered the filthy, open deck. Colourful sarongs tucked in close beside stunned chickens and giant bags of god knows what. Grizzled men gathered around impromptu games set up in spare floor space, which is to say nowhere and anywhere. I tried to look as small and inconspicuous as possible amongst the motley crowd.

Live chickens were everywhere. They scratched in the dirt around rondavels, docilely sat behind market stalls awaiting plucking and frying, or crammed into cages ready to be sold for the same treatment elsewhere. They were a common sight on buses, and here they were on the ferry that sailed south to Monkey Bay. It shouldn't have surprised me.

The large, checkered polyethylene bags were no less surprising. They could hold a traveller's entire worldly possessions, or more likely, their wares to hawk at the market. Always dirty white with a blue or red pattern, they adorned women's arms and heads. Men travelled far lighter. Heavy labour like transporting babies, supplies, or livestock was left to the women.

Babies! Everywhere you looked, babies clung quietly to women's backs or chests. They never seemed to cry or make a fuss, perhaps due to their proximity to the most important person in their lives—Mother. And god love the mothers who seemingly never noticed the addition to their load. Babies were simply a constant part of who these women were. Age was the only thing that released them from that burden.

Men, on the other hand, had it comparatively easy. No babies or children clung to them, and luggage was left to the women. Never-ending games of bao entertained them just about everywhere. Even here, I could see a few games set up in various corners of the ferry before we even left shore. Their participants were boisterous with the air of a party. I wouldn't doubt that a carton of Chibuku or two were aboard too. They loved their 'shake shake'. I myself was not a convert to the millet beer, despite having given it a go once or twice. The taste of the sludge was not worth drinking it, even for the giddy consequences. I was not offered any on this particular trip though. I sat alone, curled up on a little bench to which I greedily clung.

We left Nkhata Bay at 3:00 p.m. There were stops scheduled for Senga Bay and a few other little ports, before we would reach Monkey Bay at 6:00 or 7:00 a.m. two days hence. It shaped up to be an exceedingly long ferry ride and my white legs were the only ones on the boat. I was a ghost amongst a sea of black travellers. Curious eyes followed any movements I made, but the shy women would never dream of speaking to me. Not their place to speak? Certainly not to a foreigner. I couldn't imagine the reality into which they had been born.

Without Brett by my side, I silently watched the world go by. He was headed North with his sights set on Ethiopia, while my journey veered South again after leaving Mwaya Beach. My current working plan was to see if I could find work with an overland company, and Harare was the best place to do so. Back to familiar territory, hopefully in one piece.

As the sun sunk lower in the sky, I prayed my pack wouldn't disappear overnight. I shivered in the misty darkness on deck, feeling more alone than I had ever felt before. Luxury was not something found on this boat, and neither were familiar faces. My pack was it and for that I was at least glad. The cool night air found me digging for extra clothes to put on, to

253

add a lick of warmth overnight. The sleepy chickens now looked a little more inviting with their small, warm bodies. All I had left was the mindset to will warmth into my chilled limbs.

Jealous of chicken feathers? Yes, I was. And while I could have booked an inner cabin for the voyage, my pockets suggested otherwise. I figured if others were willing to ride on deck, why couldn't I? I looked around at the others that huddled about and couldn't help but contrast our stations though. Realistically, I could have afforded better accommodations. Elusive sleep and ever-present fear screamed my folly. It was a long, unpleasant ride, where I was ever vigilant of the filth and thieves who potentially lurked everywhere, but I had made my bed (kind of), and I stayed the course.

As long as this ferry doesn't sink, I'll be fine, I thought to myself. I hated the fact that I knew another ferry had done just that a mere month before.

"I miss you Brett," I silently whispered to myself, as the ferry bore me away from the four months we had spent together, now gone.

"City Living"

I turned this way and that in front of the mirror. The dress was pretty tight. No, scratch that. The dress was skin-tight. A leopard-print mini to be exact, with high heels to complete the image. Not exactly my style on a good day, let alone while backpacking throughout Africa.

"Oh my," I exclaimed.

"You look great," Debbie said. It was her outfit I wore, so not surprising she felt that way. I was a lot more skeptical though. I had never worn a leopard-print anything before and wasn't sure if it was really my style. The look in Ian's eyes told me I worked the outfit better than I thought though. I suddenly felt like a doe to his wildcat.

"Let's do your makeup now," Debbie gushed.

Oh Lord, help me through this night! I prayed to myself. There was no room for negotiation. Before I could protest, we were out the door.

"Off to 'The Tube' babe. You look hot!" Sure, I did...

Ian's smile was wide as he waltzed me into the club. I was his prize trophy in my vampy attire.

"Hey," he yelled to someone we passed. "Wicked beats tonight!"

"Smoking night!" he called to another.

He strutted around with me like I was a prize bauble. I was the hot white chick in town for the week, and he the stud who snagged her. Never mind that I was only there for a few days, before leaving, probably to never return. That mattered little in this status game. I didn't take well to playing a trophy possession, but he was blithe to that. My patience was quickly tiring of the charade that I was his girlfriend though. And while I didn't want to hurt his feelings, any dreams of a real relationship were slim to none.

Whether he got it or not though, he certainly took advantage of showing me off as much as he could. I was his for the night, a wandering traveller who never made any place home for more than a few days. He was a native Zimbabwean, not about to follow me far. We both knew that, but he preferred to live in the moment.

"Axle, my man!" he knew everyone and seemed to make a point of talking to them, just so he could take advantage of my arm in his.

In his defense, I didn't take many pains to wither Ian's dreams in the grand scheme of things. There I was in a nightclub as his wanton guest. I had allowed myself to play seductive mistress. While I might have decided it wouldn't go any further than that, he tried his damnedest to convince me otherwise. To his credit, he was cute, and his dogged persistence wore me down. It had been a long time since I had received such flattering attention and I guess I liked it enough it to keep the charade going. It wasn't destined to last though.

"I am going to talk to Deon," I said to Ian as I pulled my arm out from his. "Oh, and there's Phil too!"

"What about me though?" he replied churlishly. I waved over my shoulder as I wobbled across the dance floor on uncertain heels. I didn't care what he got up to and wasn't about to stick around and let him parade me around any longer. Plus, I couldn't help noticing a few other eyes follow me across the floor. I might have been unaccustomed to the attention, but it was fun, and I savoured the attention.

"Let's go," Ian insisted a little while later when he came up and grabbed my arm.

"I think I'll stay actually," I said pulling my arm away, as I turned back to Phil.

"But you came with me," he whined. "You're my date!"

"Sorry, Ian," I insisted. "I am not going home with you."

"But…" He looked from me to my other companions, and back to me. It sunk in that he wasn't going to win this battle. I was not his woman. I didn't owe him anything and refused to be badgered into anything I wasn't comfortable with. He left dejected, but not beaten.

As the days passed, it only got worse. He hung around the hostel constantly and dripped off me every chance he got.

"So, what's going on with you and Ian?" people asked.

"Nothing," I answered. "I'm working on moving on." I wasn't interested in a permanent life in Harare. It wasn't even a possibility. I suspected it might hurt him, but truly questioned how Ian could have ever put himself into such a ridiculous situation. I was a backpacker; a transient. My money belt forever grew thinner, and time demanded that I do something about it. There was no option at any point for me to stay, and I didn't want to.

"You shouldn't bother with me, Ian," I tried time and time again to say. "I'm not staying. I can't." The confirmation for my training trip finally helped him realize all was lost. I was set to leave. "I'm going to Nairobi," I said. "It's a five-week trip to get there. Depending upon how it goes, I don't know what will happen from there. Sorry Ian. I tried to tell you…"

It was time to leave behind my backpacking adventures, and the two weeks spent in Harare with friends and weird relationship statuses. Till the end, Ian hoped to win me over, but his struggles were for naught—his love shattered, never consummated.

For me, my erstwhile Harare boyfriend quickly become a memory of fun and frivolity, and nothing more. The attention buoyed my ego, but ultimately didn't win my heart. I never looked back. I was bound for Kenya. New adventures lay ahead.

"Life of a Courier"

"Fuck!" I cried. "Fuck, fuck," I spluttered, as I scrambled out of bed and grabbed for clothes and belongings. I jammed everything into my rucksack, cursing all the while.

I should have been at the Phoenix headquarters 50 minutes earlier. Five-zero! Rushing wouldn't help, but damn it, I tried. All I could hear in my head was my mother saying, "you never get a second chance to make a first impression". Well, this one was effectively buggered from the word go. So much for being the model courier in training.

"Damn Ian," I muttered, as I grabbed my toiletries from the bathroom. No time to use them now. "Why did I agree to go out on my last night? For one last 'hurrah'! Shit..."

Never mind that I either slept through or forgot to set my alarm. I couldn't retrieve those precious minutes though. I heaved my pack on my back and ran out the hostel door. Of course, I could only manage to run in short spates. Running wasn't my forte at the best of times, but definitely not with a heavy pack on. I just prayed the truck would still be there.

And it was. Loaded and ready to go, but the truck, passengers, and Kylie and Angus were still there when I ran up breathless with my tail between my legs. "I am so sorry," I gasped as I doubled over in front of my new bosses. I'm certain I deserved the stitches that needled my sides.

258

"Throw your bag under the truck," Kylie said coldly. "We have to go."

I was in no position to argue. I stowed my pack and slunk on board hoping I could eventually improve their opinion of me. In the interim, I also had to meet and impress the passengers. They were set for adventure, and I was supposed to be part of the package to offer them that. So far, I was failing miserably.

Angus swung into the driver's seat and turned to look at everyone on board, "Welcome to Africa!" he cried. "Are you ready for an adventure of a lifetime?"

A few people murmured, but most were still nervous about what lay ahead. We were in Harare and headed North via Zambia and Malawi, through Dar es Salaam, Mount Kilimanjaro, and the Serengeti in Tanzania, and to finish in Nairobi, Kenya in five weeks time. Despite my rocky start, I was on the road again.

God, I'm a loser, I thought to myself, over and over again. Time to make amends.

Over the next few days, Kylie and Angus slowly began to warm up to me. I did my best to be friendly and helpful, and worked hard to listen to everything they said. I had a lot to learn.

Being friendly was only one small part of the job. I had to share knowledge with passengers of where we were and what surrounded us; flora, fauna, and what I knew of the local socio-economic state of wherever we were. There were day trips to book, grocery shopping to undertake, road maps to navigate, not to mention upkeep of the truck. Oh, plus have fun (within reason). We always had to be able to function the next day and my track record already had marks against me on that front.

As with my previous overland trip back in December, time went quickly. In our first few days we visited a game ranch, where everyone was excited by the sight of a plethora of animals, including the elusive rhino. A game of polo cross followed, which set up as the perfect icebreaker for everyone, me included. Plus, it served to warm us up, as the weather was decidedly chilly for Africa. The teamwork and laughter were the perfect remedy for all though.

"Okay everyone, we're off to Great Zimbabwe now," Angus announced.

"Is it alright if I stay on the truck?" I asked Kylie. I'm sure I lost more brownie points by not going with the guests through a historic site, but I didn't care. I had seen the ruins with Miki and Brett, and the dreary weather had me feeling blue. It might have been the dry season, but that May was unseasonably wet; more rain had fallen than they had seen in many years. In truth though, my main complaint was that I missed my old travel companions. Returning to places we had already traversed reinforced that I missed Brett terribly, and I wondered if I had made a mistake leaving him.

Like any overland trip though, you never spend time anywhere long enough to get bored. Everyone excitedly returned to the truck soon enough and we were off to Lake Kyle, followed by Bulawayo. I had mixed feelings about the destination that followed though; Victoria Falls was on the horizon. A favourite place, but also filled with temptation.

Realistically, temptation was everywhere though. And apparently, I was prone to it. Did I really want to work with an overland truck? It didn't seem like it, as every time we came across another overland company, as we did regularly, temptation struck again. Food, transportation, and accommodation were paid for by the company. Beer was as well. And someone didn't seem to have enough good sense to steer clear of it, despite knowing I was on rocky ground with my fellow crew mates. What happened to my decorum and professionalism that was supposed to be the hallmark of a working woman? Beers around a campfire apparently dissolved the image.

By the time we got to Victoria Falls, I was amongst old friends again and enjoyed every minute of it. The first day, I bumped into Nat and Keith while I wandered with a few of the truck's passengers. The night after that, I hung out with Max and Ndaba like they were long-lost friends. My bloodshot eyes stung constantly from lack of sleep and the pax[40] laughed at me for my antics.

"Are you coming white water rafting?" Diane asked.

"Absolutely," I replied.

She was probably the nicest person to me on the whole truck, and I appreciated her kindness. Plus, I fondly remembered the adrenal rush from the last time I hit the rapids in Vic Falls. If they were willing to pay for me to go, I sure as hell wouldn't miss it. It helped me get over my awkward introversion too, as so far, my people skills were awkward at best.

How had I figured that I could shine like the extrovert required of a tour guide? I pushed myself and tried my best. I cheered on Tanya and Mette when they performed beautiful bungee swan dives over the gorge. Not me. I asked how Dave and Adrian's golf game went. Again, not my thing. My

---

[40] passengers.

thing? To see if I would last as an overland truck courier. The odds were stacked against me, but I kept going.

After Victoria Falls, life continued in a tenuous vein. I was shown paperwork, asked to help with the passengers, took my turn at cooking, whatever was asked of me. The love still refused to ooze from Kylie and Angus. My attempts felt pathetic, but I had no choice to keep going.

"Once the passengers head to Zanzibar, we need to do more maintenance on the truck," Kylie announced.

I had already varnished a table in Chitembo, while the passengers climbed Livingstonia. In Karonga, I scraped sand mats with a wire brush and painted truck pieces and stools. And as much as I would have loved to explore the famed Spice Islands, this was a working trip and I needed to earn my keep. More sanding and painting were my trade-off for free room and board.

"Sure, absolutely" I replied, trying to force more enthusiasm than I felt.

While it felt good to physically work, it didn't help the loneliness that encroached. No matter how much black and white paint I slopped around, it didn't mask the memories of my former companion's smiling face. I missed Brett.

What was he doing right now? Surely not sanding truck equipment or fake smiling at strangers who didn't care a whit about him. Even Bob Marley's crooning voice in my walkman didn't help. Bob reminded me of Arnie and freely wandering markets. I wasn't free to go or do anything more than tag along with the group or do as I was told. My labours left me with too much time to reflect and not enough opportunity to belong. I wasn't a welcome member of the crew, and I wasn't a passenger. I was an interloper that didn't fit. There were more countries to explore though.

"Malawi is gorgeous," I said to the girls as we drove along. "It has never-ending white sand beaches and water as blue as the sky. You will love it!"

Of course, it didn't have the same feel as when I had explored with Brett under our own steam, but Malawi's magic was still strong. I still loved the scenery and warmed under the tropical sun, but Malawi is only 840 kilometers long and 580 kilometers of that held the lake from north to south. Even with stops, it didn't take long to leave the lake behind. With Lake Malawi behind us, I found myself in new territory. That territory changed quickly too.

As soon as we crossed the border into Tanzania, the scenery changed. Tea plantations sprang up and stretched to mountainous backdrops. Stately banana palms interspersed the farmed land, making for gorgeous scenery with green valleys as far as you could see.

"We'll make our first bush camp tonight," Angus called back to us, over his shoulder as we drove along. "You'll get the pleasure of sleeping under the African stars!"

While I was excited about the prospect, our passengers weren't overly excited. Not quite as hardy as the group I had travelled with back in December by a long shot, but I enjoyed it anyway. The only problem was that waking to the stars winking out, as the sky moved from inky indigo to the dawn of another new day reminded me of Brett. He was the one who appreciated sunrises and I couldn't help but shed a tear that he wasn't by my side in the dark to appreciate these moments.

"Damn melancholy," I grumbled to myself. "Let me go already. You are in a new country surrounded by plenty of great people from all over the world. Be here." But my strained smile showed cracks, at least to my tired eyes.

What was going on? My dream had been to live and work on the African continent, but now it seemed hollow without a friend in the world to share it with. None of these people would be with me in a few weeks' time, but that was how travel always went. People came and went regularly, and a few weeks was like a lifetime in this nomadic way of being. But I couldn't shake the fact that my birthday steadily approached, and it didn't bode to be a cheery one. This trip would be over and who knew what would happen after that. A tiny hope guttered that I might bump into Brett once more, but our path made it unlikely. It was all I had at that point though. That and Tanzania's changing scenery.

By our second day in the country, the landscape changed from vibrant green to brittle yellow. Mealie patches and dry grasses dominated the landscape, and despite our proximity to the equator, you could tell it was winter. The fading leaves could never compare to Ontario's brilliant displays every autumn, but change was in the air and that was a good thing. I watched mud huts fly by and was reminded that this was an experience of a lifetime. I was in the heart of Africa. One more bush camp to go, but it didn't look like we would get many more of them with this group.

"We'll get to Dar tomorrow," Angus announced as we rumbled along another stretch of Tanzanian back country.

"You are going to have a great time," I remarked to Diane when she worried about the boat trip over to the island. "If I could come with you, I totally would." It wasn't a lie. I would have taken her place in a heartbeat. Sadly, it wasn't an option.

"Maybe you'll get to go on your next trip?" Diane remarked.

Next trip? Would there be a next trip? Time would tell. On this trip anyway, I was part of the work gang. We wouldn't even be in Dar es Salaam proper. After gathering supplies, we headed out of the city to set up camp. Silver Sands was our home until the pax came back. And I wouldn't have time to miss them, what with the chore list at hand. We had picked up truck stuff and it all needed painting. So, I plugged my headphones in and got to work. Hearing UB40 sing about being alone didn't help. Red wine wouldn't help either...I felt as blue as the song and when a character died in the book I was reading, tears finally spilled over. I cried for the lost lover in the story and finally for mine. Somehow, I had shut all the doors, scaled up the walls, and closed my heart to the loss, but that never works. I missed Jack.

At his side, the world looked a little different. We had shared our scars beside a moonlit pond with frogs serenading our embraces. His infectious laugh and sparkling eyes melted the fear that I was never good enough for love. He heaped it around me in poetry, silly dances, and songs, and with trust that I would hold his heart gently in my own. I hadn't even known I was capable of that level of connection, and still desperately clung to the walls that had been my home for so long before him. But he placed our love in the moonlit sky and it would always have a special place in my heart, even as we moved in different directions in our lives. Our steps were no longer in sync, but I knew now that he would always have a place in my life, even if it was just sweet memories. And accepting that he was a memory was hard, especially as loneliness was my only companion.

I missed Jack, Sebastien, Kerry, my Mum, and all my other friends from home. The people who made me feel loved, special, and worthy. No one knew me here and no one cared. Worse, the people around me made me feel like I wasn't doing anything right. Whether that was true or not didn't matter. The point was, that I was lonely. Surrounded by people, but all alone.

I just wish I could explore Dar es Salaam, I wrote in my journal. *Even the return of our passengers would be nice—the only friendly faces I know. They won't be back for a few days yet though...*

I tried not to think about the fact that our reunion would be short-lived. There would only be a day to explore the city before we left for Arusha. From there, the passengers would head into the Serengeti.

Sadly, I would not. My training would be officially done, and I would head to Nairobi, Kenya to learn my fate. There was talk of a five-week overland tour from Nairobi to Harare for me. My evaluation was the only thing that stood in the way. The question was, would my marks make the grade?

"A Taste of Kenya"

It was over. I made it to Nairobi, Kenya, but no further. There were no recommendations from Kylie. Angus gave me a thumbs down. I was not good enough. Considering our formal and distant relationship that never had a chance from the start, it was no surprise, but closure none the less. I was formally thanked and advised that my services would no longer be necessary. I was not cut out to be an overland truck courier. It was the end of the line.

Instead of being depressed by the change in plans, I was oddly relieved. It was freeing in fact. It was terribly obvious that Kylie and Angus had never thought much of me. While I tried to make up for my first gaff five weeks earlier, when I arrived late on our departure day from Harare, my efforts were never top-notch. I had been a backpacker for too long and used to living on my own timeline, with my own agenda. I seemed to hasten my demise every step of the way despite myself. Was that subconsciously on purpose? At this point it didn't matter anymore.

I was in a new country to explore! I didn't have to try to please passengers or fellow crew members. I wouldn't be responsible for other people's well-being or happiness. I could go wherever and do whatever I wanted again. I was free to make my way on my own again.

Now that I knew I wasn't travelling with Phoenix, I had to make alternate plans. The first order of business was to find a new place to stay while I figured out my next step. My current bed was still compliments of Phoenix until the passengers returned from the Serengeti. I was allowed to stay until then, but their return would mark my formal end with the truck. I needed a new home and destination. Both came to me by way of a stranger I met in a takeaway.

After being told I could stay (to say goodbye to the passengers), I ventured into the city in search of some much-needed time on my own. I went to the bank, where I met Charlotte. Her and I went for coffee, and I immediately brightened at the return of random happenings. Later that afternoon, I found myself in a small take-away sipping chai and nibbling chapati. That is where I met Amin and rediscovered my will to travel. He had noticed me sitting alone. I suppose I must have looked conspicuous in a decidedly ethnic neighbourhood. Not many white women wandered alone in those parts. He introduced himself and then sat to join me.

"Hello," he said in English. "I don't mean to be a bother, but I couldn't help noticing you. I'm guessing you are not from around here?"

"No," I said with a laugh. "I'm not."

"You are from Canada, perhaps?" he asked.

"Yes," I said, surprised. "How did you know?"

"I am Canadian too," he said. "My wife and I just moved from Edmonton three months ago."

"Neat!" I replied. I loved how you could meet people from all over the place, including close to home, anywhere you went. "How did you end up in Nairobi?"

"Work," he said. "But I still have ties to Canada. Several clients in Vancouver. It has been an adjustment though. Where have you been in Kenya?"

"Here," I replied half-heartedly. "I was working with an overland company, but things didn't work out. Now I have to figure out how to get back to Cape Town, and then home again."

"If you've only just got here, why don't you explore Kenya then?" he said. "You paid for a visa to get here. Take advantage and see some of the country. Oh! You should go to the Maasai Mara. It is connected to the Serengeti and is a major route for massive wildebeest migrations. A must see, if you can. And Lamu on the coast! It is a pretty little island north of Mombasa. A small Muslim community—no cars, only donkeys to get around. Think about it."

I was intrigued. It all sounded amazing. It seemed wasteful not to take advantage of the visa I had paid for to get into Kenya. I guess in all my loneliness and gloom being rejected, I had almost forgotten that I came to Africa to experience what the continent had to offer. And to embrace the bad with the good. Kenya had plenty of good parts worthy of exploration. Amin's enthusiasm served to remind me.

"Look at the adventure you are on!" he exclaimed when I hesitated. "I wish I could do what you are doing. The places you have been, the things you have seen. Even the most amazing people you have met—like me," he added, with a laugh. "My wife would love to meet you too," he continued in excitement. "She would be thrilled to see a fellow Canadian once again. She misses it very much."

Here I was in a foreign country on an adventure of a lifetime. Sure, I had flubbed my training trip, but Brett had warned me about that. He suggested they weren't all they were cracked up to be. I had gotten stuck on the idea of working in a foreign country to truly experience life here. I didn't take into consideration that working wasn't the same kind of travel and didn't allow for really experiencing the culture. Overland trips were alright for some people, but even if I hadn't gotten off on the wrong foot, I probably never would have really fit in. It just wasn't the right fit.

Amin suggested a much better fit. He painted culture, exploring new places, and being open to the unknown once more. It lit my sense of adventure once more. Somehow, he could see the traveller I was meant to be and knew that I just needed a push to get back to it. Here was fate giving me that nudge once more.

"Well, I have to say goodbye to the passengers from the overland trip I was on before I do anything," I said. "And find a new place to stay…"

"Sunrise!" he declared. "It isn't much, but it's clean."

"You are amazing, Amin, thank you. For everything. You have given me plenty to think about, but first things first. I might have to book a trip into the Masai Mara. You convinced me."

"Excellent!" he said.

"And I would love to meet your wife," I added. "She sounds lovely."

Before that though, I needed to say goodbye to my companions from the trip. While my tour guide trainers had never blossomed into friends, I did have a lot of fun with Di, Tanya, Cathi, Dave, Adrian, Mette, and Camille. They might have had a different experience than mine, but we had travelled together and they were a part of my African experience, nonetheless.

On their return, we ventured out for one last meal together at Carnivores. The restaurant specialized in game meats, which was a fun culinary adventure in itself. But while my enthusiasm was ramping up, theirs wound down. They made ready to return to their respective homes around the world. I happily exchanged addresses with the passengers, whom I had felt more comfortable with than any of the overland crew. I suppose I should have known better.

Now that it was over, I admitted that the experience felt wrong from the start. I should have listened to my gut but did my best to stick it out and hope things would turn around. Nope. The life of an overland truck courier was just not for me. Blame it on being too footloose and carefree in my backpack, but with a light and free heart, I wished overlanding adieu. And didn't miss it in the slightest.

My birthday was days away and would be ushered in alone. I was done moping though. I bought a bottle of red wine, a new camera, and a ticket for a safari into the Masai Mara. My 23rd birthday wasn't exactly what I might have envisioned, but it wouldn't be boring.

As I drove to the Maasai Mara a few days later, I thought about how I could capture the adventure I had been on over the last eight months. I was forever writing in journals. Perhaps I could compile them and write a book? Something along the lines of "The Road Less Travelled", but I suspected that title was already taken. How about "An African Adventure Tale"? I had time, I could work on it. In the interim, I had animals to spy.

*****

Despite my best intentions, a case of the "poor me"s greeted me at dawn on my birthday.

"Happy Birthday to me," I mumbled in my sleeping bag. "Whoop-de-doo. No one knows. No one here cares…"

I should have been thrilled to wake up on the plains of the Maasai Mara, but loneliness edged out joy. It was hard to feel cherished, when there wasn't a friend in sight on a day meant to celebrate me. No off-key birthday songs, no presents, no hugs; not even the dreaded pinch to grow an inch or birthday spankings. My 23rd birthday held none of those things. My present was spending another day in Africa. My company—the wild animals that roamed the bush around me. Honestly, what did I have to complain about?!

My melancholy wouldn't last though. There wasn't time! Breakfast awaited and another game drive lay ahead. While I didn't anticipate the previous day's game drive would be topped—we saw lions, a cheetah, hyenas, giraffes, and thousands of wildebeests—you never knew what you would see. Every drive was different. I shouldn't have underestimated the power of the Mara in July.

"Let's go," came the call.

I climbed out of my tent to another beautiful day under the Kenyan skies. How could I stay blue in such an amazing place? The Maasai Mara was not only a National Game Reserve, but it was also attached to Tanzania's Serengeti National Park. That made for over 31,000 kilometers^2 of barrier-free space for animals to explore unimpeded. Massive migrations happened between the two parks, making for huge game viewing opportunities.[41] And I was in for a special birthday treat. We climbed into our SUV and headed out from camp.

"Look," pointed our guide, after we had driven for a while. A cloud of dust marked a spot where a tussle was underway.

"What is it?" someone asked as we drew closer.

"Oh my god," someone else exclaimed. "The poor thing..."

That poor thing was an impala that had just been run down by five cheetahs. As we stared in awe, the cheetahs caught their breath. Their sides heaved from their exertions, but they were far from done. We might have missed the chase, but now it was time to tear into dinner and we had ringside seats. Our driver pulled to a stop, as everyone's cameras quickly whipped out to capture the scene.

The cheetahs made short work of the small deer. As we watched, it was savagely ripped apart. Ominous growls threatened lesser members of the

---

[41] Masai Mara Travel. (n.d.). Masai Mara Facts. https://www.masaimara.travel/discover-attractions.php#park-history.

coalition who inched too close to neighbours. It was a small meal and didn't go far between them. Even still, opportunistic vultures swooped in, waiting for their turn from the sidelines. This was life on the African plains.

Cheetahs might look like cute cats with furry tear-lined faces and streamlined bodies covered in black spots, but the resemblance ends there. These felines faces were matted with blood. They were far from domesticated, and I, for one, was happy that we were in the relative safety of a SUV. It was the perfect spot to observe the graphic display of life on the savanna. We did our best to not intrude, only punctuating the event with clicks from our cameras and hushed voices murmuring over our good fortune to come across the scene. It was truly a gift to behold.

By the time the cheetahs were done, the vultures only had the meager remains from the stomach and intestines. It didn't go far. Time stood still as we watched, but before we knew it, the cheetahs slunk away to rest and digest. The desperate vultures picked through the grass searching for any missed morsels to no avail. It was all gone in an instant.

"That was incredible," I breathed. "A little taste of the cycle of life. And a great way to mark my birthday!"

"It's your birthday?" the woman beside me exclaimed. "Happy birthday!"

The rest of the jeep chimed in too, until our driver put the SUV in gear and we found ourselves stuck. Just long enough to delay our return to camp, but enough to add another story to the day.

And what a birthday it was! The Maasai Mara exceeded all of my expectations. Tens of thousands of animals roamed the park and we saw plenty of them. The game viewing was made a thousand times better by the fact that the Maasai Mara and the Serengeti were adjoined. A political border might have separated the parks, but that meant little to the animals.

In fact, while I hadn't realized it beforehand, my timing was impeccable. I was just in time for the Great Migration.[42] Millions of wildebeests, zebras, elands, and many other species of antelopes migrate north from the Serengeti into the Mara, between July and October. I was right in the middle of it.

Wildebeests were everywhere. We saw thousands upon thousands of them, everywhere you looked. Our driver drove us into the middle of a herd one day. We were surrounded by black beasts that stretched on and on as far as the eye could see.

"When they cross the river, many of them die," Jimmy said, as we marvelled at the herds. "They do not stop though. Crocodiles attack as they cross the Mara River, but that isn't the only threat. Once they cross over to the Mara's greener pastures, they have to contend with predators: lions, hyenas, leopards, and cheetahs. The great herds number in the millions."

I was properly impressed. Another day, we came upon a line of wildebeests as they crossed a road late in the afternoon. They were lined up in seemingly orderly lines, both single- and double-spaced. When they got approximately 200 metres from the road, they started to run. They sprinted across the road until they cleared it, then slowly shuffled to a walk again. All without breaking rank.

I might have only had four days to enjoy the game park, but we were spoiled beyond belief with animal sightings during that time. They followed

[42] Discover Africa.com. (2021, May 4). What is the Great Migration? Discover Africa.com: Authentic African Safaris. https://www.discoverafrica.com/migration/.

in such a quick succession of sightings that it felt like being in a zoo. We saw a cheetah lazing in the sun with a herd of wildebeest and zebra in the background. Two hyenas munched on a wildebeest, with vultures waiting on the side lines. Even the sight of a tower of giraffes loping along in the African sun was enough to awe me. When we came across four lions stretched out under bushes to avoid the heat of the day, I almost had to pinch myself. Were we in a National Geographic show? It even got into adult-ratings when a male got a short root in. His lady friend didn't let it last long though.

Typical male: after his meal, all he wants is a nap and a piece of action. I saved the running commentary for myself mind you. The company I kept left a little to be desired as far as humour went. I had met many people while traversing the continent, but my current safari mates were a bit dry. No laughter over drinks. No social commentary to accompany rounds of beers. Not much real conversation at all.

You can't have it all, all of the time though. What did I have to complain about? All I had to do was ask and seemingly anything I wanted to see would be presented. Giraffes, lions, cheetahs, wildebeests…check, check, check, check! New animals, please. Got it!

- ✓ Topi
- ✓ Grant's Gazelle
- ✓ Thomson's Gazelle
- ✓ Dik-dik
- ✓ Hartebeest
- ✓ Masai Giraffe
- ✓ Olive baboon

How about the heat? Well, that was unfortunately not in their control. We were almost at the equator after all, and mid-day was punishing.

No matter, it was perfect time for siestas, for both the animals and people, and siestas were the perfect time to record stories from morning adventures while sheltering from the sun. When the worst of the heat abated, there was always a walk to round out the day. Happy birthday to me!

While conversation was stilted with my fellow passengers, it didn't prevent me from chatting with the Maasai people who accompanied us on our game drives and helped out in camp. Language left a bit of a barrier, but many of them knew enough English to have passable conversations. And I couldn't resist learning about everything and anything, if I could.

"How do you do your piercings?" I asked one young man. His long lobes swung loosely almost to his shoulders.

"With a knife, a hole is cut," he said. "Bigger and bigger pieces of wood are put in the hole to stretch it."

"How long did it take to get the size you have now?" You could easily put several fingers through the opening in his ear.

"Two months."

"Wow," I said. "Is there any feeling in them?"

"Yes," he laughed. "Feel it!" And, lord forgive me, but I did. Who was I to judge though? I had enough piercings in my own ears and navel. I was no stranger to the concept, just the extent he had gone. Little did I know how popular plugs and stretched lobes would become back home in the years to come!

Piercings or no, the people were beautiful. The women were stunning, as were the men. They had strong facial features, tall lanky frames, and a sense of dignity I envied. Plus, they managed to retain a measure of their traditional life, while supplementing their income with the tourism industry. A difficult task, but they seemed to manage. And taking it all in was my birthday present to myself.

By the end of the day, I topped off my activities with a luxurious shower and a bottle of Claret Select by Drostdy Hof. It was my last birthday present for the day. I might not have friends or family on hand, but I had abundant game sightings, a nature hike, good meals, and a fine bottle of red wine.

"Hakuna Matata"

'Hakuna Matata' may be a line from *The Lion King*, but I learned it in Kenya, long before I ever saw the movie. And it had nothing to do with lions, warthogs, or any other animals in Africa. No worries, indeed.

I heard this Swahili phrase everywhere I went in Kenya. While perhaps I should have had a worry or two, this phrase stuck with me. It resonated with the life to which I held fast. I had an unwavering faith that everything would work out for me, as I travelled along. So far, that faith had seen me through. I trusted it would continue during the next leg of my journey. No worries…

I gazed out the window of the Sunrise B & B. A throng of taxis waited for a myriad of passengers. Dozens of minivans idled in the square, while people stood in permanent queues in anticipation of their voyages. A constant buzz of traffic, horns, music, and people's voices filled the air.

It wasn't the best neighbourhood, but maybe not the worst either. I did know that once the constant throng of people disappeared at night, the city shut up tight. Bars and metal grates sealed all nearby businesses. Those bars didn't necessarily make me feel secure enough to venture far. Thankfully, I wasn't there long.

The 'Sunrise' had been home before my trip to the Maasai Mara. On this visit though, I was only there for a scant few hours. Long enough to squeeze in another visit with Amin and fulfill my promise to meet his wife, Nour.

"How was the Maasai Mara? As good as I suggested?" he asked when he let me into their little flat.

"It was awesome, Amin. Thank you again for suggesting it. It was the perfect way to celebrate my birthday."

"Your birthday," Nour replied. "Amin didn't tell me it was your birthday. For shame, Amin! We could have made a better celebration for her!"

"He didn't know," I said. "It's alright. Seeing you is celebration enough. I'm happy to be with friends now."

It wasn't a lie. That is how I thought of them. It felt so good to chat with people in such warm tones. Amin and Nour were lovely hosts, despite their meagre home and I cherished the brief time we spent, talking of Canada, travel, Kenya, and how life had a way of twisting on you sometimes.

It was clear that Nour fervently dreamt of her life back in Canada and sorely wished she could return. She missed family, friends, and the easy life she had lived in Edmonton. I could read her loneliness only too well, as she gamely tried to settle into her new home. I suspect I was a bittersweet reminder, but maybe my presence served a purpose too? I don't know. Nour provided me with a packet of goodies for my night bus ride to Mombasa, for which I was ever so grateful in the wee hours when I couldn't sleep. Amin's gift had already worked its magic though. He had given me a reminder to dream and to go with the flow, which restored my faith in the phrase, *Hakuna Matata*.

So, while the road that night would take me on a dangerous new adventure, I was ready for it this time. An overnight bus was scheduled to take me to Mombasa, where I would rejoin the coast. More than one person had warned me of this stretch of road. They told me stories of unlit vehicles which collided in the dark, of the ever-present danger of collisions with unseen animals on the road, not to mention the ominous threat of hijacking. While I tried to take it all in stride, I admit that it worried me. In a different way than Mozambique's hellish route had. But not enough to change my plans.

*****

After leaving Amin and Nour, I made my way back to the bus stop. I stood in line waiting for the bus to arrive. Without assigned seating, we were forced to queue early for the 9:00 p.m. departure. I looked around nervously, eyes peeled for the infamous pick-pocketers I was forewarned about. A collection of strangers surrounded me in the lengthy queue. The languages that surrounded me were foreign, and nothing seemed to link us together. Nothing, but our impending journey. We were all travellers, some further from home than others. And while I am sure some of them may have understood English, my knowledge of Swahili was limited to: *Jambo* = hello, *jambo bwana* = hello brother, and *hakuna matata* = no problem. It wouldn't take me far in an emergency. I prayed I wouldn't have to test the theory.

In that moment, all I wanted was for the bus to leave. I was conspicuously out of place with my worn backpack piled high; backpacks being an uncommon sight in that part of town. All my worldly possessions crammed the bulging pack and were topped by my motley sleeping bag. If that wasn't bad enough, my white skin shone like a beacon against my darker-skinned neighbours. It didn't make me feel any safer. The comparative security of a seat on the bus was what I craved. Of course, a seatmate would create stress too, but relatively less. I didn't sleep well on overnight trips at the best of times, so I didn't look forward to the seven-hour journey. All I could hope for was an uneventful and safe journey. There would be no border crossings, at the very least, so perhaps sleep might sneak in to lessen the hours of worry ahead of me.

I shifted from foot to foot again and glanced at the clock which hung over the platform. Dim lights illuminated the hands of the clock face—9:00 hours. Time to go. All we needed was the bus. One sat at another platform, but nothing graced ours. While Nairobi to Mombasa was a major route between two influential cities in Kenya, I also knew that I was in Africa. African time was *polepole.*

Ah, there was some more Swahili for me: 'polepole' meant slow or slowly. It had a strong link to *hakuna matata,* no worries. We might leave at 9:00, 9:18, 9:43; ultimately, we left whenever the bus finally arrived. No one sweated it or batted an eye. Women sat beside their giant red and blue checked plastic bags, crammed with goods for market, with babies strapped to their backs completely unperturbed. The snug babies slept or silently looked around with large, steadfast eyes. Not a peep was made. Men laughed and joked with other men or amused themselves with games.

I tried to embrace the polepole[43] schedule but found myself glancing to the clock again and again. It was hard to shake the regulated schedule of life back home. Plus, I was nervous of my next stop. Mombasa was a new city for me. And one I would face alone. This was the first time since arriving in Africa that I would travel all by myself. Up to this point, there was family, friends, or tour companies to coordinate the itinerary. Now it was just me.

My plans were loosely based. I had no concrete destination in Mombasa, nor beyond. Now was not the time to consider the craziness of the situation though. This was the nature of backpacking. For the time being, as with the rest of my African journey, I had to live in the moment.

The headlights of a bus swung into the parking lot, and I breathed a ragged sigh of relief. It pulled up to our platform and stopped with a release of air brakes. It might take a while to get people and baggage loaded, but we would leave soon enough. My smile returned, as I allowed myself to think about the adventures that lay ahead. Time to go! New destinations beckoned and I was ready.

"Friends Along the Way"

I loved that the process of making new friends seemed to happen at the drop of a hat while travelling, and it didn't take long this time either. Your backpack acts like a calling card and people gravitate to it, like moths to a flame. Differences disappear in the rhythm of the road, and you embrace people based on smiles alone.

---

[43] slow, slowly.

At home, you pass a million faces and don't stop to look at any of them. Or worse, you don't talk to anyone for fear of the 'what ifs' or dreaded 'maybes' that could befall you from the 'strangers' that fill the world. In Africa though, all those strangers were friends whom I just hadn't met yet. And as I ambled along in Kenya, I was ready and keen to meet them all. Stuart and Rob were my newest acquaintances.

After the long and, thankfully, uneventful night bus from Nairobi to Mombasa, I quickly moved on to the smaller beach city of Malindi. After Amin's pep talk, I planned to travel as far north as I could get, then explore anything I missed in more depth when I returned south again. Malindi was only 100 kilometers north of Mombasa and was home to better beaches, which I craved after being inland. There wasn't much beyond the beach, but it happened to be where I met Rob.

Rob was a quiet sort. It was funny that we connected at all, as he was an interesting fellow with a weird feel to him, but that was the way that travelling went. We were both on the move, staying at the same hostel, and planning a route North.

"Whereabouts are you headed?" I asked Rob. "I have heard amazing things about a little fishing village called Lamu, just north of here."

"I was going to stop there, too," he replied.

"Do you want to go together?" I asked. "Safety in numbers kind of thing?"

"The road is supposed to be kind of dodgy," he said. "I've heard that patrols stop vehicles along the route all the time. Not sure when you were thinking of going, but I was aiming to leave tomorrow."

"I can make that work," I replied, happy to have a companion for the bus ride.

I had already experienced enough public transit alone to know that it was better to have company. Even if that company was a little odd. Aren't we all weird in our own way? Ultimately, being a traveller made anyone alright in my books.

So, after two days, I bade Malindi goodbye, and Rob and I climbed on board a bus to Lamu. No fancy bus terminals here. The bus stopped on the side of the dusty highway to pick us up and then we were off again. We plunked into a seat and settled in for the three-hour drive, barring any unforeseen stops.

Ahead of us sat another backpacker. As we sat down, he turned in his seat and smiled.

"Hi," he said. "How far are you going?"

"We're on our way to Lamu," I replied.

"Me too!" he exclaimed. "My name is Stuart."

"Nice to meet you Stuart," I said. "This is Rob, and my name is Katherine."

The chitchat flowed from there. Stuart had travelled solo from Mombasa and seemed a decent sort. As we laughed and got to know each other, Rob lapsed into a companionable silence. He occasionally piped in a comment here or there, but it quickly became apparent that my rapport with Stuart was stronger.

"What do you think of sharing a flat once we get to Lamu," Stuart suggested as we neared the village. "It might help us get a better place. Stretch our funds a bit more..."

"Sounds good to me," I answered.

My dollars appreciated stretching at that point, so sharing a flat was a great plan in my books. Plus, I sensed Stu would be a better travelling companion than Rob, who was a little reluctant to add travellers to his roster.

"Alright," he added, begrudgingly.

To be honest, Stuart was more my speed as far as travelling companions went. We had similar taste in music and food, and conversation flowed easily between us. By the time the bus pulled up to the ferry dock, I felt like I had known him for years.

"I can't wait to see Lamu," I said as we waited for the ferry that would take us across to the island.

"Look," Stuart laughed, pointing across the short expanse to the island. "You can see it from here!"

"I know, silly," I laughed. "But up close..."

He stepped into my face and said, "Better?"

"No!" I said as I playfully pushed him away.

"Here comes the ferry," Rob remarked dryly, pointing to the small boat that approached.

Stuart was definitely a lot more fun, and I mentally thanked my travelling fairy godmother for placing him in the seat ahead of us on the bus. He was going to make Lamu far more entertaining.

The ferry docked and, once it was secure, we were ushered onboard. As there was no car traffic to load or unload, the process was swift, and we were across the channel quickly. In fact, the only a single vehicle allowed on the small island belonged to the local constable. The only mode of transit on the island nation was either your feet or one of the many donkeys that wandered aimlessly in the narrow streets.

We were polepole[44] bound and I was completely alright with that as Lamu shimmered in front of us, like an oasis ripe for exploring. Accommodation was cheap and travellers had their pick from the many locals who swarmed the dock to offer lodging. I was ready to slow down to island life pace.

"Lazy Days in Lamu"

"Ash-hadu ana Mu-ha-mud-ar rah-sool all-ah..."

I rolled over in bed. Lazy days in Lamu began with a call to worship. Mosques on the small island rang their bells five times a day to call resident Muslims to prayer. It was a loud, regular reminder of one's responsibility to Allah. I was not one of them, but heard the call, nonetheless.

While I didn't jump up to join, I found the island community fascinating. Just two degrees south of the Equator, the population held a rich tapestry of local history. Residents hailed from Chinese shipwreck survivors

---

[44] slowly.

from the 14th century, local Swahili people, Portuguese explorers, Turkish traders, and Omani Arabs. You could see the influences reflected in the narrow streets, numerous markets, even more mosques, and gently bobbing dhows that nestled in the harbour. Time seemed to stand still on this exotic island that begged one to slow down and stroll at its pace. The only catch— you needed to watch for donkey droppings underfoot.

During my time in Lamu, I spent mornings at one of the two balconies we had in our flat. The world drifted by, as I leisurely sat with a book in hand. It seemed hard to believe I was in the heart of Africa, as I gazed out on the vibrant culture that teemed around me. Men sauntered along narrow streets, directing the occasional kick towards wayward donkeys that refused to get out of their way. Women weren't overly visible; their presence was subtle, presumably due to strict religious decrees. It was seen in laundry strung between narrow alleys and the sounds and smells of locals going about their days—people preparing chapati, sweet tea, and numerous crafts to sell to the many tourists who descended upon the tiny island for a taste of the exotic.

The lure of the island was strong, and I spent plenty of time exploring its narrow streets. I had never seen such diminutive roads. They were no more than six to eight feet across. Once you stepped into them, you realized why vehicles were banned. There was nowhere they could go! The little island was a perfect haven for pedestrians intent on strolling nowhere.

Of course, sometimes a destination was handy. For that, I searched out Ali Hippy. He was a local who took immense pleasure in befriending tourists. That was my experience of him, anyway.

"Jambo," Ali called out from my favourite café. He was always around somewhere.

"Hello," I replied.

"No, no," he replied. "Njema[45]. You say njema—you're fine. That is the response to jambo—which means hello, or how are you?"

"Okay," I replied. "nejameh…?"

"No. Njema."

He would say it over and over, until I got a close approximation of it, then he would launch into that day's diatribe. Often, it was religion. As I was relatively unfamiliar with Islam, he took the time to explain some of the intricacies of his faith.

"You should read the Quran," he said as he pulled out his own small copy. "Here, read this…"

And we would go back and forth, me asking questions about Muslim life and expectations, and him finding passages that illustrated the faith he knew and loved. I learned much, and not just religious studies. I asked about island life, as often as not too.

"Where are the mango trees?" I inquired one day as I sipped yet another freshly pressed mango smoothie.

"They do not grow here," he replied. "They come on the ferry like everything else." Tourism and the artisan market were the only things that grew here. But it was peaceful in a way that soothed the soul and helped me recentre myself. I needed it. And Ali was a welcome part of that recentring.

---

[45] it's good.

"Want to go to the beach?" Stuart asked one afternoon.

While we could see the ocean from all sides, the nearby harbour wasn't safe for swimming. The beach was a 45-minute walk to the other side of the island, but I was game. Plus, it gave us the opportunity to see a little of the local flora and fauna, thus giving a larger picture of life on the island oasis. There were sand dunes, mangrove thickets, beaches, plenty of dhows out at sea, and a donkey sanctuary for the thousands of donkeys that wandered the island. You knew you were off the tourist track too, as no amenities were found on the dirt track that ran between Lamu Town and Shela Beach. It served to make me appreciate what we returned to; namely a reliable source of running water, ample beds for the three of us, plus room for plenty more if needed.

The apartment was a rare luxury in my journey thus far. Hostels, tents, and overland trucks were my usual fare, but there was something about coming home to our own space that I appreciated. Not that it was a five-star resort—far from it! It was a good deal at 1,050 Kenyan shillings (KES) a week, but the bugs...I could have done without them. I never got used to the scurry of cockroaches, ants, and spiders that scattered in all directions when the lights flicked on. The downside of our backpacker's paradise...

What did that matter in the grand scheme of things though? It was easy enough to let it all go over another mango smoothie or a seafood dinner at a local's home. It was a lesson in travelling, perhaps a lesson in life—if you could look past the occasional bugs and bothers, life was indeed a paradise worthy of anyone's time. It was all a matter of perspective.

*****

THE LONG ROAD HOME

"Heading South"

"I think it's time," I said to myself with a sigh.

My money belt was feeling light, and I was a long way from the airport that would fly me home. Leisurely days of sipping freshly squeezed juice and dining on seafood extravaganzas with locals and other tourists were at an end. It was relatively cheap to stay in Lamu, but I could no longer hide from the inevitable. It was time to move on once more.

"It's been fantastic, but I have to say goodbye," I said to Stuart and Rob. "Home is calling, which means I have to make my way to Cape Town."

They were headed north, so I set off solo once more. I caught the ferry back to the mainland, trudged to the dusty highway, then flagged down the bus headed to Mombasa. It seemed old hat by this point. After peaceful days in Lamu, I no longer dwelt on the threat of road-side attacks. Not even the sight of armed guards joining us for part of the journey bothered me overly much. I reached Mombasa no worse for wear.

Despite my original plan, I still only managed one night in Mombasa on my second tour through. Forward momentum propelled me along, plus the not-so-subtle reminder that time and funds were of the essence. My brief visit to Mombasa did bring one treat though—an ice cream date with Renée 'Deutsch'. As with so many other travellers, Renée was a friendly face when I needed it the most. He treated me to ice cream and even bought me breakfast the next morning before my bus left for Dar es Salaam. A gentleman through and through, I thanked my lucky stars that fate brought me so many good souls along the journey. He shared laughs and conversation and restored my faith in humanity once more. If you look for them, the universe puts angels on your path, and Renée was one of them. His kindness stayed with me as the day wore on. Many hours lay ahead of me and the bus trip was slated to be long.

The journey between Mombasa and Dar es Salaam was supposed to be 12 to 13 hours. I had a few refreshments for the drive, but you couldn't always plan for uncertainties. I should have known better, already having spent nine months travelling in Africa. A border crossing usually threw a kink into things. But I was still hit by surprises.

So, I climbed onto the bus in Mombasa and found a seat. I was the only white face aboard the bus and one of few who spoke English. Nothing new, but it still made me nervous.

"Jambo," said a man who turned in his seat to look at me.

"Hello," I responded, relieved that perhaps I might have someone to talk to on the long journey ahead. I forgot my lessons from Ali Hippy though. An 'njema' might have worked better in my favour and made the ultimate bus ride more pleasant.

The man laughed and called out to fellow passengers around us. While his face held a smile, he skipped between English and his native tongue rapidly, talking both to me and directing a whole other dialogue to the people around us. The women seated nearby tittered nervously, then looked away in embarrassment. I might not have understood the words, but it seemed obvious that I was the brunt of some sort of nastiness. His laughter was loud and unpleasant, and seemed to grow with the reaction from both myself and our fellow travellers.

I turned to the window and tried to ignore the taunts, hoping he would lose interest in the sport of abusing the mzungu[46] amongst them. But the fun was just beginning, and the road lay long in front of us. I plugged into my headphones to drown out his churlish barbs.

Unfortunately, the journey grew longer than anticipated though. After two and a half hours on the bus, we reached the border, and everyone was ushered off to go through customs. Again, I was singled out by the obnoxious man, but this time there was no place to turn. I did my best to ignore him while I waited my turn in queue like everyone else. We all had enough to worry about with border guards glaring down at us, let alone from someone intent on making me feel scared.

"Pasipoti yako iko wapi[47]?" a uniformed man demanded of me roughly once I got to the front of my queue.

I might not have understood the words but knew enough to hand over my passport. Everything was in order, so I was quickly stamped and moved aside. Now though, I was at the mercy of the rest of the passengers on the bus. Them, their paperwork, and the goods they carried. We couldn't go anywhere until cleared customs.

Officials rifled through women's enormous shopping bags as they unpacked the stowed luggage. Border guards checked and double-checked documents. Queues seemed to stall out, as the wait got longer and longer. My tormentor continued to heckle me throughout, until I finally wandered away to look for a bathroom. An outhouse stood not far off, but I almost threw up when I opened the door.

---

[46] traveller; derogatory term for outsider.
[47] where is your passport?

"Nope," I said to myself as I backed away from the feces smeared hole.

No amount of hovering could induce me to step inside that fetid box. I wasn't above squatting a bush pee like everyone else. Plus, the escape gave me the opportunity to move further away from where my bully stood. I preferred being alone to dealing with his passive aggressive behaviour while we waited.

By the time the border agents finally finished, I wearily re-entered the bus and looked for a new seat. A young man shyly smiled and ushered me to the seat beside him.

"You sit here?" he beckoned. I gladly took him up on his offer.

"You speak English?" I asked hopefully.

"Not so good," he apologized. English might not have been his first language, but he managed well enough for us to have a conversation.

"Where you go?" he asked.

"Today, to Dar es Salaam," I replied. "But I am on my way to South Africa."

After we had talked for a while, I couldn't resist asking about the other man who had badgered me earlier.

"He say not so nice things," he said. "Make many people uncomfortable, but they no want say anything. I am sorry he make bad impression of Tanzania. We not all so... rude."

"No, no, not at all," I reassured him. "You have been lovely, very polite and helpful. Thank you!"

We chatted for a while, but the hours ran long, and conversation lulled into sleep around us. Eventually our driver gave in as well and pulled over to rest for a few hours himself. No one could keep their eyes open, after the long border crossing and extended day. By 6:00 a.m., we finally pulled into Dar es Salaam.

"You have room to stay?" my seat mate asked as we slowed on the outskirts of Dar.

"No," I admitted. "I figured I would find someplace once I arrived."

"I take you to good place," he insisted. "Then we go breakfast." I was too exhausted to protest and was grateful for his help. We dropped off my backpack and he took me for a simple breakfast of chapati and tea. It was delicious, but I couldn't stop yawning.

"I'm sorry," I said, as I hid another yawn. "I really need to get some sleep. Maybe we can meet up later, but right now, I need to crash."

"Yes, yes," he answered, embarrassed to have apparently put me out in the slightest.

I was too tired to correct him and gratefully followed him back to the hostel. I waved goodbye, then headed straight for my room where I briefly scribbled an account from my last few days in my journal. Some much-needed sleep curtailed too many words though and my eyes slipped closed despite myself. Dar es Salaam would be there to explore when I woke up.

"Dreaming in Dar"

I turned out the light and figured I would be asleep before my head hit the pillow. My two-hour nap on the extended bus ride from Mombasa left me feeling more ogre than beauty queen, and I planned to sleep the day away to try and remedy that. It was nine o'clock in the morning, but I figured Dar es Salaam could wait. I was exhausted and needed sleep pronto. No sooner had my head touched down, then a knock roused me back to the land of the living.

"Ugh," I grumbled to myself. "No." I scrunched my eyes more firmly shut and whimpered, "Go away…"

I needed sleep! Who was at my door? Was it the Good Samaritan from the bus, hoping that I was exaggerating my need for sleep and maybe thinking he could get an invite in? Perhaps the front desk wanting to impart some imperative missive about the hostel they had forgotten to share? I knew no one else in Dar es Salaam. And I was exhausted! Perhaps if I ignored it, they would just go away?

A second knock cheerily tapped on the door, and I rolled over with a sigh. Fine! Hold your horses! I pulled open the door and my grumpiness melted. There at my door stood a jovial, red-haired giant. At 6'3", this stranger immediately dazzled me with his beautiful, hazel-green eyes. A smile lit up his face.

"Hello," he said. "I saw your name on the register when I signed in. You got here just before me. I wondered if you would like to explore Dar with me?" His thick South African accent charmed me back to fully awake, and I found myself smiling up at this beautiful man. Was it love at first sight? Damn close!

"I would love to," I replied, suddenly self-conscious of my rumpled clothes and sleepy gaze.

"Neale," he said, as he held out a hand in greeting.

"Katherine," I said, as I took his warm hand in my own.

Yeah, it was love. I would gladly wander to the ends of the earth with this man. Whether it was the lack of sleep or general good manners though, I paused. Maybe I was being hasty? Should I really throw myself at a stranger, when I was little able to use my best judgement? Sure, I wanted to spend more time with this handsome man, but I also needed sleep.

"I'm sorry," I fumbled. "I'm exhausted. I was on a night bus from Mombasa and just got in. I would love to see Dar with you, but I really need to get a few hours of sleep first. Could we poke around the city this afternoon?"

There was no way I wanted to miss out on getting to know Neale, but a little sleep would definitely make me more engaging, if nothing else. A shower wouldn't hurt either.

"No worries," he said with an understanding nod. "I'll hold you to it though. I'll be back in a few hours to pick you up?"

"Perfect," I said as I eased the door closed. "See you soon, Neale." Oh my god! Did that just happen, I wondered? But sleep won out. I plunked back on the bed and drifted off to sleep almost immediately.

Dreamland didn't erase the memory of my visitor though. I woke a few hours later with a luxurious smile playing across my face. My brain might have needed sleep, but it vividly remembered my new friend, Neale.

Oh, sweet promise, what would the day hold? I stretched, cat-like, in my little cot, then jumped out of bed.

"I have to have a shower!" I cried. "What am I going to wear?"

What could I wear indeed? I rifled through my scruffy backpack but found scant options. Everything was almost worn threadbare. And none of it seemed fit to impress the South African lad I had promised to meet that afternoon. There wasn't time to do anything about that though. It would have to be my slowly fading gypsy skirt: the most feminine thing on offer, not to mention that it still fit. Somehow a few pounds had begun to creep up on me and my body was beginning to show it. My hair hadn't been cut in months either and any makeup I may have had at the beginning of my trip was long since gone. All I could do to gussy myself up was brush my hair and put on my sparkliest smile. It would have to do. And you know what? I think it was perfect!

Once the mirror gave a half-hearted nod of approval, I took a big breath and headed downstairs. Neale sat downstairs in the common area of the hostel patiently waiting for me.

"I hope you haven't waited long," I said, while I secretly hoped he felt his wait was worthwhile.

"Nah, it's alright," he said with a smile. "Shall we?"

"We shall," I answered.

We headed out into a bright afternoon and leisurely meandered through the city; markets, side streets, wherever our feet took us. Conversation flowed between us like we were long-lost friends. We talked about where we had been, where we were from, and everything in between.

I giggled like a schoolgirl at his witty sense of humour. His dazzling smile lit my cheeks with a natural blush that money couldn't buy. I forgot my tired appearance and bubbled to life in his presence. He seemed honest and truthful, which was a breath of fresh air after some of the conniving men who had tried to woo me in other ports. I was present in a way that I didn't want to stop any time soon.

"What d'ya think of grabbing a drink?" Neale asked as the afternoon wore on.

"Sure," I replied eagerly. "That sounds great. Where do think?"

We had passed plenty of stores and restaurants, but honestly, I had seen little more than his smile. It felt like so long since I had been genuinely charmed, that I didn't care where we went or what we did. I was in the moment and didn't want to be anywhere else.

Neale pointed out a local pool hall, "How about there?"

"Looks good," I replied. "Looks like a place locals frequent." That was always a plus in my books. It made the experience more authentic somehow, and this was nothing if not that.

"Do you want a beer?" Neale asked. "Maybe share a pitcher?"

"Sounds good."

"Right," Neale replied with a smile. He steered me towards a table, then raised his hand to get the servers attention.

"Do you prefer a lager, ale, something heavier?" he asked.

"I'm easy," I answered, then blushed madly at the implications. "I mean, I will drink anything. Whatever is on offer..." Oh man, lush alert! And easy? What was I thinking? But Neale took it in stride and soon enough a frosty pitcher lay between us. He poured me a glass with a flourish and offered it to me, before pouring one for himself as well.

"To Dar es Salaam," he offered, with a raised glass.

"To Dar es Salaam," I agreed, as I clinked his glass with my own and smiled over my glass at him.

"This is really lovely," I offered. "I am so glad you knocked on my door. I am having an amazing afternoon."

In fact, I couldn't remember the last time I had felt so pretty and doted upon in such a sweet manner. Neale pulled out my chair, rested his hand on the small of my back to steer me around obstacles, and seemed genuinely interested in what I had to say. I was smitten and that was long before the alcohol started to take effect. I wanted more than just an afternoon with Neale and prayed the day would never end. Our eyes were locked on each other, and I couldn't tear my gaze away.

"Habari," a young man said with a smile, as he stopped at our table. "Excuse me for interrupting, but my name is Nimesh. I couldn't help but notice you and felt it my duty to say hello. How do you like Dar es Salaam? Is our beautiful city living up to the expectations of you and your lovely wife?" I wondered for a moment who he was talking about, then realized he meant me! Ha!

"Oh," I laughed. "No, no, I am not his wife."

298

Neale winked and said, "Not yet. We've only just met today. My name is Neale. Nice to meet you." They shook hands, and Neale turned to introduce me as well.

"Really? Just today?" Nimesh replied in surprise. "I cannot believe that. Oh well, I do not think this will be the only day you spend together."

"Nah, brother," Neale said. "I hope not either." I hoped he was right too. The chemistry that flared between Neale and I was heady. But Nimesh's friendliness was a welcome addition to our afternoon as well.

"How about a game of pool then, my friends," Nimesh challenged us. "I want to hear what brings you to our fair city!"

Several games of pool later, we tottered out of the bar, bidding our new friend Nimesh good night. Neale held me close, as we headed back to the hostel arm in arm. I couldn't believe the events of the last 12 hours and still didn't want it to end, but the day had slipped away on us unawares.

The next morning, I lazily stretched and cracked an eye onto the new day. An unfamiliar room greeted me. Not surprising really, as most nights I rested my head in different locations. Today was different though. A warmth in bed beside me brought back the day before. I was not alone. Neale breathed deeply beside me, still blissfully asleep.

Oh my god! I thought to myself. *Frig, what have I done? Jumping the gun a little bit, Girlfriend. Shit! Ok,* I reasoned in a panic. *Maybe I should just quietly slip out before he wakes up and this gets awkward?*

With a pang of regret, I slowly eased a leg towards the edge of the bed. Just as I was almost free and trying to figure out how to quietly find my things without waking my sleeping companion, a strong arm reached out and drew me back. Neale pulled me back into his warm embrace and gently kissed my bare shoulder. That was it. I blissfully melted back into him. With a sigh, I cuddled into Neale's chest and closed my eyes again.

"Morning," he said.

"Good morning," I replied, as I opened my eyes to gaze into the brilliant green pools of his eyes. How could these joyful thoughts be a bad thing? I was the happiest I had been in months. Neale's generous grin filled my heart and more.

"Thinking of going somewhere, Beautiful?" he asked teasingly.

"Not anymore," I said with a smile. Not on your life. I was quite happy to stay like that forever.

"Leaving on a Jet Plane"

Neale and I were constant companions over the days that followed. After I spent a second night in his larger room, we decided to pass on keeping up appearances and I moved in with him. There was no point in us both paying for rooms if we were only going to use one. You couldn't separate us if you tried. We wandered city streets, chatting, laughing, holding hands, and finding quiet corners to share a passionate kiss or two. We met back up with Nimesh for a personalized tour of the city as well. Neither Neale nor I had much cash available in our pockets, but that did not dampen our euphoric spirits. Burgeoning love fed our souls.

The problem was that the more time Neale and I spent together, the less we wanted to be separated. In Dar es Salaam that wasn't a problem, but neither of us had the money to stay put and the city was quickly losing its appeal. We were both travellers and our feet itched to move on. Neale was headed north. After my failed attempt at being an overland courier, I still drifted and sought direction for which way to go next. I felt like home vaguely called my name, but Africa was in my blood, and I loathed the idea of leaving. Temptation arose and I had no good reasons to turn it down. Neale's hearty laugh and generous compliments had me in favour of pretty much anything he suggested.

"Come with me to Cairo," he asked one morning.

I had always wanted to see Egypt, but while the idea of it was exciting, a few worries crept in. Was it really a good idea to traipse across the continent with a virtual stranger? Hmm. Well, I had done that for the last nine months with a steady stream of strangers, many of whom I knew even less than Neale. So that was easy enough to write off.

If we went to Egypt together though, how, and when would I get back to Cape Town, or Canada for that matter? A harder question to answer, but Neale's enthusiasm was infectious and erased any doubts I may have offered. Be present and trust in the miracle of the moment. I had travelled long enough to know that you needed to trust your instincts when the fates presented new opportunities. If it felt right, then it was meant to be. How could I not jump on board?

"Okay!" I cried.

All that stood in the way, was the means to get there. So, over a cheap beer in our favourite pub, we decided that we would leave for Cairo as soon as we could muster up plane tickets. Giddy with anticipation, we finished our pitcher and wandered home arm in arm for the night. The plan was to find a travel agent in the morning and leave on a jet plane to Cairo as soon as we were able.

Excitement got the best of us in the morning. Luxuriant snuggles were temporarily curtailed, as we had a bigger plan—we were in search of plane tickets that day. Cairo waited for us. That was just the tip of the iceberg though. Israel was a hop and skip from there. Europe was on its doorstep. We could travel the world together! The sky was the limit!

It all started with a trip to the travel agent though. Actually, it started with a phone book—to figure out where to locate a travel agency. It wasn't something we had noticed in our wanders. Address attained, we dressed and headed out.

I felt like a naughty teenager arranging to skip class but didn't stop to think about the consequences. We would fly to Cairo and figure life out from there. What fun!

"I've always wanted to see the Pyramids of Giza and the Great Sphinx," I said as we made our way across town. "Not to mention the bazaars, the people, the food..."

I could barely contain myself. We would be stepping onto a plane heading north in a matter of days, if not hours! I squeezed Neale's hand at the thought of all we would see and do together. Across town, we found the travel agent and stepped into a small, clean room, covered in travel posters. Two desks sat waiting for clients to dream of adventure.

"Hello," a pleasant-looking young woman said. "Can I help you with anything?"

"Yes," Neale replied. "We want to go to Egypt."

"As soon as possible, if we can," I added. "And um, maybe as cheaply as possible?"

"Of course," she said with a smile, as she waved us to one of the waiting desks. "Please, take a seat."

She poured through timetables and looked at price tags, then turned to us with a smile. "Would tomorrow do?" she inquired.

"Yes!" we replied in unison, as we smiled at one another at our good luck.

"Oh my god!" I squealed. "I'm so excited!"

"I'll just need your information and we can go ahead and book everything."

I pushed my passport across the desk to her and squeezed Neale's hand. We would be headed for Cairo the next day! A measly six-hour flight would touch us down in a whole new country, as well as a new hemisphere in Africa for me. It was over 4,000 kilometers, and I had no idea how I would be able to get back to Cape Town (where my plane ticket back to Canada departed from), but none of that mattered. Tap, tap, tap, went the keyboard, as she typed in my particulars.

"And how would you like to pay?" she finally asked, as she looked up at us.

I dug for my credit card and pushed it across the desk to her. The tapping stopped, then she punched numbers into the credit card machine. It buzzed and beeped and groaned for ages. Finally, the woman frowned.

"There appears to be a problem with your card," she said.

"What do you mean?" I asked. *What the...?*

"I can try again," she said in apology, but shook her head once more as she handed me the machine, so I could see the explanation.

"CONTACT CREDIT CARD COMPANY," it read.

Oh, oh. This wasn't part of the plan.

"No problem," she said, as I now looked nervously on. "I will call to see if we can solve this."

The travel agent dialed the phone number on the machine, and explained the situation to the representative, then handed me the phone. After a round of identification questions, a handful more questions, plus some of my own, the answer was presented to me—INSUFFICIENT FUNDS. Our plans rapidly started to unravel. My credit card was at its limit. I could not use my debit card in Tanzania, and I only had a $50 USD travellers cheque left, as well as small amounts of currency from the last half dozen countries I had been to. Essentially, I was broke.

"That's alright," Neale said. "I can pay, and we'll figure it out later." He handed over his credit card to pay for both tickets.

"I will pay you back as soon as I figure out what's going on," I promised.

Once I got a hold of my mom, I knew I could sort out my finances and pay him back quickly. It shouldn't take long at all, and the money would be back in his pocket in no time. Fate had other plans though. Our beleaguered travel agent shook her head once more.

"It too has been denied," she replied handing the card back.

We were both flat broke. We couldn't even afford one ticket to Cairo between the two of us, let alone tickets for both of us to go. No phone calls or other desperate measures would help. Forlornly, we walked out of the travel agency empty-handed.

"What are we going to do?" I said, abjectly.

"We'll figure it out," Neale replied gamely with a squeeze, but I wasn't so sure.

So often I had listened to fate as I travelled, and this time it didn't seem to lean in my favour. Our dreams of Cairo were fizzling miserably. Without plane tickets, the distance loomed large. There were 6,000 kilometers between Dar es Salaam and Cairo. Only 5,000 kilometers stood between Dar and Cape Town. As much as I fought against it, the odds leaned towards heading south and my original destination.

"Let me see if I can make a few phone calls," Neale said as we wandered towards a public phone booth. I nodded and gazed towards the crowds around us. Everyone seemed to have a purpose, as they bustled around us. It was just us cast adrift, I mused sadly.

"You're looking lost," a voice broke into my thoughts. I turned to a gentleman standing beside a jeep. His accent was American, and the logo splashed across the vehicle marked him as a tourist, like me.

"Waiting for a friend," I replied, forcing a smile. "Where are you heading to?" I added, gesturing towards the jeep.

"Just finishing up a tour. My passengers are doing the last of their sightseeing and I'll be saying goodbye to them tomorrow. After that, it's back to Zambia for me to pick up a new group. What about you?" he asked. "It doesn't sound like you are from around here. What's your story?"

"No," I laughed. "I'm not. I was going to go to Cairo, but there's been a change in plans. Cape Town might be my new destination. I just have to figure out some finances."

The man paused for a moment considering. "My name's Eddie. I own Tusker; this American safari company," he said gesturing at the jeeps. "I've got two vehicles heading to Victoria Falls the day after tomorrow. If you are in a pinch, I can get you that far. Just cost you for food."

Neale walked up at that moment and said hello. I looked from him to Eddie and instinctively knew that my plans had changed once more. I was being offered free transportation south. Victoria Falls was halfway to Cape Town. As much as I didn't want to agree, it didn't feel like I had much choice under the circumstances. How could I say no?

"Thanks, Eddie," I said. "My name's Katherine. Can I get back to you this afternoon?"

"Sure," he said. "Think about it. I'll be here again around 4:00 p.m."

"Think about what?" Neal asked.

I turned to him and my heart sank. It was no good. I knew the fates had butted in once more and I couldn't refuse. We weren't going anywhere. It was time for me to go home.

"Hindu Celebrations"

"I'll find you," Neale said with a kiss. "I'll call…"

My arms dropped to my sides, as he stepped onto the bus. A moment later, it turned a corner and disappeared. Nimesh stood beside me and respectfully let me have a moment. In the end, it had been him who lent Neale enough money to catch a bus north. Neale was off to Nairobi in hopes of finding a cheaper flight from there. I was not. And with Neale gone, my heart no longer thrummed with adventure.

"Let's go home," Nimesh said kindly, breaking my sad thoughts.

"Yes," I replied, as I wiped the tears from my cheek.

Home, my mind echoed. *It was time.* Nimesh led the way.

Home wasn't a bed in my mother's house, nor was it anywhere at Neale's side. It was somewhere in between for the time being. Today, it was Nimesh's house.

Nimesh had swooped in with a protective wing when he heard mine and Neale's dilemma. He offered Neale a loan and me a place at his family's place for my last night before I left Dar myself. Home would be a piece of floor in the corner of their living space. The next day I planned to hitch a ride south with Eddie. So, with heavy heart, I followed Nimesh through the familiar streets of Dar es Salaam, now a little emptier without Neale's warm heart beside me. We headed towards the outskirts of the city.

Despite my sad spirit, I recognized the honour it was to get an invitation to stay with Nimesh. He lived with his parents and brother in a small home which consisted of two bedrooms and a kitchen. It was comfortable, if not spacious. There was no running water inside, but a tap stood handy outside to fetch water for all their needs. No real water closet was available either, but they did have a private latrine. I had been in Africa long enough to not balk at their primitive hole in the ground. Their "toilet" was cleaner than many I had seen along my voyage.

In fact, I was overjoyed that Nimesh's family agreed to take me in for the night at all. For them, a visitor was a cause for celebration, so as soon as I arrived, the party began. There was no time to entertain sad thoughts, as I was dragged into the centre spotlight of a grand hoopla. It was shoes off and time for festivities. Jasvanti, Nimesh's mother, took me in hand and hugged me warmly.

"Nimesh has told me so much about you and your husband," she said. "How did you meet? He is South African and you Canadian, yes?"

"Uh, yes," I stammered, staring at Nimesh in confusion. What had he told his mother about Neale and I?

"How long have you been married? When will you meet up again?" The questions had me scrambling for answers, but I did my best to answer.

"I am going to South Africa now and Neale will meet me there," I said. "From there, we go to Canada." I hoped no Hindu Gods would strike me down for the little white lies that seemed necessary to maintain a sense of decorum for my generous hosts.

"Here, have some tea," Jasvanti offered, as she bustled back and forth between the kitchen and living space. She poured me a steaming cup of sweet chai and returned to dinner preparations for the feast ahead. It was a feast like no other. Dish after dish materialized from the kitchen offered in their finest wares. The people present seemed to grow with every course, as brothers, cousins, and neighbours joined us on the mats on the floor.

"Eat, eat," she cried as hands flew to the various dishes laid out on the floor. There were sauces, rice plates, vegetable platters, and more. It was all delicious, but I could only eat so much! There didn't seem to be a way to politely say I was full.

"You must try this one," she encouraged, as she pointed to yet another spicy dish. When the meal was finally declared done, I hoped we could rest, but there were other plans yet for us. Now it was time to dance!

What have I gotten myself into? I wondered.

"We must change," Jasvanti declared. "I have just the thing. We will get you pretty. Come!" She bundled me off to one of the bedrooms where yards of silk were produced. A sari was the only thing fit for the occasion.

"Oh Jasvanti," I exclaimed. "They are beautiful. Are you sure?"

I didn't feel worthy of the finery she pulled from her wardrobe, but she shushed me as she set to work. I obediently stood there, as she stripped me, then handed me a light blue top to put on. This was followed by an intricate wrapping of one of her own saris. She chose a length of pink checked silk, lined with blue and a band of white, and decorated with squares and circles throughout. It was wound around my waist and then tucked across my shoulder. I was transformed.

"Now we need makeup!" Jasvanti declared.

I suspect she would have loved to have had a little girl of her own to dress, but she made do with me that day. She produced bangles and a necklace perfect for the occasion. My lips sported a bright pink to match my sari, but there was still one missing piece—a bindi. I had to have one. Jasvanti found a pretty, oblong one that was attached with an adhesive backer. I had

309

no idea that bindis could be stickers! Hers was a simple red dot painted in the middle of her eyebrows, by comparison. Once she was finally finished, I was a sight to behold.

"Go get the camera," Jasvanti urged Hemendra when we finally emerged. Nimesh's brother ran off to find the missing camera, as I looked at my transformation.

"You are beautiful," Jasvanti declared. I certainly felt special but wasn't sure about pictures. Before I could protest though, Hemendra was back with the Polaroid, and I was placed in front of the altar for a photo shoot. Picture after picture was taken, all a combination of me with every member of the household, in every combination imaginable.

"Here, one for you," Jasvanti said handing me one of the precious Polaroids. "You must send the picture to your husband. Show that we are treating you right."

And then the music began. It was time to dance. I laughed and whirled and embraced every moment of the special evening, but eventually it came to close.

"Thank you so much," I said to Jasvanti as I returned her precious sari to her. "You don't know how much I appreciate everything you have done for me."

Indeed, she had taken a sad moment and infused it with joy. A goodbye had been balanced with a celebration of life. Wasn't that the way life was meant to be? I couldn't help but retire for the evening with a smile on my face.

"You take the bedroom," Jasvanti admonished when I turned to the corner of the room. "Hemendra and Nimesh will go to the neighbour's."

She wouldn't hear my protests and I was secretly pleased for the privacy. I longed for Neale's arms around me once more, but the gift of an evening spent with new friends was a precious moment I would never forget. Sleep claimed me, as I quietly reflected that the next day was the start of my final road home.

"Views from the Window"

The world flew by the SUV's windows. I was headed south, re-tracing my steps back to South Africa, and eventually home. Gone were Neale and Nimesh, now just fond memories. Previous travel companions flitted through my mind's eye, as the miles clicked by. Miki, the one who unexpectedly started me on the road in the first place. Brett, my constant companion over many months and countries. Stuart and Rob, my flatmates in Lamu. Unwavering Ian, my ardent admirer in Harare. Oliver and Taro, van mates along the way, and so many more. I remembered, Max, Karel, Marjory, Eric, Sue, and Bubs; all from my overland trip into Botswana so long ago. Luke, Catriona, Kurt, and Enar at Bob's Backpacker in Cape Town, encouraging the mad adventures to come. All friendly faces who filled in the memories across a continent ready to embrace me. Not to mention the many family members who didn't think twice about welcoming their long-lost cousin from Canada! But as we drove south, it also meant that my time in Africa was coming to a close. It left me feeling hollow, a little lost in the grief of realizing that I would have to say goodbye to an amazing adventure and the many people who had been a part of it.

The only people currently in my world were Eddie and his crew: Mark, in the SUV I rode in, and John and Catherine in the other. None of them made any great efforts to befriend me, but my efforts weren't incredibly overt either. I was more content to sit in the back of the vehicle and capture my mind's wanders. Our stop in Karonga, Malawi was no different.

"Mark and I are going to get supplies," Eddie announced.

"John and I need to stretch our legs," Catherine declared. "We are going to poke around Karonga. We'll meet you back in an hour?"

"Good," Eddie said. "What about you Katherine?"

"I'll just stay here and watch the vehicles," I offered lamely. I had no money to spend, so what was the point in tempting myself? I could have explored the bustling market, but it wasn't my first market, and my spirits were low. I contented myself with my journal.

Despite my lack of socializing, I knew the gift that Eddie brought. Like so many instances along the way, I knew a sign when I saw one, and meeting him was an incredibly glaring one. An offer of a free ride to Victoria Falls when my pockets were tipping towards empty couldn't be ignored. He was my path home.

In a week's time, 1,500 kilometers would pass under the vehicle's wheels. That left plenty of time for reflection, but I was also a guest in Eddie's world. As such, I tried to help as much as I could along the way. When Eddie and crew returned, we repacked the jeep and hit the road south again. When Malawi's coast crept into sight, I couldn't help but smile. It was like coming home to the mesmerizing azure shores.

"Do you see that hazy cloud?" Eddie asked as he pointed to a dark mass across the lake.

"Is it smoke?" I asked.

"No," he declared shaking his head. "Those are lake flies."

"Lake flies?" Catherine asked. "Ew! What's that?"

"They are a local delicacy, is what they are," Eddie replied. "When they swarm across the lake, people catch them by the handfuls. They squish them into balls, then fry them up into fly cakes."

"Hunh," John remarked. "I've never seen that before. Are they any good?"

"Well, you won't get them now," Eddie said. "Not the right time of year. But let's just say, you aren't missing anything."

"No good?" Catherine asked with a laugh.

"Not especially," he replied.

"Anything like grasshoppers?" I asked. "Not that I grooved on those much myself…"

"Meh," Eddie shrugged. "Protein is protein when you can't get other sources."

"I guess," I agreed, but was secretly happy our timing didn't prove his point either way.

I preferred to just hear the stories and see the view from where we were. Lapping waves on a pristine beach with not a mosquito or lake fly in sight to bug us as we slept under a star-strewn sky. The only other light was from fishermen stringing nets across the serene waters by the moon's soft glow in hopes of catching a meal for the next day. The long row of lights that marked each fisherman along the net, painted a line of humanity in my mind's dark eye. I was mesmerized and fell in love with Malawi all over again. Before I knew it though, the lake was behind us.

"I can drop you at a hostel once we hit Lilongwe," Eddie said.

"Sure, that would be great," I replied. They planned to stay in a nicer hotel than I could afford, so I was back with backpackers again. To be honest, I relished the camaraderie found at cheap waystations and Annie's Guest House was the perfect spot for stories. By noon the next day, I was back in the SUV to cut across the continent with Eddie and his crew. The miles flew by now, as conversation ebbed and flowed. We crossed the border at Chipata, then made our way across Zambia to Lusaka.

"What are your plans," Eddie asked me as we drove past long stretches of dry plains dotted with rondavels.

"Ultimately, I need to make my way back to Cape Town," I replied, "but I am not 100% sure which route I'll end up taking. I am thinking of going through Harare again on my way south, just because I have been there before. I can say hello to a few people on my way through…"

"If you have been to Harare already, why not cut through Zimbabwe at Kasane and go south via Namibia?" he suggested. "You could travel along the coast and see places you haven't been yet. The roads are good and if you haven't seen them, there are plenty of interesting sites along the way."

That gave me pause. Why not indeed? And with that, plans changed again. I silently bade my Harare friends goodbye and perked up at the idea of another new country to explore. I had been all around it but had yet to explore Namibia.

Silence filled the vehicle, as I thought back to the many places I had been and people I had met along the way. I had been in Africa for nine months and travelled through nine countries. At the beginning of my trip, I may have felt forlorn at leaving behind family and friends, but now I found myself desperately trying to hold onto every last piece of my African adventure, as it slipped between my fingers. I had been on dhows, crowded buses, rickety taxis, rusty ferries, and even hitched rides in the back of bakkies, but I still delighted in everything I saw along the way, including the beautiful people who waved as we passed. Their enthusiasm never ceased to bring a smile to my lips, even after so long on the road.

While Lusaka neared, my own path shifted on a new trajectory. What else was in store for me before I made it to Cape Town? Time would tell, but a few days in the capitol of Zambia were in store for me before I would get to that.

"I have to get some welding done while we are in Lusaka," Eddie announced. "We'll be there at least one night, if not two. But I have a friend who has an apartment there and you can stay the night if you want." I didn't have to check my finances to know that saying yes was my only option. Plus, I had access to a bed in a safe space? Sign me up, please!

"Thanks, Eddie," I said. Again, I thanked my lucky stars to have met him. I don't know what I would have done otherwise, as there was no way I could have afforded the journey south on what little money I had left.

"We are going out," Eddie said after introducing us all round. "Do you want to come with?" As much as I didn't want to appear rude, I looked

315

around at my surroundings. Not only did I have a comfortable, clean bed to slip into, but access to several other luxuries I hadn't seen in a long time.

"I think I might hang back, if you don't mind," I replied.

"Help yourself to whatever you find…"

"Thanks," I said, as they left. "Have fun!"

I looked around, as the door closed and sighed at the luxury of being in an apartment all alone. I planned to take him up on his offer. A candle-lit bath was in my future. I hadn't seen a bathtub since… since when? Cape Town? Plus, there was a stereo and library filled with music and books!

I fired up classical music, then discovered a treat from home— Leonard Cohen. I browsed through poetry collections, then selected a book of short stories from Roald Dahl. It felt like lifestyles of the rich and famous for me, and I loved every minute of it. I sighed as I slipped into the warm tub and let my road-weary body sink into the warm suds. Heaven.

Since the next day was repair day, I was left to my own devices again. It allowed more time for reflection, but this time I was transported back home. It was Jack's birthday, my erstwhile boyfriend. Thoughts of him seemed unreal, memories from an ancient history. But the miles I had put between us had softened my anger and shifted my mindset. I allowed myself to reflect on who he was, what we were, and how things had ended up the way they did. I knew nothing of where he was or what his life looked like now. Was he still bumming spots on people's couches? Did he have a place of his own or a job? Was he still with the woman whom he had hooked up with when I left? Did it matter? Not really. I hoped he knew I thought of him on his birthday and realized that noting the date at all still spoke volumes of the relationship we had had. I might have told myself that I had moved on and was fine, but he still held a piece of my heart, despite all that had happened.

"Happy birthday, Jack," I murmured to myself. "I wish you well my friend. I hope happiness and clarity visit you on this day and in the days to come."

If it mattered, I knew he would hear my thoughts. And I truly hoped he was in a good spot. We had experienced a deep spiritual connection that had strengthened my sense of self in a lot of ways, even as I had struggled at his side. He might not have been able to be alone, but I could. Yes, it hurt to say goodbye, but it had been for the best for me. And I could not begrudge him finding happiness after me. At this rate, odds weren't in our favour to ever see each other again. And finally, I realized I was okay with that. I could never have flourished walking a path with him and would have found myself dragging or becoming disillusioned with all the beauty we had shared. My trip was my escape. It was my opportunity to discover me, and the journey thus far had been incredibly life altering.

Jack was not with me. No one was. I was in Lusaka and had another night to look forward to with a roof over my head and running water at my fingertips. I had no money to spend, but nothing I had want of either. Food and drink were readily available. A real bed and pillow would catch my dreams that night. We would depart Lusaka in the morning and by evening, I would be back in Victoria Falls, Zimbabwe—a place I hoped to be able to access depleted funds once more.

There was so much to be grateful for; so many blessings poignantly illustrated along the way. How could I not appreciate life when my physical needs were met, good people were around me, and my transportation was taken care of? Life was good. And I was all too aware that tomorrow was always a different day, with a story all its own.

"A Pitstop"

I had slept rough often enough during my travels, but my stiff and achy body proclaimed the previous night's rest as one of the worst. My thin, orange sleeping bag gave little protection against the rocks, roots, and rough ground that served as my bed. The view was less than appealing as well; a barbed wire topped rusty chain link fence, sparse patches of grass scattered across a dusty expanse, reaching for the protection of random trees. The relative luxury of a spot underneath one didn't offer many redeeming qualities. Despite the shade, I was still awake at dawn.

"Made it," I murmured, with a luxurious stretch and smile. Despite the many miles that had stood in the way, I had returned to Victoria Falls, Zimbabwe. It felt like coming home. Victoria Falls was where I fell in love with white-water rafting so many months before. My first trip to Mosi-oa-Tunya in December was with my first overland trip and it was packed with adventure from beginning to end. We explored the beautiful, misty park that surrounded the top of the gorge, watched friends plummet off the Great Zambesi Bridge on bungee cords, and tipped a few beverages back on a booze cruise. It was non-stop laughs and brought a smile to my face upon remembering.

In March, I returned to the largest waterfall in the world for a canoe trip along the Upper Zambezi with Miki. We paddled along the river with not a care in the world, before returning to camp to be pampered with soft beds and mosquito nets, plus luxurious outdoor showers to wash the toils of the day away. Once Brett and Oliver arrived, another booze cruise wreaked havoc on our woozy souls. By June, I returned to Victoria Falls once more, this time with another overland company as part of the crew. More white-water rafting, bungee jumping, visits to the park, and the obligatory booze cruise ensued. Vic Falls was a rocking fun place, and it felt good to be back where so many good memories lingered.

This trip to Victoria Falls was different though. I wasn't with an overland truck, neither as passenger nor employee. I had no friends by my side. Even Eddie was gone, having said goodbye as he dropped me on the bridge from Zambia to Zimbabwe. I was solely responsible for my own actions once more. I was the only one to guide the way and the thought left me a little fearful of what might unfold from here. As if reading my thoughts, the morning sun peaked forth to burn some of those trepidations away.

"First things first," I thought. "Get up and get clean."

The campground didn't offer much, but the bathrooms were reasonably clean. And the barbed wire and glaring light I slept under were meant to be security measures. It was about reframing the story and it helped with my outlook, even as I splashed water on my face. Plus, the camp stored backpacks during the day for those who needed the service. Shedding its heavy straps for a few hours promised to save a few new knots from forming in my grateful back. So, with my "home" rolled up for the day, I strapped the sleeping bag onto my pack and stowed it away.

"Now to see if I have any money," I said, as I headed to the bank machine in town.

There had been no bank machines since Tanzania, and I was down to little more than dust in my ravaged money pouch. My last traveller's cheque was sacrificed to pay Eddie for the provisions I had shared en route from Dar es Salaam to Livingstone. I felt like desperation's door was at hand, knowing that my remaining Rand (ZAR) wouldn't be enough to get me to Cape Town. The thought wasn't worth entertaining until I slid my card into the machine though.

"Please, please, please..." I whispered. Rejection wasn't an option. I slid the card in, punched in my magic numbers, and held my breath. After a painfully long wait, the machine whirred to life. The sweet sound of gears churning released the breath I held, as money slowly slid into my waiting hands.

"Yes!" I cried. Money. That cold coin that I needed so badly, was mine once more. Without it, I was destitute. But with it, I could continue to travel. Even better, *I could afford breakfast!*

"Time to go shopping," I happily sang, as I tucked the precious bills away. I needed staples for my depleted backpacking larder; cheese, bread, and cucumbers being a start.

"Hey," a voice rang out, as I turned in the direction of the grocery store.

"Glenn!" I said with surprise. I hadn't seen him since I left Harare. "How are you? How're things? What have you been up to since I saw you last?"

After catching up for a few minutes, I headed off to pick up my much-needed supplies, only to bump into more familiar faces. As I stood there trying to remember where I knew these next people from, it hit me. Miki and I had met Craig and Nina way back in March when we were on our canoe safari right there in Victoria Falls. The world became smaller again.

"We just got married," they bubbled. "There were only 10 of us, but it was perfect. The ceremony was on a small island in Lake Tanganyika in Tanzania.

"Oh my God!" I exclaimed. "That sounds so romantic!"

"It was," Nina replied.

"Both our parents came and a few close friends," Craig added. "Now we are on honeymoon backpacking through Africa. Everyone else headed home, but Nina's parents are still with us."

"Nice!" I said. "That's cool that they can handle backpacking." I loved the spirit of backpackers and how our fortitude bonded us together so readily. After saying goodbye, I walked down the plaza stairs, only to see another familiar face. Try as I might, their name escaped me, but as our eyes locked, we both knew that we had met before. Where had I met them though? Was it here in Victoria Falls? Elsewhere in Tanzania? Nope, our connection wasn't even from the continent.

"Hallo," the woman cried as we crossed in the middle of the street. "I know you. Where do I know you from? Wait... Yes, I know!"

I stayed at her house in Enschede, Netherlands two and a half years earlier. Her name was Barbara and while we stood there trying to figure out our connection, her husband Jap walked up to us. It all came flooding back. One of the last places I stayed while travelling through Europe was their house. Their cousin was my then travelling companion's ex-boyfriend, and they opened their home to us for a few days to use as a home base while we poked about the Netherlands. It was incredible to bump into them almost 12,000 kilometers away.

"Come," Jap cried. "Let's go for a beer. You must tell us all about your travels and what you have been up to!"

"Sure," I agreed. "The camp bar is probably better than the middle of the street."

"Where are you going?" another voice asked. Nina, Craig, and their parents materialized as well.

"Nina, Craig!" I cried. "These must be your parents? You should join us. We are headed for a drink."

And with that, we set off to find a table at the bar. We pulled together chairs and regaled each other with stories of our various travels around the globe. After being alone for several weeks, it felt amazing to reconnect with people I had travelled with before. It was a balm on my soul, and I revelled in the camaraderie, as dancers thrummed out a beat on the patio in front of us. We talked and laughed and had a marvelous evening all around. I felt a warmth that extended beyond a mere round or two of beers. I was amongst friends, and it felt good. This was what travelling was at its best.

Add to that bumping into Ndaba and Keith, locals I had met on previous visits, and Victoria Falls quickly became a lifeline for me. I hoped to spy Max too—my first white water rafting guide whom I had a soft spot for from way back in December—but was happy with all the familiar faces who now surrounded me. At the end of the night, I wobbled home to my sleeping bag on the ground underneath my sparse tree. It was far from luxury, but still felt like coming home none the less. The familiar patch of dirt was like a return to a long-lost friend. Nothing could wipe the smile from my face, as I drifted off to another night's sleep in Zimbabwe.

"Thumbing a Ride"

"Hi, from Victoria Falls!" I cried into the phone. Not only could I access money in Victoria Falls, but I could make telephone calls again too.

"Oh, Katherine dear," my Aunt Elsa exclaimed. "We've been so worried about you, not having heard from you in so long. How are you?"

There were so many stories to tell, but only so much time available on the phone. I gave her the Coles notes version of my trip up to Kenya and back to Zimbabwe, mentioning highlights like my birthday game drive, Lamu, and some of the friendly people I had met along the way. She in turn shared that Uncle Sammy had passed away (his long-time illness actually made it a blessing), and their plans to go to Springbok shortly.

"Where are you bound for now?" she asked. Always an interesting question to someone with limited funds and only a loose destination in mind. Cape Town was the final destination, but I was still 3,300 kilometers from there, and still without a solid plan.

"I have met a few people here and might be able to get a lift with some of them," I replied. No need to give her too many details, as I know how worried the family already was. Better to have them think I was with fine and with trusted companions. It was partly true anyway. I did have a ride lined up with an Orthodox Jewish couple and a vegetarian Seventh Day Adventist. The Jewish couple had a rental car and were looking to split the cost of their trip to Namibia with other travellers. Worked for me!

"I plan to go to Namibia and then make my way back down to you!" I cried.

"Very nice," she said. "Keep us in the loop of when you think you'll be back, luv. Can't wait to hear all about your adventures. It all sounds very exciting!" I promised to do my best and signed off. No one answered the phone back in Canada, so I returned to present day issues. Saying goodbye to the last of my friends in Victoria Falls. And that is when I saw Max.

"Hey there, stranger," said a familiar voice as I turned from the pay phone.

"Hello yourself, Max," I replied with a smile. The soft spot I had for him grew a little more just gazing into those sparkling eyes. His magnetism and charm worked their magic all over again.

"What brings you to Vic Falls again?"

"Oh, you know," I laughed. "I missed your smiling face." We chatted and I caught him up on the whirlwind that was life as a backpacker in the continent.

"Where are you staying?" he asked.

"The campground," I said. "Luxury at its finest with my very own skylight."

He laughed but got a new glint in his eye. "How long are you here for?"

"Was trying to sort out a ride today," I replied.

"It's too late to sort out a ride today," he said as he gestured in the late afternoon sunshine. "Why don't you spend another night? You can stay at my place." He was right. It was late to set out. And I never seemed to be able to resist his charms. This was the first I had seen him this trip through

324

the Falls and to be honest, I wanted to see more of him. Was it prudent? I didn't care. I would have a roof over my head for a night and that made it worthwhile.

"Alright," I said. He gave me the address and turned back to work.

"I'll be a few hours, but you can head there whenever," he said as he left. Before I knew it, it was morning and I was saying goodbye. So many goodbyes.

"Wasn't that the point," I reminded myself, as I crammed my pack into the trunk of the waiting car. "Making friends?" I was on to the next ride down the road and saying goodbye to friends again. While the goodbyes added up, I was beginning to realize that they weren't all bad, as the memories travelled with me into the future. Max was just the most recent one to add to the many friendly faces I had met in my travels.

"Goodbye Max," I murmured, as I climbed into the back seat. His memory was a welcome companion, as I realized quickly that my newest travelling companions were a strikingly different group. I was thrilled that they were gracious enough to allow me to accompany them, but I felt decidedly out of place.

Erik had just come from a volunteer position in Rwanda. He spoke fervently of the actions he had taken there and the profound effect they had had on him. Gavri and Freeda were on a month-long vacation. Their rigid dietary restrictions meant that eating out was next to impossible, so renting a car and carrying their own kosher food—and dual sets of plates and cutlery—was essential. One set of dishes was for meat. The other for everything else. I didn't feel like I carried that level of dedication or drive, but listened politely to their stories, nonetheless. Here were two groups of people that both held vastly different versions of god and how to live a life.

Their level of faith was a new experience for me on the road, and a revelation all over again. I had met Hindus, Muslims, Christians, and a fair share of roughneck folk along the way. They held different beliefs, but wasn't that a part of the journey too? We may have been inherently different, but they were no better or worse than me. They held religious and moral convictions that left me silent. What did I have to offer in the face of that? I was a heathen traveller out to see new lands, experience different cultures, and meet new people. But wasn't this another experience? Just found in a rental car puttering across southern Africa.

I reminded myself of that, as I did my best to understand my newest travelling companions. The world was made up of an infinite number of souls. I might not have completely understood these ones, but I had to hand it to them for their convictions. Where I had found it difficult to find fresh water at times, they took their faith one step further and held out for kosher and vegetarian food. I didn't envy them the challenges they faced while travelling in foreign countries. That included finding someplace to pray. While "God" is everywhere, how do you find any church, let alone your preferred church, temple, synagogue, or mosque, when the only structures to be found for miles were a collection of trees or dusty rondavels? God is in the heart though, right? Faith is part of your soul. You carry that everywhere, regardless of where you find yourself in time and space. I might not have stepped foot into many religious temples in the last several months, but I kept the faith in the goodness of humanity. I saw proof of that everywhere, regardless of skin colour, language spoken, wealth, or stature in the community. That deserved dignity and respect. Including, for my newest travelling companions.

So, as we left Victoria Falls behind, I looked ahead to a new country and the experiences that I would find along the way. Namibia awaited, after a brief half hour hop through Botswana.

326

"Passports," the border guard barked, as we pulled up to the Botswana border. Erik and I handed our passports up to the front, where Gavri passed them to the guard. The guard scanned them and stamped them with a flick of the wrist, then turned to Gavri and Freeda.

"You. Israelis," the man said, shaking their passports. "Where is your visas?"

"What visa?" Gavri asked.

"You need visa to enter Botswana."

"Can we purchase one?" Gavri asked again, as he reached for his wallet. "How much?"

"No!" said the now offended border guard. "This is not a consulate. You cannot buy one here! You must go to Lusaka or Harare." Both cities were hundreds of miles away. If they were forced to backtrack, it meant that myself and Erik would be crossing the border on foot. It was the Israeli couple's car after all, and I couldn't afford to go back with them at that point. Thankfully, it was not my battle to wage. Gavri calmly negotiated his case and finally managed to arrange for the essential stamps. I marvelled at his calm demeanour in the face of the angry guard. It might have only been a half hour trip between borders, but the many veiled threats and eye rolls left me highly nervous in the back seat.

"Next time, you get stamps before you come to border," the guard criticized as he handed all our passports back, stamped and ready to go once more. There wouldn't be a next time for me, and I doubted that anyone else cared to retrace their steps again either.

We sailed through the next border, and I soon found myself in a new country once more. Namibia was the tenth and last new country for me to explore. The road ahead was gravel, but in good shape despite the dust which kept our windows closed. The thin Caprivi Strip was a gateway to the rest of Namibia. And we made Popa Falls that night before the rest of the country opened up to us. The chilly ground embraced me once more under a star-filled sky, as I looked to the heavens above. Trillions of miles away, they winked back at me—no different than anyone else who gazed upon their stark beauty. We were all laid bare under their light. It was a humbling thought as I fell asleep.

*****

After another day spent on the road (hitting every petrol station between Rundu and Grootfontein for some reason), we ended up in Tsumeb. Money dictated that the ground was my cot under another chilly, cloudless sky. I was stiff and getting cranky as a result. That probably didn't help when Freeda suggested we veer off to Etosha for a game drive.

"Honestly," I said. "I can't afford it. I'm sure that it's incredible, but I'll have to jump out if you are going that way." It was a good excuse, regardless. Awkward conversations had run dry, and my funds were heading that way too. Nope, I had had enough.

"You are sure?" Freeda asked again.

I nodded.

"Your share for gas and rental fees is NAD $122.50," Gavri added, as he quickly tabulated what had been spent in the two days we had been together. It seemed exorbitant to have slept rough, but I wasn't about to argue. I had seen him outtalk a border guard and knew I wouldn't win. I was happy enough to say totsiens[48] to this round of travel mates.

"Okay, Girlfriend," I said to myself after they drove off. "It's just you and your thumb now. Let's go!"

I plunked my backpack on the side of the road in high spirits and stuck my thumb out heading west. The Atlantic coast was calling with a vision of one toe in the ocean and another in the Namib desert. It was only 700 some-odd kilometers away. Nothing as compared to some of the jaunts I had undertaken. It didn't take long before a motorist stopped. It was not the ride I had been hoping for though.

"You nee da'ride?" the driver slurred.

"Yes, please," I exclaimed, as I scrambled into the car. I didn't notice the fumes until the driver aimed his car back onto the road. 'Aim' being the operative word. It was the best description of his attempt. I was quickly horrified to discover that he was obviously three sheets, or more, to the wind. He reeked of booze and swerved all over the road.

"Where you headed to?" he asked. As he looked over at me, the car veered in the direction of his head. I was terrified.

"Swakopmund," I managed, as my hand snaked out to clutch the door.

Every oncoming vehicle spelled disaster in my eyes. Lines blurred, as the driver drifted from the soft gravel shoulder to the middle of the other lane. Horns blared mercilessly, as I panicked trying to come up with an

---

[48] until we meet again; goodbye.

excuse to be let out. If I didn't get out of the vehicle, I feared death would find us or fate would flip us into oblivion. Suddenly, religion didn't seem so far-fetched, as I prayed to my guardian angels after every near miss. Their wings worked overtime that day. But finally, they had enough.

"I 'ave to let you out 'ere," my driver apologized, as he pulled over at a crossroads in a small village. "Good luck on your rest or ya journey…"

"No worries," I mumbled hastily, as I gladly scrambled out of the car. "Thanks."

I was down a life or two, but grateful to feel the road under my feet once more. Hopefully he didn't kill himself, or anything else, on the last of his journey, but I was certainly thankful to be rid of him. Of course, there was still miles to go before I could call anyplace home and fewer options now. Whether I liked it or not, hitchhiking seemed my only option.

With a little less swagger and a lot more trepidation, I clung to the side of the road once more, praying my angels would forgive my former transgressions. Cars zoomed by and I remained where I was. With my last ride fresh in my memory, it was only half-discouraging. But as a transport truck approached, it appeared to slow down as it neared. Was this my next ride?

"Big Rig Rides"

"Where to?" asked a man perched high up in the big rig.

"I'm headed to the coast," I replied, cautiously.

"Hop in then," he said with a smile and a wave. "I am going to Windhoek. That will get you most of the way there."

330

"Thanks."

I grabbed my pack and pushed it up in front of me. Plenty of room for me and my bag in the big sleeper cab. And plenty of room between me and the driver too, which gave some piece of mind, as I ventured into a new wave of hitchhiking. My guardian angels approved and breathed a sigh of relief for a moment. As the driver geared back up, the road ran smooth in front of us. Unlike my last drunken ride, conversation flowed easily between us. He asked about my adventures and shared stories of his own life on the road. Slowly, I relaxed into the journey and enjoyed the sunny day that shone upon us. We even stopped for a bite to eat and he bought me a burger and soda, before getting back onto the road once more. Everything seemed rosy, until conversation paused. A worried look crossed the driver's face. I looked between him and the dash and tensed. A slight tremor hitched into the smooth ride. Was that a noise? Where was it coming from? Was it anything to worry about?

"Everything alright?" I asked cautiously.

"Mmm," he grunted. "Maybe not. I am going to have to stop. Sorry about this..." He geared down and edged to the side of the tarmac. Silence filled the cab, as he focused on controlling the 18-wheeler. The wheels crunched onto the side of the road, and we stopped.

"I have to call dispatch," he said as he picked up the CB. He gruffly relayed what was going on, then turned to me. "They are going to send a mechanic," he explained. "I have to stay with the truck until someone can collect the trailer, but I will contact one of the other drivers to pick you up."

"Oh," I replied. "You don't have to do that."

"Ack, yes. I do. I feel awful and don't want to leave you stranded out here in the middle of nowhere." I looked around. It was true. We were in the middle of nowhere and my options were limited. He was already on the CB once more. Without tools, mechanical knowledge, and a space to work on the unwieldy engine, his hands were tied. Even if he knew what was wrong with the truck, he couldn't fix it on the side of the road. He had to wait for the mechanic, and I had to switch rides once more.

"Once the sun sets, the temperature drops," he added. "You don't want to be stuck out after dark." I remembered my recent nights on the ground and shivered in memory. This would be worse, with not a tree in sight to protect me from the desert chill. "Right then," he said after signing off the CB again. "The truck behind me is going to pick you up when they get here."

"Thank you," I replied. "I appreciate your help." Despite engine woes, it looked like he would get me to the coast after all. Sadly, I hauled my backpack down out of his truck to wait.

As I stood waiting once more, a young woman appeared on the highway near me. She appeared to be about my age; perhaps a little younger, maybe a little older? I wasn't a great judge of age and all we had for common communication was shy nods between us. She had the large utility bag that marked her as a local, minus the usual live chickens. My bag was no smaller but was a dead giveaway that I wasn't from these parts. We appeared to be heading in the same direction though, so found ourselves gravitating towards each other. Strength in numbers...

When the newest big rig appeared and rolled to a stop, we both ran together to jump in for the next leg of our journeys. I prayed that this ride would prove to be less eventful.

"Onda Pumbwa Olefa[49]," the woman said to the man who rolled down the window.

"Oto Yi Peni[50]?" he replied.

"Swakopmund."

"Itule[51]," he said as he opened the door. She turned to me and motioned for me to follow her. I had no idea what was just spoken, but figured it amounted to her getting us a ride. She climbed into the back bunk, as the second driver climbed in after her.

"Thank you," I said, as I climbed into the vacated passenger seat with a nod. I quickly fell silent, unequipped to carry on a conversation in anything other than English, but not feeling especially chatty anyway.

The road rolled out underneath us, as the last of the day's rays trailed out behind the truck. I was headed west again. It was good, but my happiness was on shaky ground. The luxury of the front seat wasn't the perk I had hoped, and the driver wasn't nearly as amenable as my last ride. He had a certain tone to his voice that made my smile falter. I tried to gamely focus on the road ahead but found it hard to ignore the noises which began to drift forward from the back bunk. No curtain blocked the view, but my eyes laser pointed forward. With the sun set, we drove along in darkness. Few other vehicles passed. The desert enveloped us as we drove towards the coast and the feeling of isolation grew without the sun's encouraging rays. The only thing that illuminated the night sky were the truck's headlights carving a lonely path through the murk. With two drivers, it meant that the truck wouldn't stop until it reached its destination. They would drive all night long,

---

[49] I need a lift.
[50] where are you going?
[51] let's go.

swapping out as necessary for the second driver to rest. Except it didn't seem like the man in the back was getting much sleep. A rustle of bodies was hard to miss in the cramped quarters. A muffled grunt, even more so.

"Mwena[52]," the man grumbled.

"Aawe[53]," she responded, as more shuffling reached my ears.

I might not have understood the words, but I got the feeling that the young woman was not interested in the advances thrust upon her. I wracked my brain trying to figure out how to help the poor girl, when I suddenly found a hand on my leg. I instinctively shoved it away, but my hackles were now raised. Things had just taken a decided turn for the worse.

How the hell am I going to get out of this truck? my brain desperately cried, as I flicked a glance at the driver. A lascivious smile returned my glance.

This was so not good. Not good at all. The girl in the back seemed to be keeping the second driver away from herself, but things were getting decidedly dangerous. It was dark out. We were literally miles from nowhere and our apparent saviours had turned into fiends, intent on extracting their fare for passage in flesh. Then the drivers switched places. As did myself and my fellow hitchhiker. Now she was in the front seat, and I was the one on the bunk. Sleep was the farthest thing from my mind though. I was young and vulnerable, a female traveller at the mercy of strange men. As fingers began to crawl up my leg, I kicked and began to pray. God wasn't someone I had

---

[52] be quiet.
[53] no.

ever turned to, but I hoped that maybe a guardian angel or two might intervene on my behalf. In the interim, I did what I could.

"No!" I said, as I shoved creeping fingers off me. "Stop it!" My foreign words were hollow, but the implied meaning was ignored. The hands kept coming.

"Leave me alone," I cried, as I tried to make myself as small and inaccessible as possible. Desperation kicked in. I began to silently beg favours from whatever omnipotent beings were around.

Let them have an attack of integrity, a thought of honesty, a whiff of decency. Something, please! My body strained with the struggle for resistance, as I continued to will any kind of positive energy to intervene.

"No!" I yelled again, as I jammed my foot into his side, desperately trying to push him away. While my brain projected images of worst-case scenarios, a new voice crept into my head.

"You shouldn't always trust strangers," my mother's warning rang out. "You never know what they want or how they might try to connive to get it."

I get it! I cried in my head. *I'm sorry. You were right! Just please don't let things get any worse! Please!!!*

And slowly, I realized I was winning the fight. My protests must have bored him, or perhaps sleep seemed more appealing the longer the struggle went on. Or, just maybe, he felt a twinge that what he was attempting to do was the wrong thing. Whatever it was, that night my Guardian Angels earned their places in the Heavens for eternity. I wanted to cry, sob, or scream, but my fight or flight response had me wired into a ball ready to attack if necessary. I occasionally felt a hand explore to see if perhaps I was asleep or had changed my mind, but a swift shove let him know that I was not up for a night of 'fun'. Long after he turned over and curled up to go to sleep, I lay tightly wound in the corner of the bunk, my breath ragged in my chest. I no longer considered hitchhiking to be the free and easy ride I once thought. I somehow felt like I used up one of my lives that night. But it was a life I never wanted back.

"A Toast to Swakopmund"

I was never so happy as to touch solid ground in Swakopmund. Despite all odds, I made it! To be honest, I had my doubts, as I grappled groping hands throughout the night at the hands of the two persistent drivers. As soon as I stepped out of the truck I turned away, grateful I would never have to see those men again. Good riddance! And shame on them for shaking my faith in human goodness. Their only redeeming qualities were that they didn't push the point and extract whatever they wanted from myself and the other young woman at their mercy. It was a story I didn't care to share with my worried family and one that brought me a sense of humility as a single female travelling alone. I was not infallible. Far from it.

The best way to shake the dark vibes was by finding a safe haven. Another city, another hostel, and this one with a bar. First measure of business after stowing my pack was toasting my desert drive survival with an icy cold Windhoek. Heaven! I don't know if I exactly earned the beer (should I have been hitchhiking in the first place?), but by god, I wanted it anyway. Anything to take away the sense of feeling tainted and dirty. Nothing could change the past though. Better to let it go, learn from the experience, and hope that a new day would bring more positive moments and a bigger measure of happiness. The ocean awaited. I could feel the salty air on my lips and skin, even if I could not see the South Atlantic waves from where I sat. It was a new coast for me, and I was happy to be by the water once more.

A bed was the bigger draw in that moment though; my first one in three nights, with the added bonus of a roof over my head. I was stationary, solo, and safe. Pen and paper were my companions as I acknowledged the lessons available to learn in life, if we take the time to notice. Adventure was still there. The sun would rise again tomorrow. And I was blessed to be its witness. That was always worth toasting.

*****

"Do you accept a collect call from Katherine?"

"Yes!" came the excited response from my sister. I hadn't talked to anyone in over two months. Even my written communication had dropped off, leaving them all wondering if I was safe and where in the world I might be. The last they had heard from me, I had sent pictures of Nimesh and I dressed up in my stately sari and accoutrements back in Dar es Salaam. No explanation. For all they knew, the pictures were wedding photos. My mother had fretted that might happen from the day I left. She always claimed it would be her mother-in-law's revenge for stealing her precious son; my father left home to travel and never returned after falling in love with my mother on the road. That wasn't the case here, but they didn't know that. And, as I was always on the move—erratically over the last few months especially—no one had any clue where to track me down to confirm or deny. So, the first question of course was…

"Where are you?!" I laughed and explained that I was in Namibia and was slowly making my way back to Cape Town. Almost there! Only

1,600 some-odd kilometers to go. After sharing some of the condensed stories of the last little while, I turned the conversation to home.

"How is everyone? What's going on in Canada?" Kerry's voice became quiet. I was suddenly concerned and uncertain that I wanted to hear the news she obviously had to share.

"Grandpa passed away…"

"What?" I cried. My brain reeled trying to process the loss. "What happened? When?"

"July 5th." My birthday. Just over a month before. And coincidently, a month after he visited family in Ontario. If I had returned when my original plane ticket left, I would have had a last visit with him in person. There was a piece of me that felt like he might have held on just long enough to hear some of the stories from my travels. But I had changed the ticket long before and that visit never happened. I was crushed.

The rest of the conversation blurred with details of his death, the memorial service they had just come back from, and how they had wanted to protect me from all the details while I was too far to do anything. My excitement at talking to family ended on a bittersweet note, as I cradled the receiver back onto the base. My pen took over where our voices left off. It was high time I wrote a letter home. This one didn't require postage though.

*****

Dear Grandpa,

As I sit reminiscing, I think back on your long and full life. You brought three daughters into this world, and I know you are proud of all their accomplishments, not least of which being the grandchildren they presented you with. The better to spoil and cherish every chance you got! You even got to meet a great-grandchild before leaving this world. How blessed! Know that we are all indebted to the legacy you leave behind.

What is that legacy? You saw so much in your lifetime; it is hard to capture it all. The television came into existence, along with VCRs, fax machines, and now the internet. You fought in World War II and served for years after in the Air Force. You sweated in steel mills too, but I remember you sweating in the garden. That lovely garden you built on Pender Island, along with a beautiful house to go with it. My memories of that house and garden will stay with me for a long time to come.

I clasp my hand around a smoky quartz at my neck which you polished and set. It wasn't specifically made for me, but I cherish it nonetheless for your toils. You always worked with your hands, creating something, whether it was a greenhouse, the 'discomboobulator', a 'gotcha stick', or your famous peanut butter sandwiches. You were always doing something.

Even in your later years you were president of your local legion, played bridge once a week with friends, and still had time to advise your children and grandchildren on major life decisions. I recall my mom asking for advice on job offers. Your other children also turned to you for guidance during life's struggles. You had a good head on your shoulders, and everyone knew it.

Grandpa, you were the father I never had. You taught Kerry and I (your favourites, you always teased) how to spit, and collect wood and stones. I have the stones to prove it on this trip. You taught us how to gather eggs when you had chickens, fish, play crib (and count via muggins), and

339

blow my nose (which I should do now, sniff, sniff...). All that, plus so much more, including the manners I rely on today. I have iconized you (I know you would tell me to look that word up!) in many ways--in speeches (remember my grade five speech on your inventions!) and in memories of the summers Kerry and I spent with you and Grandma (integral to my growing up and formation of personal beliefs and traits, and as a teacher). I too have asked your opinion many times. It seems you had a hand in everything. Whether you were an expert or not, your general knowledge was broad and in-depth, and always sought by many.

I love you for your hat and suspenders. I picture me snapping them and... "aggh"! Despite your military breeding (that I did not necessarily always agree with—Front and Centre!), it taught me respect for my elders and authority figures. But oh, when we finally got you to start using a 'please' now and then...success! With repeated effort from us army of kids.

Time clicks forward. Now I recall helping you on with your socks and can see your varicose veins in my mind's eye; snakes or worms, you called them. I picture you in your rubber boots, with a chainsaw in hand, sticking out your dentures at us kids ("arrh!"), and Grandma complaining, "Geordie!", all the while.

Oh, you could make us laugh! I recall you tapping the blunt edge of a knife into elbows, curtly saying "elbows off the table" or "are you tired?". Those elbows were a huge no-no and sign of disrespect. Tears were chased away with your famous pout-catchers also, which almost always got us laughing again, despite even the most stubborn tears. The dreaded whisker rub made us shriek worst of all though. Every. Single. Time. I could go on and on.

Grandpa, I love you dearly and always will. I carry you with me wherever I go. You are a part of me, as you are a part of everyone you touched. I cannot even begin to paint a complete picture of you, as the colours I have available are insufficient and drab, compared to the rainbows you left on people. The respect you earned from the world, I flaunt as a memory to you. Many will pause, as your spirit touches the wind.

To SGT George McLeod: husband, father, grandfather, great-grandfather: The 23 years I have known you are not enough, but as the hurting flesh is laid to rest, your essence carries me on. May your heart be felt forever in those that pump your blood. Go well, strong warrior. Stay well.

Love

And with that, I raised a scotch to my lips in memory of a great man. My eyes stung as the ice clinked against my teeth, but I valiantly swallowed my sorrows along with the libation. Teardrops littered my journal, as I paid homage to him. The hugs I needed and craved for release were over 6,000 kilometers away, but there was nothing to be done about that now. I was alone with a grief that needed to be heard by someone, but all I could do was talk to the wind. So, I did.

*****

I couldn't resist. I slipped my shoes off. My toes needed to wiggle in the sand and feel the delicious sift of the Namib Desert touch me. My aching soul needed it too. I was alone, but not lonely with my company. The world was all around me. I was in the desert. The Atlantic Ocean stretched out before me, as behind me sands shifted and drifted, as far as the eye could see. Life surrounded me and it was beautiful. The lapping waves reminded me that home was closer than ever. The mighty Atlantic Ocean kissed my feet here, then travelled to the East Coast of Canada to deliver my love to the wind. Perhaps it would whisper its secret message to my mother, as she stepped out of her car when she arrived home that evening? Who knows? But its music filled me with peace in this moment, making us one. I lifted my face to the sky with a smile.

As I listened to the Earth speak to me, poetry surged through my mind. My grandfather lingered there and offered his blessings. With a tear, I picked up a pen and offered thanks.

> *Now all I hold is a polished stone*
> *And a picture in my hand,*
> *But your loving glow*
> *Pumps my heart to go,*
> *Eternity is yours for all time*
> *-Love in a circle-*

Every day is a good day, in the fact that it has been.

"Write my Way Home"

My journal entries got longer and more verbose as the days went by. It was to be expected I suppose, as I spent much of my days alone. It left more time to think, reflect, and subsequently write those thoughts down. After having travelled with so many people, through so many places, it was kind of nice being alone. But in truth, it also kind of scared me too.

I should better understand global dynamics, social constructs, race relations, and more, I thought to myself. Instead, I still struggled with what I wanted to be when I grew up. I had gone to university to expand my mind and come up with ideas for what the future might hold but left its hallowed halls with a degree and no further direction. Not true. I had direction—Africa—but not the exact life path for which I had been hoping. No career had materialized as the golden cure to life. At university anyway.

Now with my travels winding down, I still wasn't any closer to life's inherent answers though. I hadn't become an overland courier. I hadn't found a lasting romance to give me purpose and a new path. I had met family, but it didn't seem to change my life's trajectory, from what I could tell. I was still set to return to Canada in a few weeks' time, with no clue what I would do once I got there. Were all those days and kilometers all for nought?

Far from it. While I might have continued to squeeze in as many side trips as I could before hitting Cape Town, there was still plenty of time to ponder all I had experienced and seen. While I poked about in the Alte Feste in Windhoek, learning about the animals, people, and history of the area, I filtered it through my new lens. I wasn't the same young woman who left Canada behind nine months earlier. Time and experience had changed me, altered how I looked at education, waste management, and adventure. Even if I couldn't see it yet.

From Windhoek, a train whisked me further down the continent. The swaying compartment was a new luxury in travel, but the 11-hour journey left me a little less than impressed. More time to think about all I had seen: the fear that still existed between the races, the inequality between men and women, the differences in how first and third world countries functioned, and what truly made for happiness (and in case you were curious, happiness seemed so much easier to attain here than what could be bought in stores back home). Life was harder—toting water for household use from long distances—but happiness could be as easy as having access to clean drinking water. Helping others wasn't just a quaint theory, but a way of life that helped whole communities. And money spent in local communities stayed there, benefitting those who lived there. Why was that a novel concept?

I learned that fear was based in history, but that the future can be re-written. Likewise, adversity doesn't always break you; instead, it provides a window for creatively forging a new way through life. And most importantly, I discovered that there are so many people out there who are worthy of my time, attention, and friendship. Those moments don't have to last long to leave an impression, but making space for them can be life changing, usually for the better. If I had never paused to notice Miki across a crowded airport, so much of my trip through Africa might never have happened. That alone was mind-blowing. As time stretched into the wee hours of overnight, the rocking train lulled me to sleep.

The reality was, there were few pages left to write. My plane ticket had been changed for the last time. In a little over two weeks, I would fly out of Cape Town for Germany, then home. A stop in Keetmanshoop would punctuate my travels before I arrived in Cape Town. The people I met along the way were now memories. The places, little more than pinpoints on a map. As I poured through the memories, my mind knew one thing for certain. It was finally time to go home.

"Mango Delivery"

As I left the hostel behind, I swung my pack onto my back for the last time on the road. Keetmanshoop was a small town and acted only as a short rest stop for me. Time marched on and so did I. There was now less than two weeks left of my African adventure. Every moment was precious. There was no time left to play idle tourist when I had a finite amount of time to get back to Cape Town and squeeze in final visits with relatives. It was time to go.

"Damn it," I cried when I calculated what was left of my funds. "That won't get me to Cape Town. That won't even get me to Anne's house in Springbok."

Don't even think about alternatives, my conscience pleaded. *Have you already forgotten your last hitchhiking experience? How dangerous and foolhardy that ended up being?*

"How else do you suggest we get anywhere?" I countered. "I've got almost no money left. What else can I do?"

My conscience didn't have a good answer to that one. Options were indeed limited. So, armed with my recent renewal in faith in the fates, care of Swakopmund, I focused on the end goal. I double-crossed my fingers that I wouldn't run into any rides reminiscent of my last hitchhiking fiasco. Or worse, for that matter. With a prayer to my angel wingman, I turned from the train station and headed to the highway.

I couldn't resist taking a quick snap of my dusty, beat-up old pack that had seen thousands of miles pass under it. There wasn't much left of it, or in it, besides the thin orange and brown polyester sleeping bag, and an assortment of even thinner clothes. It was hard to believe I would hang it up soon. Even harder to think about leaving this beautiful land. I still felt like I was only just beginning to unearth Africa's secrets.

When I thought of the family and friends whom I would soon see, I was spurred to action though. I slid my camera back into my pack, just as a big rig approached. I valiantly stuck out my thumb and the truck slowed to a stop.

This is it, I thought to myself, as I swung up into the cab. *Please don't be more than I can handle.* And as the truck lumbered back up to speed, I met Mango.

*****

Think of yourself as small, inconspicuous, and less than attractive, I repeated to myself, as I leaned in my seat toward the truck door. Was I pushing my luck by hitchhiking again? Especially getting into another big rig? I was committed now but took solace that there was only one person in this truck.

Maybe that's a bad thing... my brain whispered to me. *Shush!* I demanded. *Nervous thoughts will only make me look more vulnerable than I already am.*

The heated dialogue in my head continued, as we drove along. Mango didn't seem to notice. He also didn't seem overtly threatening. His eyes stayed on the road and small talk was minimal.

"Where you headed?" he asked.

"Springbok," I replied. "Ultimately, I am going to Cape Town."

"Why stop in Springbok?" he wondered. "When not just go straight through to Cape Town? I'm headed there. I can take you all the way if you want." I thought about it. One continuous ride from Keetmanshoop to Cape Town was over 1,000 kilometers. Staying with Mango meant I wouldn't have to chance other more questionable rides, or long stretches waiting on the side of the highway for them. For him, it meant he would have company along the way too, which I assumed was a welcome break from his regular monotonous run.

"I charge you RTGS 50."

You couldn't beat the price. A bus would have cost me at least double that. If I got out of the truck any time before that, I would have to scavenge god knows how many more rides in order to get closer to Cape Town. And I only had two weeks to get there now. The sooner I got there, the more I would be able to squeeze in, like visits with aunts, uncles, cousins, a trip up Table Mountain, out to Cape Point, my Dad's birthplace of Hermanus, or perhaps even another wine tour!

Of course, I could stay in the truck. Watch Mango turn into a super sleaze ball or worse. I did not know the man, and from experience, was leery about trusting anyone now.

"I kind of wanted to see my cousins in Springbok…" I said, stalling for time. Were my guardian angels still in place? Was it time for me to be tested again? If I fell asleep, would I wake up? My mind raced as my butt inched to the far edge of my seat. What should I do?

"Think about it," he said. "You don't have to decide until after we cross the border. After the border, the road to Springbok veers off to the west. You decide then, okay?"

"Okay," I agreed. I breathed a little easier once more. Most of the time, the fates had not steered me wrong. I had learned to trust my gut and make snap decisions based on the options presented. I knew that plans could be changed in an instant and this was no different. Mango's offer could be another gift presented, perhaps Africa's final offer of faith? Time would surely tell, but was I willing to wait and see? For now, I was.

As the miles flew underneath the truck's wheels, conversation ebbed and flowed between Mango and me. He smiled, but hands did not cross

347

over to my side of the truck. We chatted, but it was sparse due to language barriers between us more than anything. He seemed a simple man, doing his job and nothing more. My presence in the truck was a kindness and the norm for travel on African roads. I suspect that some ladies paid their fare in "favours", especially when they travelled alone, but I continued to hold out hope that I would not have to pay this fee for my passage. My hope was that I served more as company, extra pocket money for his troubles, and distraction to keep him from boredom or falling asleep. Accidents along African roads were legendary in traveller's tales everywhere I went. Keeping a solo driver alert was more than just a perk at times. It was often a lifesaver.

The border approached and decisions needed to be made. You never knew how long you would be held up at the border, but once across it was only a few hours further to Springbok. The longer I travelled with my new companion, the more comfortable I became. Was it worth it to skip Springbok altogether, and a potential visit with cousins, in order to get to Cape Town faster? A deep breath, take one step at a time and enjoy the world going by my window until the universe told me different.

Namibia flew by. So did the border. And so did the turn for Springbok. It felt like the right decision, and I stuck with it. Before I knew it, darkness stole over us, as was the way in Africa. The difference between light and dark was fleeting and negligible. Springbok lay behind us, and Cape Town was still a long way to go. I was committed now. There was no turning back and the night made sure of that. The highway was no place for idle hitchhikers after dark. I knew that all too well. So, for better or worse, I was Mango's passenger for the night.

When dinner became a memory and eyes fought for purchase to stay open, I began to release the day. I was not the only one who fought a battle with sleep. I tried to chat with Mango to keep us both awake, but conversation gradually ceased, and we drove along in silence. Reflective lines flashed towards us in the dark. My eyelids bobbed under the mesmerizing display, dangerously close to staying shut, until Mango's voice jarred me awake.

"I am going to stop," he announced. "I need sleep."

"You're the boss," I thought, as I nodded in agreement. The truck geared down and eased to the side of the road for a much-needed break for both of us. We were in the middle of nowhere. No lights twinkled in the distance, near or far. While there could have been people hidden in the depths of the dark, essentially, we were alone.

"Do you want to join me," Mango half-heartedly suggested, as he crawled into his bunk. "No charge for the ride?" This was what I had dreaded and hoped against hope would not happen. I was instantly awake and tense.

"No," I stated firmly.

"Sure?" he pushed, but I shook my head emphatically. He waited a second and then lay down. He flipped over with his back to me, apparently unconcerned by my rejection. I remained rigid in the passenger seat. Long after Mango slept, I listened for his even breathing, to assure me that I too was safe to snooze. Needless to say, it was less than a sound sleep that night.

Before morning light, we rolled along again. The sky outside my window was steely gray and rain broke on the windshield as we drove. My eyes were dry and gritty from having slept in my contact lenses, but Cape Town approached. After spending almost 24 hours in the truck with Mango, he geared down once again. Where the N1 and N7 intersected, I alit from the truck into the pouring rain. I thanked him for the ride, gave him the promised money, and watched him drive away.

"Thank you, my guardian angels," I whispered. "Thank you, Africa," I said with a smile. Within minutes two lovely ladies stopped to scoop me out of the downpour.

"Oh, you poor thing!" they cried. "You're soaked through!"

I didn't care. They could fret all they wanted. A little rain couldn't hurt me now. Next stop was downtown Cape Town. After nine and a half months of meandering almost 10,000 kilometers between Cape Town and Lamu, my travelling days were finally at an end.

"The Return"

"You have returned!" Terry exclaimed, as I signed back into Bob's Backpacker.

"Yup," I replied.

"You've put on weight," Terry continued. "It looks good." His eyes dipped briefly to the most obvious spot that the aforementioned weight had landed. Yes, my thread-bare bra was now stretched to the max.

Yeah right, I thought, but could not deny it. My chubby cheeks and straining pants were a tell-tale sign that not everyone is starving in Africa. The many days and nights spent in the passenger seat of a moving truck had taken their toll. Not to mention all the food I had scarfed along route. In fact, before I hit the hostel, I had stopped for breakfast at Nino's. I decided I deserved to splurge on breakfast after having survived the questionable transportation I had endured over the last month. A RTGS 20 English breakfast was no match for this eating machine and my servers were thoroughly impressed. The only thing left was a mere croissant, which I slipped into my bag to save for later. The lady can eat folks!

I made a mental note to cut back on the carbs when I finally hit Canadian soil again. And yes, a little exercise might not hurt either, especially after I watched the arm on the scale swing wildly back and forth under my tread. Even with my shoddy conversion of kilograms into pounds, I was shocked to note that I was the heaviest I had ever been in my life. No wonder all I wore was my stretchy peasant skirt! It was definitely time for some exercise. With that in mind, I stowed my pack and headed out to walk around the city. Over the days that followed, I wandered through art galleries, perused the Cape Town Museum in a downpour, and did some last-minute shopping on my limited budget. I desperately tried to cram in as much culture as I could in my remaining hours.

Now that the days were numbered though, the hours flew by. I realized that I would not make it to the top of Table Mountain, nor out to wander around Robben Island. There was time enough to visit with relatives and as that was the reason why I came to South Africa in the first place. I returned to the arms of my kin. Indeed, when I returned to Brackenfell, my father's brother greeted me with all the warmth he possessed, as if we had known each other my whole life, versus the short few months that I had been on the African continent. In the grand scheme of things though, I suppose that my life in Africa was a lifetime in and of itself. And the adventure certainly created enough memories to last me many more lifetimes as well.

*****

"The spring flowers are a sight to behold," promised Uncle Jock. He didn't have to sell me on one last excursion though. The suggestion alone was all that was required to convince me, and with that I was travelling again.

This time, I was in the back seat of my aunt and uncle's car though and we headed to Springbok to stay with my cousins for a few days. I would not have to carry my pack, nor stand at the side of the road in hopes that a ride would soon materialize. And I certainly did not have to worry about anyone's hands or where they tried to put them. This was an adventure much more to my liking.

Namaqualand was well worth the drive. Just as my uncle had promised, the desert had blossomed into a multi-coloured patchwork of blooms. Orange, purple, yellow, and white flowers filled the eye, as far as one could see. We wandered up on the dusty hillside behind Anne and Pieter's house, but the trip to Namaqua National Park blew me away. Everywhere I looked, the daisies turned their pretty faces to the sun, and I was in awe. The normal brown and dusty green shoots that struggled to exist during the rest of the year, exploded into a brief, brilliant rainbow after winter rains gave them a fleeting taste of life. Just as quickly though, the blossoms would be gone, burned away by the hot South African summer sun. During those few days in August, I was blessed to behold the desert miracle of life for its season of rebirth and renewal. The pictures I snapped were flat compared to the beauty I was surrounded by. I took them anyway though.

One prickly plant drew my eye in the midst of the blanketed foliage. Where most of the other plants were tucked close to the ground, *Pachypodium namaquanum* stood tall, if not quite erect. When I asked my uncle about the curious cacti, he gave one of his hearty laughs and launched into a tale of folklore.

"Do you see the bend at the top," he asked.

"Yes," I said.

"So, the story goes, a local tribe was being driven south by another bloodthirsty tribe. Attacked and suffering in numbers, they retreated from their homeland and made their way towards the Richtersveld mountain desert. In grief, a few of their numbers turned back to gaze north towards their former homeland. The Gods felt sorry for these poor folk and turned them into *halfmens*, the plants you see there. In that way, they could always gaze towards their homeland and find some small comfort in the view," he explained. "The *halfmens* always grow with their tips bending north."

I listened to his tale and stared at the tree. It was a delightfully sad tale and one that resonated with me, as I gazed north towards my own homeland. Would I always be frozen in time, as I looked back at my days spent in Africa? The answer of course is yes. It will all stay with me forever.

"The Final Trip Home"

The last of my days in Africa slipped through my fingers. We returned to Cape Town, and I managed to sneak in a few more visits here and there. I visited with my cousin Greg, went out to my aunt's house for a last cup of tea with her, and enjoyed a final braai with my uncle's clan. It was heart-wrenching to let go of the continent that I felt like I had just begun to know, but it was also time. I had been gone for 10 months and my birthplace called to me. I longed to see my mother's face, to feel my sister's hug, and to hear my friends' excited banter. To know that this new continent that I had come to love would be so far away in a matter of days was bewildering, but acceptance had to tame my qualms.

A phone call arranged a layover in Germany to visit with a friend on my return flight. I would have a week to decompress and adjust to life away from Africa before I winged back to Canadian shores. It all felt so lacklustre, but I tried to muster up a little excitement at the prospect of seeing a long-lost friend and catching up on her life and times. I wondered though, how I would process stepping onto European soil after my earthy African adventures that spanned the southern half of the continent. Europe would be like a different world. Of course, Canada would be an adjustment all over again a week later. For the time being, I tried to imprint every image, taste, feel, and smell of this land that had gotten under my skin. The concept of leaving was akin to abandoning a homeland that I dearly loved and feared I would never see again. Africa was home to my soul, and I ached at the thought of leaving. The fates refused to give me reason to stay though, and I begrudgingly packed the last of my things, adding last minute trinkets to my battered backpack to keep Africa close forever.

On August 29th, the last full moon I saw in Africa arose to wish me adieu to the continent of my dreams. The following day, I drove to the airport with kin who would forever hold a piece of my heart. With a few strings pulled, I was upgraded to the luxury of business class and slid into the ample seat with a sad sigh. A flight attendant materialized with a champagne glass topped off with orange juice and a smile. I peered out the window of the plane, tipped my glass to Table Mountain and let a tear slide down my cheek in farewell. Tears ushered Africa in and bade me go well as I left. It was cyclical, but the journey would never truly end.

I was going home. All the moments I had lived in this amazing continent seared into my brain as the jumbo jet lifted off the ground. Just like my first flight, there would be no sleep on the return journey. With an aching soul, I left a piece of me behind but more importantly, took a bigger piece of Africa with me. It will always be, to this very day, a part of my heart.

*****

2021: THE 25TH ANNIVERSARY

In 1995, I graduated from university and headed to Africa. My plan to stay six months was altered and extended several times, and ultimately lasted a total of 10 months. Upon returning to Canada, my goal was to stay only long enough to earn some much-needed funds to continue my travels. I temporarily moved in with my aunt to serve as a live-in nanny, then made plans to move to Japan to teach English for a year. When my aunt became pregnant again, I got a job at a lodge in Central Ontario to help fund my trip to the other side of the world. A week after moving to that lodge, I met my future husband and plans changed once more.

Skip forward 25 years and life has changed several times since then. I never did make it to Japan and haven't been back to Africa but hope to change that one day. My time there got under my skin and helped me look at the world through different eyes. That journey stayed with me, despite every change that happened along the way. I started and stopped writing this story several times, but the words just never came out right. That began to change a few years ago.

It should be of no surprise that with all that practice writing letters and journaling my way across Africa, I ended up in a career 'playing' with words daily. I started blogging over a decade ago and the world of social media helped me to hone my writing skills. With every post published, I learned how to massage and wring nuances out of strings of prose. Those words weren't always as solid as they could be, but time has a way of helping us find our footing and I think I needed that time to improve my craft before my travel memoir could see fruition. A certain level of confidence in that ability has also grown too.

With confidence comes the knowledge that you need to push yourself, if you want to get better. Writing, rewriting, and editing my story occasionally wasn't ever going to see my story completed, so I joined a writing group a few years ago. My weekly meetings force me to get my butt in the chair and write, if only for an hour. We share what we are working on and update the other group members of our progress, creating a sense of responsibility. It doesn't matter what you write, but when it comes time for you to share, the pressure to have achieved something usually forces some words into place along the way.

That all changed a year ago. As 2020 opened, there were rumblings of an illness lurking on the other side of the world. Many people poo-pooed it, thinking it was too far away to worry about. But the power of travel made the world shrink in an awful hurry and soon enough a global pandemic had us all on lockdown. Everywhere. The entire planet. What happened in one small city had a major ripple effect that changed how everyone lives their lives. Pretty powerful stuff; the speed and ramifications of a few people stepping onto a plane, and unbeknownst to them, bringing an invisible virus in tow—Covid-19.

But you know that. Everyone has been touched by the coronavirus in one way or another. My writing group went online in March. While our numbers plummeted, a few stragglers remained, and we kept on writing. I was one of them. And as the days turned into weeks, then months, jumping back into my travel memoir was an unexpected boon. I might not have had the opportunity to leave my house, but I could fly back in memory and relive experiences from another lifetime and another world. Every week, I met with old friends and laughed, cried, and gasped over shenanigans undertaken while I was in my footloose and fancy-free 20s. I didn't have to leave my chair to be reminded that human connection was more important than material goods, and that the future might be uncertain, but that something good was always lurking somewhere in the future. You don't have to know what form it takes. You just have to have faith that there are good people out there who will cross your path when the time is right.

Interestingly enough, the timing aligned for me and my book this year. A friend virtually introduced me to a colleague who had ties to the publishing industry. We shared a snippet of our life stories, and I told her a little about my travel memoir. She was intrigued, so I forwarded her the first few chapters to see what she thought. She wanted more. And now we are here at the end.

So many people have heard fragments about my travels through Africa over the years, but I knew I wanted to share the whole story. It took the world slamming to a stop to finally carve out more time and some serious determination. I have lived a few lifetimes between when my plane touched back down in Canada and today, but my story is finally ready to be shared. Any errors in dialogue, details, or description are the fault of time and my flawed memory, but that is the joy of storytelling. It is my story to tell from my perspective. And this is the version that I have decided to share. Hopefully, you have enjoyed travelling with me as I explored my roots, many roads, and an indulgent revelation or two along the way.

One last thing. For those of you reading this and thinking that you could never take on an undertaking like this: why not? I grew up a painfully shy girl who lived more in books, than adventuring with friends. I do not have any magical super-powers that kept me safe, although I swear that there must have been guardian angels watching over me at times. What I did have was an idea, timing, and faith that I could do this thing. We can all do a thing if we put a little effort in and are open to what life has to offer. Keep your eyes open. Life might be knocking. And if it is, go for it!

ACKNOWLEDGEMENTS

First and foremost, I owe great thanks to my father and his spirit of adventure which inspired my own. To be fair though, it was my mother who had the strength of character to let me go and the faith that everything would be alright, no matter the path I took. While not all the paths I have taken in life have been safe or stuck to the original plan, I have met so many interesting people along the way that I welcome the twists and turns I have made and continue to stumble through. Those twists and turns have brought me so many new people, like my publishing agent and new friend Marcia Allyn Luke. New experiences, like my writing group that inspires me to return to my writer's chair every week. And new inspiration, like my cheerleaders who have been encouraging me to get these words down so I can share them with the world—thank you to my sister, Kerry, Aunt Leslie, and friends: Joe, Corrie, Laura, Darin, Rick, Nancy, Rebecca, Jon, and Daisy-Mae, for always asking about my book! I cannot forget to thank my family in South Africa who took me in while I was overseas, nor the love they showed me despite my long-lost status. Lastly, thank you to my beautiful daughters for giving me the space to write and having absolute faith that my story is worth writing. You have heard the tales a million times, but I love that you are always willing to listen again when I slip an African story into the mix once more. Love you all!

ABOUT THE AUTHOR

Katherine Krige is a Freelance Writer and Social Media Manager living in London, Ontario, Canada with two daughters. She graduated from York University with a B.A. in English and has taken several writing courses through Western University Continuing Studies. She fell in love with words at a young age and learned to manipulate them through regular journaling. These practices stood her in good stead when it came time to capture a journey of a lifetime in Africa. While nowadays she doesn't get much further than her own backyard, her mind is still touring the world via memories, and she is always happy to share. You can find her on Facebook, Twitter, Instagram, and LinkedIn, plus the local coffee shop when they are open, scribbling in her latest journal.

www.katherinekrige.com
krigek@katherinekrige.com
https://www.facebook.com/KatherineKrigeFreelanceWriter
https://twitter.com/katherinekrige
https://www.linkedin.com/in/katherinekrige/

PRAISE FOR ROUGHING IT IN AFRICA

"This book is both engaging and incredibly well written. You can actually feel, touch, taste, and see her experiences as she takes you on her amazing journey through Africa. I would highly recommend this book to anyone who enjoys a great read."

- Suzanne Boles, Writing Instructor and Coach, Award-Winning Feature and Content Writer

"Not all of us are brave enough to head out on our own, travelling halfway around the world to discover our roots. Katherine Krige's *Roughing it in Africa* lets us travel across foreign landscapes from the comforts of home. Part coming of age tale and part adventure story, this love letter to Africa will keep you turning pages. Equal parts excitement and introspection, this book takes us there and back again with a joyous enthusiasm and wry wit. A truly enjoyable tale!"

- Corrie Haldane, Award-Winning Short Story Writer

"Katherine Krige's new book takes readers on a wild adventure through 10 countries in 358 pages! One might think that this book is just a travel memoir—but it is so much more than that. This true backpacking story, *Roughing it in Africa*, tells of a once-in-a-lifetime journey many could only dream of.

Katherine's story is about family connection, being in love (and losing it), being swept off one's feet in quick and unexpected romances, and facing near death experiences. But other powerful topics are also addressed, such as white privilege, stereotypes, poverty, gender dynamics, bias and discrimination, and quite literally, the meaning of life.

Roughing it in Africa will feel like 'a movie you can hold in your hands' and just the trip that readers have been waiting for!"

- Daisy-Mae Hamelinck, Founder of Your New Leaf, College Professor, and Author

"Katherine's words paint a wonderful picture of her adventures in Africa. Her book definitely entices me to visit many of the places she travelled to. Although, I confess, 'roughing it' is not so appealing, but I might consider 'glamping' in Africa.

I also love how Katherine was able to connect with relatives that she had never met. It was like she had a home-away-from-home, even if she was a whole other hemisphere away from her own bed.

Reading these personal tales has stoked the fire I have in me to return to Scotland and discover my roots. As a sixth generation Canadian, it might be a wee bit more difficult.

Congratulations on the launch of your book, Katherine!"

- Darin J. Addison, Parallel Creative Enterprises

"*Roughing it in Africa* grabbed my attention right from the first line. Katherine's writing feels like a comfortable conversation between friends. I laughed, I cried, I learned, and now I'm inspired. I felt like I was right there with her!"

- Rebecca Summerfield, Career Services Consultant at Fanshawe College

"I'm 50 pages in and I'm hooked! The author has a way of taking you by the hand and leading you on adventures that you would swear were your own. I can't wait to see what's in store for us next!"

- Rick Stamp

"At a time when travel has been shut down and our homes have become the outer limit of our world, *Roughing it in Africa*, a travel memoir by Katherine Krige, is a wonderful adventure and much needed escape.

Roughing it in Africa transports us back to a time of youth and innocence as Krige ventures far from her home in Canada to South Africa, the birthplace of a father she never got to know. Her trip to South Africa is a journey to discover her roots, to leave behind a broken love, and to explore an unknown land that has called to her all her life.

Though Krige draws you in through her vivid descriptions—from the shanty towns of Cape Town to white water rafting on the Mighty Zambezi and the game parks of Zimbabwe—she leaves her mark through her recollections of friendships formed and bonds forged. Krige and her fellow travellers build connections through a mutual commitment to living in the moment, and to exploring and experiencing Africa to the fullest.

As Krige relays her adventures we see her growing awareness of the poverty and racism that continues to haunt South Africa to this day. And we see the beautiful awakening of a young traveller growing up and becoming a resilient, mindful, and compassionate young woman. *Roughing it in Africa: Roots, Roads, and Revelations* is a journey well worth taking."

- Nancy Clarke, Owner/Artist at Acme Animal